HANDBOOK
FOR
CARE
ASSISTANTS

A pra

to caring for
elderly people

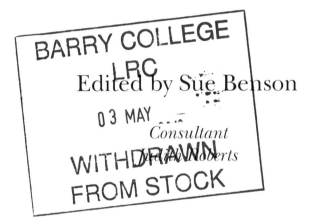

Edited by Sue Benson

Consultant
Amelia Roberts

HPL

A Care Concern Publication

This fifth edition printed in 2000

First published in 1989 by
Hawker Publications Ltd
13 Park House
140 Battersea Park Road
London SW11 4NB

Reprinted 1990 (twice), 1991
2nd Edition 1992, 3rd Edition 1993
4th Edition 1995

© Hawker Publications 2000

British Library Cataloguing in Publication Data
*A catalogue record for this book is available
from the British Library*

ISBN 1 874790 50 7
(ISBN 1 874790 19 1 4th Edition)

Designed by
Richard Souper

Phototypeset by
Hawker Publications

Printed and bound in Great Britain by
Butler and Tanner, Frome, Somerset

*Illustrations demonstrating the Heimlich Manoeuvre in chapter 13 are redrawn from How to Save a
Life by Alan Maryon Davies and Jenny Rogers, BBC Books. Other illustrations by Eve Morris*

Other titles in this series:
The Care Assistant's Guide to Working With People with Dementia
Third Edition 1998. ISBN 1 874790 37 X
The Handbook for Community Care Assistants and Support Workers
1994. ISBN 1 874790 18 3
A Practical Guide to Working with People With Learning Disabilities
Second Edition 1994. ISBN 1 874790 12 4
The Handbook for Hospital Care Assistants and Support Workers
1993. ISBN 1 874790 10 8

Contents

Contributors

June Andrews RMN RGN MA is Director of Nursing, Orth Valley Acute Hospitals NHS Trust. Her clinical experience has been in nursing elderly and elderly mentally ill people.

Rosemary Ashbee is manager of the Royal National Institute for the Blind's Westcliff House, Westgate on Sea, Kent. She began her career as a care assistant with RNIB 14 years ago, and has trained in social work and communication with the deaf-blind.

Karen Bryan PhD BSc MCSLT is a lecturer in acquired communication disorders at the National Hospitals College of Speech Sciences. She is currently involved in developing a communication training programme for care assistants.

Margaret Cheetham is Inspector of Homes with Scarborough Social Services, Yorkshire. For eleven years until 1988 she was officer in charge of a voluntary home for 79 residents in Scarborough.

Alan Crump BSc (Nursing) RGN RMN, is charge nurse in the Nursing Development Unit, Seacroft Hospital, Leeds, and an executive member of the Royal College of Nursing membership group, *Focus: on older people, nursing and mental health.*

Stuart Darby RGN RMN RHV DPSN wrote this chapter while head of the Community Nursing Development Team, Camden and Islington NHS Trust. He worked as a health visitor, as a clinical nurse specialist in mental health care of older people, and was chair of the RCN group *Focus: on older people, nursing and mental health.*

Anne Eaton RGN RM RCNT RNT Cert Ed is NVQ Coordinator at the Mid Trent College of Nursing and Midwifery. She teaches on NVQ courses at Levels 2 and 3, and is an Internal Verifier and External Verifier for BTEC.

Paul Julian Fletcher BSc MA CQSW is Head of Care Services for the Fremantle Trust, providing residential care for elderly people, people with learning disabilities and those recovering from mental illness, in Buckinghamshire. Before this he has worked in service planning, been a team manager, managed a group of homes for elderly people and been an officer in charge.

Claire Hale BA PhD RGN RNT is a research associate at the Centre for Health Services Research at the University of Newcastle upon Tyne, and a senior nurse (research) at the Royal Victoria Hospital, Newcastle.

Brenda Hooper MA, wrote this chapter shortly after her retirement as manager of Libury Hall, a residential care home in Hertfordshire. She was previously a training adviser for the Centre for Policy on Ageing.

Karen Hynes CSS was formerly a manager of a residential home and is now a Staff Development Officer with Wirral Social Services. She is an internal verifier for care NVQs and is involved in the training of candidates and Work Based Assessors.

Mansour Olawale Jumaa MSc BA DipNEd PGdip Hon Psych RN RNT is the director of continuing education and NVQ co-ordinator at the North London College of Health Studies, and associate colleague of Middlesex University.

Judith Kemp MSc SRCh wrote this chapter while a chiropodist with City and Hackney Health Authority and research officer for the Age Concern Institute of Gerontology, King's College, London.

Alastair Kent MA MPhil DipCG wrote this chapter while director of residential, education and employment services for the Royal National Institute for the Deaf.

Sue Knell SRN SCM wrote this chapter while Matron of Aynsley Nursing Home, Wallasey, Merseyside.

Sheila Mackie Bailey BA SRN RCNT DipNEd RNT is a freelance lecturer, consultant and author. Her interests include elderly people, nursing ethics and complementary therapies.

Jane Maxim PhD MA DipCST MCSLT is a senior lecturer at the National Hospitals College of Speech Sciences. She is a speech therapist whose research area is language change in dementia, and she works with elderly stroke patients.

Teresa Mearing-Smith BSc MB BCh DCH MRCGP wrote this chapter while working as a clinical assistant in geriatric medicine and dermatology and dermatology at St Peter's Hospital, Chertsey.

Eric Midwinter is a past director of the Centre for Policy on Ageing. Now "retired" he works as consultant to projects in a wide variety of fields, including old age and education.

Sue Millward SRN is senior clinical nurse for the National Society for Epilepsy at Chalfont St Peter, Buckinghamshire, where she is in charge of the Nursing Unit and teaches on the in-service training course for care staff.

Joan Mitchell BSc BA MB BCh studied medicine at Newnham College, Cambridge and The London Hospital, Whitechapel. For the last 26 years of her career she was a general practitioner in Crayford, Kent, and is now retired.

Tracy Packer RGN is development nurse for dementia services at Frenchay Hospital Bristol. She is involved in training and developing strategies with staff to improve the well-being of people with dementia. She previously worked as senior staff nurse and acting ward manager in the acute elderly care unit at St Mary's Hospital, Paddington.

Helen Ransome (Dip. Physio. Victoria, Australia) wrote this chapter while district physiotherapist for Lewisham and North Southwark Health Authority.

Gwyn Roberts DMS was Associate Director with Court Cavendish – the nursing and residential home operator – where for seven years, she was closely associated with the care for elderly people with dementia. She now works for Hastings and Rotherhithe NHS Trust in the field of patients' services.

Judith Roberts RGN RSCN Cert Health Ed, wrote this chapter while lecturer at Wirral Metropolitan College, and joint co-ordinator of Wirral Social Care Assessment Centre, a joint partnership between Wirral Metropolitan College and Wirral Social Services.

Sue Thomas SRD is a dietician with special interest in the nutrition of older people. She is currently working part time for Richmond, Twickenham and Roehampton Healthcare NHS Trust.

Helen White RGN RHV is continence adviser with Disability North at the Dene Centre, Newcastle upon Tyne Council for the Disabled.

Deirdre Wynne-Harley, lately deputy director of the Centre for Policy on Ageing, is now an independent consultant/adviser. In 1982-84 she co-ordinated the DHSS sponsored working party which produced *Home life: a code of practice for residential care*.

Foreword

*By Peter Millard, Eleanor Peel Professor of Geriatric Medicine,
St George's Hospital Medical School, London.*

Ageing is universal. Nothing escapes. Animals, motor cars, buildings, bridges and elastic bands age. Why ageing occurs is beyond the scope of this book, but the fact that all of us have aged, are ageing and will (if we do not die first) become old is inescapable.

To live to be old one must not die young. The number of old people in our country is increasing because at the turn of the century children stopped dying in the first year of life. Yet the number being born did not decrease until the 1930s. As well as an increase in absolute numbers, the proportion is increasing because for the last twenty-odd years fewer children have been born. Thus we have more old people with a decreasing labour force.

Most do not need care. Reflect that much of the voluntary work being done in the homes, churches, clubs and societies of our country depends upon the enthusiastic contribution of those who are chronologically old. Their bodies show age but is is not the years they have lived but the sickness they have had which hampers them.

The ill-informed say if only we were like the East we would have no need for care homes. Yet those who say that, betray their ignorance of life in both parts of the world. People in Western society are in care mainly because they have no families. You cannot slaughter a million men in the First World War and expect all the eighty and ninety year old women to be married and have families. Nor do all married couples have children.

I used to think that others should change their attitudes. Later as my knowledge increased I realised that people's attitudes reflect their knowledge. Unless they are sick in mind, people do not willingly harm others. Therefore if people in care in rest homes, nursing homes, and hospital wards are being badly treated it is not because the people employed to look after them don't care, it is because they don't know how to care. Ignorance is nothing to be ashamed of.

At one time I knew nothing about geriatric medicine. At school the subject was not mentioned. Indeed even at my Medical School, which in the 1960s was the only London teaching hospital with geriatric medical wards and a consultant, I still did not know, for I was not taught. I was taught anatomy, physiology, biochemistry, obstetrics, medicine, surgery, paediatrics, and psychiatry, but no one mentioned old age.

By the age of twenty four I had gained sufficient knowledge to be given sole charge of a 100-bedded African Hospital. There I made many mistakes but I knew what had to be done. However, two years later as a junior doctor in a geriatric ward in this country, standing with four others around a cot-sided bed, I did not know what to do.

Thirty years later as a Professor of Geriatric Medicine I now know something, but not everything, about the care of elderly people. I research and study because I want to do the job better.

Age changes are universal, intrinsic, progressive and deleterious. Yet the rate of deterioration is influenced by genetic, nutritional, environmental, social and psychological factors. Elderly people when they are admitted to hospital usually have something wrong in at least seven systems of the body. Therefore to practise my subject one must know a little about ageing in all systems: skin, eyes, ears, teeth, feet, hearts, lungs, bowels, kidney, bladder or brain. However, in addition to these organ changes that are relatively easy to understand, one has to deal with a person who has lived their life. Each one is different. Each a unique person with their life. To help them requires skill, tact, patience, and understanding.

In homes, in residential homes, in nursing homes and in hospital wards staff have been developing better ways of caring. Because a better way is possible we can see the poverty of management in other places. To improve standards nationally we must teach others.

Over the next decade there is no doubt that a universal training system will be established for those who tend elderly people. Throughout the country there is a hunger for that knowledge. Gradually courses in gerontology and in geriatric medicine are being established, and as we teach we learn. This book represents a beginning, and I feel privileged to be asked to write its foreword. Yet in reading the chapters, each contributed by a different author, I recogise the depth of my own ignorance, the debt I owe to others and the gulf of knowledge that still exists.

I wish the book well. It represents the effort of many people who have tried in their professional lives to benefit elderly people. Within its pages you will find the perceived wisdom of many people. In reading their thoughts you will gain an understanding of the problems and how to cope with them. Each writer comes from a different professional discipline. You, the reader, will have to use the knowledge they give to build on the understanding you have already gained.

That you have read this far in the foreword shows that you have a quest for knowledge. I hope that through the pages of this book you gain further insight and understanding of your work, and that through ventures such as this the home, residential home, nursing home, or ward in which you work moves towards the better world that you know awaits it.

Peter H. Millard

Introduction

to the Fifth Edition

Education is about enabling people to think for themselves. Training is imparting the particular skills a job requires. We hope this book will help provide both education and training for everyone who cares for older people, especially those staff who have had no previous training but on whom managers, relatives and residents depend for high quality person-centred care every day. The book's focus is on the residential or nursing home (and we have used the terms *care assistant* and *resident* for simplicity) but its content applies equally to any long-term care setting.

No book can replace practical instruction and work experience; rather it adds an extra dimension of knowledge, and the resources to question and challenge some of the assumptions and attitudes you are all bound to meet.

One of us was told by the matron of a luxury nursing home, "They're just 80-year-old babies really". Think about it. The people in your care are not babies: they are individuals who have lived long, varied, stressful, boring, rewarding, frustrating, joyful, tragic, selfish, valuable, utterly different real lives. In other words, each one needs and deserves to be treated with respect and careful attention to their individual needs and preferences, *especially* those least able to make their wants known. This is the message which we hope sounds loud and clear through the pages of this book. It is also the reason why you will not find words like independence, dignity, autonomy, individuality, self-esteem, choice, opportunity or equality in the index; these themes are central to every chapter.

In this new edition, considerably expanded and completely revised, we have aimed to retain the individual voices of our authors, and their wisdom distilled from years of practical experience. At the same time we have planned the book to cover all the demands of National Vocational Qualifications in Care, especially Level 2 Direct Care, and beyond – well on the way towards Level 3 in many instances, and relevant to many other endorsement areas. At the end of each chapter we have listed the main units covered, and on page 206 is a chart showing how each chapter relates to the units of NVQ in Care Level 2 (Direct Care). Chapter 27 also explains how NVQs are structured and how the system of assessment works in practice.

Previous editions of this book have been very popular, and we hope this Fifth Edition will continue to meet the needs of both care assistants and those responsible for their training, as a practical teaching resource to further the aim we all share, of high quality individualised care.

Sue Benson and Judith Roberts

CHAPTER 1

A healthy old age

Eric Midwinter

• Taking a broad view • Active older people in the community • Statistics • Old does not mean ill • Encouraging independence, but allowing eccentricity

Being old is normal. What is, if anything, abnormal is being old in a residential care setting.

Nearly 12 million people in the United Kingdom are over 60 years of age; almost a fifth of the population. Contrary to popular belief, the number living in care is very small. About 330,000 older people (less than three per cent of those over 60) do not live in their own ordinary accommodation, but in residential homes, nursing homes, sheltered housing and so on. So, first of all, you are dealing with a very small minority, whether privileged or unfortunate is a matter of circumstance and opinion. But they are not, basically, different from the norm.

It is true that they tend to be older and more dependent than the wider cohort of older people, and this you would expect, for of course many residents of homes are there because of difficulties in managing alone. Nonetheless, being very old as opposed to old is not so exceptional. Nearly four million people are over 75, and there are 180,000 over the age of 90.

For every thousand people aged 65 to 74, just over six will be in residential care: for every thousand who are 75 and over, the figure is nearer 49. In effect, you are likely to find up to four-fifths of residents will be 75 and over.

How dependent?

Until recently dependency levels in residential care settings were actually better than many believed: in any hundred residents you would have probably found about 17 severely dependent, 42 moderately dependent, and 41 reasonably independent. One reason for this was the decision in 1979 to make social security payments available for private residential care. However, the government became worried about paying for expensive places where the resident was not dependent.

The 1990 Community Care Act addressed that issue, and was implemented in 1993. The bulk of expenditure on community care, including residential and nursing homes, became the responsibility of the local authorities, in the hope that more support would be given to people staying in their own accommodation, and leaving the residential sector to those most in need. Local authority social workers have become much more involved in assessment for service eligibility and individual "care management", and the local authorities themselves are encouraged to be "enablers", granting contracts to a diversity of agencies, rather than just providers.

Although it will take some time for this

to work its way through (obviously, residents already in residential care were not re-assessed and ejected) there are already signs that dependency levels are rising rapidly. The same thinking, indeed, the same act, has led to a decrease in long-term geriatric care, and there is evidence of people with severe clinical conditions finding themselves in residential care homes, something for which they were never intended.

This raises a serious debate about the basic role of the residential care home. It creates a dilemma, for care homes appear to have two distinct functions: caring for those unable to look after themselves, and providing a rational habitat for those able to look after themselves.

There is no simple answer to this. It has to be accepted that this is a fact of residential care life. What should be recognised is that the two camps – dependent and independent – are not, in practice, quite so definite in composition. In some respects, the "severely dependent" resident might be fiercely independent, and rightly so, insisting on this or that personal need. A "reasonably independent" resident, on the other hand, might be temporarily incapacitated or be absolutely dependent in one aspect of lifestyle. In the end, the blurring is such that it is much safer to take each resident on his or her own terms.

A word of warning: for all sorts of reasons, such as the number of places locally available in the public sector or the demand made evident locally in the private sector, these figures of age and dependency vary crazily from area to area. There is no prototype – the "average" home probably doesn't exist.

You will find that women outnumber men in residential care, in the ratio of at least three to one. This reflects what happens in society at large where women gradually grow in numbers compared to men as they age.

Old does not mean ill

Although many people are in residential care for reasons of ill health, it is worth recalling that "old" does not mean "ill". By the very token of increased survival into older age, it follows that a decline in health should not automatically be associated with an increase in years.

Consider the following statements, based on an over-75 yardstick, because, as we have already noted, most residents will be of that range. These are, of course, national figures, for all over-75s. Let us assume a sample group of 100 people over 75 years of age.

This 100 were asked whether they had suffered any "restricted activity" during the previous fortnight, any time they had been inhibited from getting about in the ordinary way. Seventy five of them had not been so restricted.

Asked if they were housebound or bedfast, 90 of them said they weren't.

Asked if they were able to climb the stairs without assistance, 86 said they could manage that in reasonable comfort.

You see, if you put the figures the other way round, they do look a little sunnier and more optimistic. Of course, it is bad enough that 25 out of every 100 people over 75 have been limited in activity during the last two weeks. But it's not a complete tale of woe.

It is just too risky to assume that everyone over 75 is automatically declining in health and capability at some alarming rate. Take dementia. The popular view is that people crumble mentally with age, and that the older you are, the dottier. But 78 per cent even of over-80s do not suffer from any form of dementia.

Let us not be mistaken about this. The fact that 22 per cent do suffer from dementia amounts to a million tragic victims, just as 13 per cent of over-65s being unable to move outdoors readily is a grave social issue. This is not whitewashing, but it is a matter of perspective.

Of course, in the residential care home, there will be some accumulation of those with needs of a mental and physical, as well as a social, kind. The lesson of perspective is that you should begin with the stance that they are all right, that they are, so to speak, normal – and then adapt according to degrees, if any, of ill health and impairment, some of which may or should be temporary. In short, treat them as residents, not as patients.

A long retirement

Remember then at all times that we are living in an "old" society. The chief reason why the proportion of older people has risen dramatically, is because the proportion of younger people has dropped dramatically. A hundred years ago near enough to two-fifths of the population was under 14; that has halved to a fifth. It is unlikely to change significantly.

Many more people survive beyond 60 to enjoy another swathe of, one hopes, pleasant years. Some people are retired for as long as they have worked.

This means, in turn, that residents crossing the threshold into residential care homes, increasingly, spent a long time "at leisure". They are not coming to you direct from work, as would have sometimes happened in the past, nor equally, from completion of the happy chores of parenthood. Their children, did they exist, will be grown-up and away, and their jobs, did they have one, long ago over.

This raises an important issue. You should understand that, over the past years, the involvement of retired people in sports and pastimes, education and recreation, has been remarkably low. People take retirement all too seriously. They retire. They withdraw. They do very little.

You can see that it may not be easy for them to adapt to the public business of living cheek by jowl with ten, twenty or forty others, with staff hopeful that they will "join in" and be one of the large family. Many have been "counter-institutionalised": they have been ingrained into a lonely and negative lifestyle. Don't be surprised if they are not eager for bonhomie.

Choice and opportunity

Opportunities is the operative word. If one is a believer in giving maximum dignity and independence to older people in residential care, then the critical thing is choice. Old people must choose to do this or that. If, acting with all the sensitivity to their previous perhaps negative background and offering the most tastily tempting of chances, the resident still hands you the frozen mitt of refusal, that is her or his right.

If they do not want to do keep fit (to improve and maintain their physical suppleness), if they do not want to join in the quiz about World War II (designed to keep them mentally alert), if they do not want to create an Easter bonnet and process in an Easter parade (in the interests of social cohesiveness), so be it. They have made an informed choice, offered proper opportunities, and that is their civic right.

Some residential homes, rebounding from the autocratic model of yesteryear, have gone to another extreme, practically forcing residents to do things, either by ruling, like the washing up, or by social pressure, like joining in collective activities. That is wrong. You cannot twist people's arms into dignity. You cannot frogmarch people into independence.

You can request, persuade, even plead, but self-determination involves the resident's right to say "no" and lead a life as eccentric as is compatible with the safety and comfort of others.

That also entails the need for as much

consultation as possible with residents. They are citizens, not clients. As far as possible, they should make the decisions, either the individual ones, like when to take a bath, or the collective ones, like what should be the character of the Christmas party. Chapters that follow go into practical detail on this subject.

They are not children

There is a tendency to see normal ageing as a decline rather than a continuation. But frailty and weakness are not vices. Unconsciously, sometimes consciously, some treat very old people as children, as being in their "second childhood". This too has its attractions, but unluckily it is misleading. In any event, people do not always treat children as if they were "normal" and human: they do patronise them and assume responsibility for their rights; at worst, they humiliate them.

When this is applied to equally normal older people, the insult is compounded, for here are experienced veterans of life, who have grappled with all kinds of problems, and who have perhaps remained resilient in the face of hammerblows – losing spouse, home, income; suffering pain, hurt and indignity – each of which would floor many "ordinary" individuals.

One observes the trait in the forced ebullience with which residents are sometimes approached: in the use of forenames and endearments in a discourteously familiar way; in the presumption of decisions; in entering rooms without knocking; and in a score of tiny ways. By all means develop a close and warm if not sentimental (they are not "family") relationship, but do not assume it before it occurs, any more than you would in the work place with a forty-year-old or in the local tennis club with a thirty-year-old.

Saints and sinners

Old people are normal. They are saints and sinners; more usually, mixtures of both. Some are cantankerous and quarrelsome and bloody nuisances, not because they are old, but because they probably always were. Old age does not confer a second childhood, and it does not convert to a benign mellowness. There will be rows. There will be good times, and bad.

The pundits say to architects now that the acid test is: would you live or work in the building you designed? The rule of thumb for staff in residential care is sometimes said to be: do you look after the residents as you would look after your own mother? That's fine, but another question must be put: have you, as a person, the self-critical faculty which enables you to assess how well or badly you did or do look after your own mother. For a kick-off, did you or do you *like* your own mother?

This is important. Please be honest. Care is about the whole person, not just about washing that bit or bandaging this bit. It is about enabling the full person to be as free, independent and yes, as happy as possible.

We should emphasise the old saying that every age has its compensations. This is very true. It should be the aim of the care assistant to help guarantee that each resident's compensations are entirely realised.

NVQ Level 2 Core Units
O Promote equality for all individuals.
Z1 Contribute to the protection of individuals from abuse.
W2 Contribute to the ongoing support of clients and others significant to them.
U4 Contribute to the health, safety and security of individuals and their environment.
U5 Obtain, transmit and store information relating to the delivery of a care service.

CHAPTER 2

Coming into care

Gwyn Roberts

• Imagine how it feels • Welcoming a new resident • Preserving self-respect • Relatives
• Personal belongings • Pets • Leaving the home • Respite care

Have you ever tried to imagine what it is like to go into residential care for the first time? From being surrounded by your own belongings, living life according to your own rules, you are suddenly catapulted into a new environment where everything and everyone about you is strange and different.

This is not easy for anyone, regardless of age. We all tend to be suspicious of strange places and people. It is not surprising then, that many elderly people initially find the transition from their own home to a residential home quite a difficult one to make.

It is undoubtedly one of the major decisions people make in life– and almost certainly the last major decision. Going into care is surrounded by all the fears and doubts that everyone, young or old, feels when they are faced with a momentous change in their way of life.

All elderly people are not the same, any more than all young people are all the same. They have different hopes and aspirations, uncertainties, capabilities, intelligence, background and indeed everything else that distinguishes one human being from another. It is crucial that we do not lump our residents together as being simply "old".

Gains...

Of course, "going into care" is not all bad. For many it represents relief from worry about cooking, housework, dealing with finances and loneliness. From time to time, most of us feel pressured by modern life and the thought of being cared for by other people is idyllic. Imagine never having to worry about putting aside money to pay bills or going shopping when it is bitterly cold outside. These can be positive benefits of going into residential care, especially for those elderly people who are physically frail.

...and losses

On the other side of the coin are the losses people endure when they make the decision to leave their own homes for good. They will never have quite the same freedom of choice or action again; they may miss their gardens or their pets, or having meals whenever they feel like them.

Those of us who work in care homes should be constantly aware of these feelings of loss and try to strive to minimise them as much as possible. Perhaps it is possible for the resident to help in the garden; maybe there is a pet belonging to the home that could be "adopted" by the resident (or could they keep their own pet?). Keeping one's mind and imagination open can provide all sorts of possibilities for reducing a person's feeling of loss.

Staff should be aware of the circumstances leading up to the admission into care. Why was it felt necessary for this person to leave their own home? What were the problems? How were they failing to cope? Who was involved in the decision? Answers to these questions give valuable clues to the future happiness of the resident.

For example, they may be feeling inadequate because they have been told they are unable to look after themselves. It is quite a shock to people who have spent a lifetime looking after their families to be told they can no longer even look after themselves. As carers, we have a responsibility to try and reverse this feeling of inadequacy. We should try to support and encourage the things that they can do for themselves, rather than emphasising their frailties.

It is important for all people to feel needed and loved, to have a place in the world that is recognised as their own. Therefore, all carers must be aware all the time of the individual needs of the people for whom they care.

As an exercise, try and make a list of "losses" and "gains" you personally would feel about going to live in a large house with a number of other people who are strangers to you. It can be very enlightening!

Before admission

Many homes offer the opportunity for a visit before the planned date of admission. This can be very valuable if it is handled properly because it will obvi-ously give the new resident the chance to see the surroundings and meet some of the people with whom they will be living. Make the most of this opportunity. Make sure the visit is informal and friendly. Include a meal if possible and ensure that the care team use the time to introduce themselves and to involve the potential resident in appropriate arrangements that could make their stay more satisfactory.

Receiving a new resident

The first few days in the home are very important in setting the scene for the future, and in making the resident feel comfortable and at home. Even more important in some ways though, are the first few hours.

Try to think how you would feel leaving your own home and moving to a totally strange environment where people seem preoccupied with their own activities and hardly notice your presence. It does not take much imagination to realise how sad and vulnerable you would feel.

When someone comes into care there are always various administrative tasks that have to be carried out and it is easy for staff to become absorbed in these and seem to forget the new resident. It helps a lot if one member of staff can be designated to sit with the resident for a while; to help unpack clothes and belongings; to make a cup of tea or even to introduce other residents if this is appropriate. How you behave on the first day can make all the difference to the long-term wellbeing of the person coming into care.

Do not try to give new residents all the information about the home that they are eventually going to need. All that matters in the first instance is vital and immediate information like where the toilet is, and what time and where the next meal is being served. Everyone going into strange surroundings needs to cling on to familiar things, and helping to unpack or even just sitting in the room while the new resident unpacks, gives the opportunity to talk about items being brought out of the suitcase. Of course, some people may actually prefer to be alone when they are unpacking. Give the new resident the opportunity of being alone if that is what he or she wants, but be on hand in case there are any queries or problems.

It is important also not to assume that new residents are unable to help themselves. People come into care for all sorts of reasons; many are able to undertake daily tasks of living quite independently and this ought to be encouraged. So, again, on the crucial first day, try to establish by observation how much new residents can do for themselves and let them do those things. If it takes a little longer, so what?

A calm, relaxed atmosphere will help in settling in, rather than one of bustling efficiency. Remember that a care home should be a substitute for the person's own home and should provide the same sort of relaxed and homely environment with opportunities for independence and choice.

Of course, some residents will need more help than others; this is dependent on their level of physical or mental disability. Good observation and listening skills at the start should make it reasonably clear how much help is going to be needed.

Having said that, however, do not forget that people change when they become more comfortable and used to an environment and it may be that they are capable of doing much more after a few days than you had first thought. The trick is to review constantly and update your impressions about the residents. Nothing is cast in concrete!

Independence

It is tempting to try to do everything for people in care, especially if they are very slow or very forgetful. But if we do not think carefully about how much we are doing, it is possible to make people entirely dependent upon us for every aspect of life. Naturally, there is a fine line to draw between neglecting people and allowing them an appropriate degree of independence, and only by careful assessment of their capabilities can we draw this line with any accuracy.

For example, give them the chance to wash themselves, to choose which clothes to wear and to make their own hot drinks. Obviously, in many homes this is self-evident – many residents are quite capable of undertaking all self-care tasks without supervision and for these it is easier to organise a programme of care that suits both carer and cared for.

However, it is not always so clear cut. Where people are physically frail, staff are inclined to offer a great deal of help, perhaps without thinking how much those people may be able to do for themselves. But standing back instead of helping is not cruel or hard-hearted: it is a common-sense approach to helping people keep their independence as long as possible.

Even with mentally frail residents, we may underestimate their ability to do simple tasks. Of course, the end result may not be as good as we would like, but at least they will have put some effort into their own care. For example, people with dementia may have poor eating skills; their table manners deteriorate and they may forget how to use a knife and fork properly. It is often easier and quicker to place people like this on the "feeders" list, and once this is done it is unlikely that they will ever return to feeding themselves.

Instead, have heated plates, give them spoons and leave them to get on with it. Does this sound hard? It isn't really – it is giving those people the opportunity to do something independently.

Dignity

Perhaps the most important aspect of all of residential work is the preservation of dignity, or self-respect, for each individual resident.

Of course, many elderly people going into care are in need of help and supervision, particularly if they are suffering from mental confusion. In particular, people who have a dementia may be incontinent or prone to behaving in a sexually uninhibited way, and it is difficult to help them maintain dignity in these situations. However, the fact that it is difficult is no excuse for not trying **at all times**.

Indeed, if the carers regard the need to preserve dignity as a constant challenge rather than as a problem, the whole thing takes on a different perspective. Remember that the confused resident could be your grandmother, your mother or even you, one day, and act appropriately. Ensure that residents are always properly and cleanly dressed (even if that means their being changed several times a day); that they are led gently and quietly away to privacy if there are signs of sexual disinhibition and that incontinence is dealt with quickly and patiently when it occurs.

Another all-pervasive human need is that of privacy. Living in close proximity to a lot of people can be stressful and most of us (particularly those with unimpaired mental faculties) will need time to "do our own thing". Do not push people into joining in – perhaps they have never been the type to join clubs and mix socially with others, or prefer to just sit and watch. Everyone deserves to make their own choices about their daily lives.

It is worth thinking about how you will address a new resident. Never assume that using their first name is acceptable. Many of the people now coming into care are from a generation that used formal names even with long-standing acquaintances. They may be used to being called "Mr" or "Mrs" and may resent the use of their first name by a total stranger.

Certainly everyone should be asked what form of address they would prefer. Calling people "darling" or "love" should be avoided at all times unless they themselves use such expressions and are comfortable with them.

Friends and contacts

Don't forget that there may well be others who have significant involvement with your residents. Older people have friends just as younger people do. Don't assume that the relatives are the only people who are part of the resident's life. Find out as much as you can about those who may wish to have a continuing involvement and build up a picture of this person's life and who is important to them.

On the other hand, there may be people the resident does not wish to see. In our own homes we have the right to decide who will or will not be invited in. In the residential setting, the care team becomes, in a sense, the gatekeeper. Give residents the opportunity to say "no" if they do not wish to have visitors. It is their right to exercise choice in this as in every other aspect of their lives.

Belongings

The fact that a new resident is moving into strange surroundings has been mentioned several times already, but it is important to remember just what this means. A lot of elderly people have lived in the same house for many years (their generation tended not to move around quite as much as we do nowadays) and leaving treasured possessions behind can be very upsetting.

Fortunately, most homes allow people to bring in some items of furniture and this should be encouraged. Even just a favourite chair and a small coffee table may help transform the room (no matter how nice the room) into that individual's "space". If furniture cannot be accommodated, at least pictures, photographs and ornaments may give a feeling of homeliness.

People's belongings are important to them; they are all that is left of a lifetime and must therefore be respected. Remember that losing one's home is a form of mourning: a time to reflect on things past and, perhaps, to feel anxious and fearful of the future.

If the resident is confused, it is just as important to have familiar things around. For example, it is very useful if the family can provide a photograph album of holiday snapshots; all clearly labelled so that they can be used by staff in talking to the resident.

People with dementia should also be afforded the dignity of wearing their own clothes. This can be very difficult sometimes when they have no recollection of which items belong to them, but having all clothing name-tagged is a small price to pay for helping them to look good. Appearance is important and every personal item that surrounds them helps to add meaning to their life (see also chapter 20).

Pets

When people live alone they often have pets to help combat loneliness and perhaps to give them a feeling of being needed. The love that is felt for the animal should not be underestimated and any decision about going into care will obviously have to take account of the future of something that has become a very important part of that person's life.

It would be easy to say that all residential homes should be prepared to take pets – and, in fact, many already do – but the fact is that there are practical issues that must be considered. Firstly, cats and dogs have to be cared for. Who will walk the dog if its owner is not able to? How will the cat get out and if it cannot, who is going to clean the litter tray? How can we ensure that the animals cannot stray to the food preparation areas where high standards of cleanliness are required by law? It is important to discuss with potential residents the full implications of having their pets with them and come to a shared decision about how they will be cared for.

Of course, there are some pets that are easier to accommodate – such as budgerigars or goldfish – and it is possible that staff at a home are willing to accept at least a supervisory role in the upkeep of these animals.

But it is clear that in some instances, the beloved animal may not be able to accompany its owner into care. It is important for staff to realise that there will be a period of mourning just as acute as mourning for a person who has died. Sympathy, patience and understanding will go a long way to easing the grief, and you should provide opportunities to talk about the lost animal.

Photographs are useful, but by the time the person comes into care, it may be too late to organise these. The family

The older person's love for their pet should never be underestimated.

may, of course, be able to provide snapshots, and it is a good idea to use these as conversation pieces to try and reinforce the new resident's feeling of belonging to someone or something.

Leaving the home

Of course, not all people who move into a residential care setting stay there for the remainder of their lives. Some residents may be returning to their own homes after a planned short stay (respite care). In this situation, there will probably be staff from other agencies like social workers or district nurses who are involved in providing a package of care. You and the other members of the care team in your home will need to work towards supporting the resident in a care plan that maintains the resident's independence and ability to return to their own home after their stay.

Sadly there are other residents who, through deteriorating physical or mental condition, may have to move to a nursing home and it is important that this situation is dealt with sensitively and with patience. It is a decision that is never easy to make, but it must be remembered that to keep someone in an inappropriate care setting is not doing them any favours.

Family, friends and the residents themselves should be involved in the decision-making process and, if possible, the new home and its staff too. Perhaps you could help prepare a dossier of background information, likes and dislikes, etc, to pass on so that the resident starts life in their new setting with all the familiarity they felt with you.

Whatever the circumstances, there should always be a policy for discharge planning that ensures a consistent approach is taken. This will include discussing and supporting the resident and any members of the family (including friends) regarding the impending transfer, as well as practical aspects like packing belongings and arranging transport.

You should also, as a care worker, have the opportunity to discuss your own thoughts and feelings about the transfer because there may be occasions when decisions about a resident have been taken that you disagree with. You have every right to share your concerns with the care team and to have explained to you the reasons for the transfer. Having said that, however, it is important that the resident is not made to feel uncomfortable or drawn into discussions that are inappropriate.

Points to remember

The prospect of entering a care home means different things to different people. It can range from relief from everyday domestic worries to total supervision in every sphere of living. There are no hard and fast rules – only guidelines.

Every resident:

• is an individual with different needs

• has led a life that is at least as full and interesting as our own

• is right to feel strange when first coming into care

• needs privacy and the right to choose

• is a customer and should expect good service.

NVQ Level 2 Core Units
O Promote equality for all individuals.
U4 Contribute to the health, safety and security of individuals and their environment.
W2 Contribute to the ongoing support of clients and others significant to them.
W3 Support clients in transition due to their care requirements.

CHAPTER 3

Attitudes, feelings and the risk of abuse

Paul Julian Fletcher

• How your behaviour is seen • How your attitudes show • Rules ruled out • The trouble with routines • What to do about bad practice • Handling abusive situations • A framework for care • The keyworker role

L et us begin with an example: the old lady who comes to a home for a two-week stay while her family, with whom she lives, goes on holiday.

The family bring her with a packed case at 11.00am and it's a busy morning as mornings usually are. It takes a few rings of the bell before someone can get down to answer it. She is welcomed with a smile by a care assistant who shows her and the family into the hallway, and then shoots off to fetch the manager who is busy elsewhere. She looks around warily while the family try to reassure her.

The manager arrives and welcomes her, again with a big warm smile, but quickly gets into conversation with the son and daughter-in-law, reassuring them that she'll be all right, asking about her clothes, her tablets, her money and when they will be collecting her again. Our lady gets distracted by the care assistants and other residents that pass and as someone else is helped by in a wheelchair.

The manager asks her if she would like to see her room, adding that it's on the first floor but she's sure to be able to manage the lift. It's a slow walk with her walker to the bedroom and it seems a long way down great corridors and around many corners to get there.

Forty people live here, the manager mentions, and she also talks about the mealtimes, the buzzer system and the laundry arrangements as they walk along. She talks in a nice friendly way and introduces her to other care assistants and residents as they make their way. The lady catches glimpses into sitting rooms, other people's bedrooms and a bathroom with a hoist as they go.

They arrive at her room which is OK though not like a bedroom in an ordinary house. The manager leaves them for a moment while her son and daughter-in-law unpack and talk to her about the room. She mentions that she will never remember how they got there!

Everyday event

For most of us this is a familiar picture. I am sure we have all shown someone new to their room at some time. It's not an example of how not to do it either. It's just a familiar event in our work, though

	What she might have thought
The packed case	they are going without me: I must be a nuisance.
Few rings of the bell	they are not ready for me – we're too early.
The hallway	it's so strange...
Manager talking to son	I'm as much use as that suitcase...
Care assistants/other residents	so many faces, and none familiar. Do they think I'm like that?
The lift	does she think I can't press a lift button?
The long corridors	it's no use; this will never work.
Other rooms and bedrooms	it is strange... it's frightening.
The hoist	I'm frightened.
Unpacking	they will be leaving soon...

we know it's special for this lady and for her family. But let's go through that again and think what some of those events might have meant to the new lady: what could she be thinking while we would be talking and showing them around? (See table above.)

What has happened is that this lady, like all of us would do, is making sense as best she can of what she sees around her. She makes sense of it by relating it to what she has known in the past, from ideas that she has, and to how she feels at that time. She is interpreting what she sees and hears, making her own sense of it, as we do all the time.

Picking up clues

In just the same way we all interpret the attitudes of other people towards us – what we think they think about us. We interpret attitudes from what someone says, how they say it, from their "body language" (with a smile or an outstretched hand, or looking away with their back turned) and from what they actually do.

So we pick up someone's attitude towards us in many different ways from the clues we are given. The attitude can sometimes be quite clear, or it can be open to misunderstanding. Either way it can be very powerful, and quite change the meaning of something that is said.

For example, if someone says to us "Nice to see you again" it can be enthusiastic and sincere, or it can be said routinely and without much feeling, or it can be muttered while they roll their eyes up to heaven. The words are the same, but those are three quite different attitudes.

Some attitudes demonstrate positive feelings and make the day nicer for anyone, like:
- respect
- interest
- affection
- patience
- kindliness
- willingness to listen.

There are lots more. They make people feel comfortable about being with whoever they are with, wherever they are.

Other attitudes will be understood to show less kind feelings. From this we will believe that other person:
- is not interested in us
- does not like us
- thinks we are worth nothing
- has no time for us

• is unkind
• is mean
• can't be believed
• is bored
• does not want to help
• is condescending and thinks they are better than we are.

In our work our attitude towards residents is crucial – either what we mean, or what others think we mean. People we help may be frail, vulnerable and dependent. they may need our help and may need it every day that we are there. If a request is met by a negative attitude, how can they ask for help again? How crucial to self respect and dignity to feel worth something, that people do care, and that they really will help.

Actions speak louder

What we say and how we say it is vital if we are helping someone, but many small actions imply an attitude too. For instance:

• Do we knock on doors and always wait for a reply before entering?
• Do we close doors? This is crucial to self-respect and privacy, especially in bedrooms and bathrooms.
• Do we make time for people? Showing that they are worth our time?
• Are we polite and respectful – even when we are rushing to do something else?
• Do we look happy to be doing something, even when it is not our favourite task?
• Do we sit with people, or stand and "talk down" to them? Do we talk to other staff over residents' heads?
• Do we always treat old people as adults and equals? Nothing else is ever enough.

The "positive" attitudes are positive and the "negative" are negative whoever the resident may be. The most able, alert, independent and jolly person to be helped deserves no different an attitude from someone who may be disabled, confused, demanding or "unresponsive". All are adults and deserve our respect whatever the assistance they need.

Elderly people who are confused deserve special mention. Too easily attitudes can creep in which suggest that it somehow "matters a bit less" how they are helped or treated. It sounds shocking but it's true. For example, the bedroom or sitting room that is bare and unattractive; less careful attention to clothes or hair or personal possessions; undignified toileting routines; less patience; less attempt at conversation or finding out their pleasures; fewer outings; less knocking on the door before entering...

For the most confused residents there is sometimes the terrible tendency to "babify". Baby talk, baby bibs and baby nappies are strictly for babies – not for handicapped adults. There are decent adult solutions to adult disabilities.

Consider the messages that treating someone like a baby contains: you are not an adult any more; you no longer have the rights or the respect that an adult can expect; to be helpful I expect you to behave like a "good baby". The devastation of Alzheimer's disease does not need to be compounded by loss of dignity, respect and civilised behaviour by those around you.

The rot spreads

It is also worth considering two other points: what are the effects of attitudes also (i) on other people being helped, and (ii) on us, the helpers.

For other residents, it is degrading and frightening to witness a fellow resident being treated as they would not want to be treated themselves. The phrase "I hope I never get like that" also means "I hope I never get treated like that". It also encourages other residents to adopt negative attitudes towards a confused person: "Poor thing, she's no idea what she is doing".

This also serves to justify poor staff behaviour, like asking in a loud voice in a room full of other people, "Have you been to the toilet this morning? Have you wet yourself again? Come on, come with me". We can all think of more discreet, adult and respectful ways of asking, or places to ask this, once we accept that it does matter how we do it.

For us as staff or helpers there is also the danger that treating one person inappropriately can spread so that all residents being helped get similarly treated; everyone gets cared for as if they were incapable of thinking for themselves or doing anything properly. A simple but common mistake is to always speak loudly, assuming everyone over eighty is deaf. Just think how many negative attitudes this demonstrates and what its effect on people must be, even when it is well-intentioned "caring".

This is far removed from the attitudes expressed in the practice of many enlightened homes, that stress the rights, individuality, independence, personal choice, abilities and strengths, privacy and dignity of every single person, regardless of their specific disabilities.

After all, our role as helpers is only to assist residents with the things that they cannot do for themselves. We are not in the business of somehow changing people into what we think they ought to be, or doing what we think they should do. Our role is about helping to fill in the gaps in what residents or their families and friends can manage, it is not about taking over and running other people's lives.

That is why I have never had any time for the rules and regulations that some homes have dreamt up, that say what you can/can't , or must/mustn't do, or where you can or can't be at any time. These are repressive, institutionalising and unnecessary. A set of rules can be a set of negative attitudes too.

The trouble with routines

A special difficulty that we as helpers face is that so many things that are crucial to residents become routine to us. It is just normal to us to do things in the way we usually do – without checking first that that is what is wanted of us.

We cannot assume that a resident wants us to do what we think they what us to do, or what we would routinely expect to do for them. If we do, our attitudes are showing. We are giving them a message about what we think of them – or what we think they are capable of – and these are probably negative attitudes. Perhaps this is the difference between "doing to" and "doing for" the client.

If something is wrong

The attitudes of our colleagues will affect us as well. We too can be pleased, upset, amused, saddened, infuriated by the attitudes of our colleagues.

In an ideal team all the members would be sharing broadly similar positive attitudes to the work, but it does happen that one member of the team may be expressing attitudes, and demonstrating them in their work, that you feel are clearly going against the interests of residents. It might be about their behaviour to a particular resident or in a particular task.

What can you do about it? Firstly, if you are sure you are right and you really care for the people you help, you know you cannot just forget it or pretend it didn't happen. You cannot keep it to yourself and stay worried or unhappy about it;

that solves nothing. You have to do something about it; you must confront bad practice even in the face of "group pressure" from colleagues. But how?

The only answer is by talking to someone who can do something about it, although it may not be easy. Can you talk to the person who did whatever it was? If not you must talk to your supervisor or manager. Do this as quickly as possible: it can be very difficult to do anything positive about something that happened weeks before.

If you feel bad about doing this you must remind yourself of why you came into this work, of what you believe in and why. We all have a duty to safeguard the rights of residents and to maintain the professional standards of our work. If your boss will not listen to you, you must go to the boss's boss, and so on. You may feel you need support in this, and may find it helpful to enlist the help of another colleague, a friend, another "professional" you may know (nurse, GP, vicar), or a representative of a professional organisation (Social Care Association, British Association of Social Workers, Royal College of Nursing) or a Trades Union.

Large organisations these days must have grievance and complaints procedures, and all private or voluntary homes for elderly people are inspected by a Registration Officer of the Local Authority Social Services Department who can be consulted.

If you are an outsider to the organisation go straight to the manager or the director of that organisation. You may not be able to change the world, but you must satisfy yourself that what you have to say has been fairly heard by a person who is in a position to do something about it. Try and deal in facts as far as possible, not in personalities or "rumours", and find someone you can talk to for your support. You may want someone else to come along with you to speak on your behalf; that is perfectly reasonable.

Rights and abuse

There is a lot to be said for the old shop saying "the customer is always right" because somewhere in the history of institutional care this got completely lost. With it dignity and a sense of self worth got lost too, only to be replaced with powerlessness. This is no foundation on which to build a life. It may just about be justifiable in hospital as everyone understands that they go there for a limited period for treatment to be made better – "Doctor knows best"! – and so may be willing to temporarily allow someone else to make decisions for them. It has no place however in a care home. People are there to live their lives, they haven't just come for treatment.

No one has any right to make decisions about someone else's life just because they are living in a home, and no one has a right to make people do anything they do not wish to. They may suggest but they may not rule.

Perhaps this is the commonest form of abuse in homes: gradually taking over the resident's life, even with the very best of intentions. If every day someone is made to feel powerless and passive, all the personal care, or physiotherapy, or activities or medicines in the world will be worth nothing to them.

If their dignity and sense of self worth are intact though, it can make all the difference. The key to this is providing what people want, and not "what is good for them" – so the customer should always be right. Living in a home does not give anyone any fewer rights.

Living in a home people are more at risk from abuse because they come into contact with so many other people. By

The best homes stress the rights, individuality, independence, choice, strengths, privacy and dignity of every single person.

scrupulously observing residents' rights (the normal adult rights that everyone takes for granted in their own lives) we are taking the first and biggest step towards preventing abuse. Every organisation or home should have a clear "Equal Opportunities" policy that everyone understands and which actively promotes anti-discriminatory practice. After all, fairly and fully providing care and support to every resident as a unique individual is at the very heart of social and nursing care.

Abuse can come in many forms. For example, it could be verbal, physical, emotional or sexual. It may be what the carer does to the cared for (from being overbearing, to bullying, to worse...), what one resident does to another ("Get her out of this sitting room"), what a resident does to themselves (like a tragic overdose), or what an environment does to that person (like squalid surroundings, no personal possessions, or none of the aids that person needs).

In all probability one residential worker alone cannot deal with these situations. An earlier section of this chapter

("If something is wrong") suggests how to involve important people who can help.

Handling abusive situations

There are times though when the residential worker on duty will have difficult situations to deal with. Say, when one person takes a crack at another with a good swing of the walking stick. You must stay calm and even in the heat of the incident treat people as adults. Diverting the protagonists and deflecting them from their outburst is often a good first course.

Then perhaps a chance to think through just what triggered this – to know that, is to know how it can be prevented. Physical, psychological and environmental reasons should all be considered. For example pain, being bullied or a change in routine could be causes. It needs to be accurately reported so that others can be watchful, but also because incidents may form a pattern that helps us understand them. But like all personal information this must be factual and held in the strictest professional confidence.

The things not to do are to tell people

off, apportion blame or invent punishments and penalties. These are entirely unacceptable. Effective communication means helping someone to understand the effect of their actions on others. Minimising abuse means thinking of all the steps that can be taken to try to prevent this happening again. And no one should imagine for one moment that they have the right to be judge and jury.

No one feels good after an incident like this, and the more serious the incident the greater the trauma it will cause. This will affect the person who has suffered the abuse of course, but it will certainly affect the abuser and the member of staff who was immediately involved. Other residents who may not even have been present but who get to hear of the incident may be anxious and worried when they do. The only way out of this is to talk it through with the right people, in the right place and at the right time. This means involving senior staff right away to decide how and when this should be done.

A framework for care

In this chapter we have looked at a number of pitfalls. I hope that nevertheless my own attitude to residential work is clear. As someone who has worked as a care assistant, assistant officer in charge, deputy officer in charge, officer in charge and as a manager of a group of local authority homes for the elderly, I can say that I have a great respect and admiration for the many people I know who are engaged in it at every level, and a true belief in the positive opportunities it provides for the people who choose to join a comfortable, stable and unrestricted community, where they can find the services and companionship they seek without being diminished as individuals.

Attitudes and feelings however do not exist in a vacuum, and for the best service to residents they need to be harnessed together in a "framework of practice" where every helper is clear about their role and the overall aims of the establishment. If we are trying to establish a professional framework, here are fourteen key features of it that I would list first. None is imaginary; each is well developed in one of the homes I know well, and all are in everyday practice in a few excellent establishments. Compare the home you work in with these:

1. Planned **admission procedures** built around each new resident (including relief care and day care clients) also involving their family, friends and community services that have helped them. The thing to think about is how that person is going to transfer their lifestyle, and all the things that they enjoy, to this new setting, and what new opportunities can be added too.

2. A **care plan** for each resident. This is a description of what the resident wants from the home to help them lead the life they would like to have, and how the home is going to provide this. Some people will need more help with this than others. It is all about that person's wishes and how these will be met. It is not a prescription of what other people think that person should have or the life they think that person should lead in the home. It goes without saying therefore that the resident is involved every step of the way, that they have a copy when it is written up, and no one else gets a copy without their say so. It is their life and they must have control over it.

3. **Annual reviews and meetings** – with the resident and perhaps family/friends: a friendly but "formal" annual meeting with staff of the home to discuss just how far the services provided meet the wishes of the resident.

4. **Home as "home".** This is about power. It is a rejection of all the old ideas about "rules" and do's and don'ts, and is seen in returning decision-making to the resident. This is observable in the ways residents use their rooms, what they bring with them, flexibility in meal times/bedtimes/bath times, how residents and their families come and go about their own lives and have their own unique lifestyles within the home with our support. Residents' meetings are also a part of this.

5. **Programmes of social events.** Although some residents will choose to avoid these, as they are free to do, for others they provide stimulation, entertainment and fun. They can also foster a feeling of belonging, a sense of community and something to look forward to. The contribution of voluntary organisations or individual volunteers can be invaluable in this. Without these diversions life in a home can be boring and empty, unstimulating and uninteresting.

6. A clear **delegation of duties amongst staff** – real responsibilities allowing for real satisfaction and opportunities for creative working.

7. **The key worker role** to offer individual support to each client, balanced with the wider care assistant role (the shared team responsibilities).

8. Regular, well established, personal **supervision** for each member of staff.

9. Properly planned **induction programmes** and probationary interviews for each member of staff, introducing them to their individual and team responsibilities. Ongoing staff development courses, to continue this process. **National Vocational Qualifications** (see chapter 27) can meet needs not only for training but personal supervision and staff appraisal as well.

10. **Annual staff appraisals.** A discussion sheet prepared by the care assistant and their supervisor provides the basis for this annual review of their work by the manager; a chance to thank and congratulate staff on all their good work and to help work on areas of weakness. Similar systems are just as necessary for senior staff.

11. **Communicating and recording.** How best to use staff meetings, co-ordinating work "as a team", the value of written records, and making the best use of them. Regular senior staff meetings are essential too.

12. In an attempt to bring all these together in the form of a policy for the establishment, homes are increasingly writing **Home Policies** to define clearly just what it is they are aiming to achieve, and how they intend to set about it. These must be written in a sensitive and straightforward way so they are easy to read and meaningful to residents and visitors. They should be freely available and everyone should be given a copy, along with the complaints procedure, when they first move in.

13. **Annual Establishment Reviews.** A cycle of meetings brings together discussions with residents' families and friends, fellow "professionals" (doctors, nurses, occupational therapists, physiotherapists, social workers etc), volunteers and staff.

14. Many homes are involved in **Quality Assurance** programmes to standardise and improve the quality of care.

NVQ Level 2 Core Units
O Promote equality for all individuals.
Z1 Contribute to the protection of individuals from abuse.
W2 Contribute to the ongoing support of clients and others significant to them.
W3 Support clients in transition due to their care requirements.
Level 3 Core
Z3 Contribute to the management of aggressive and abusive behaviour.

CHAPTER 4

Homes are for individuals

Brenda Hooper

• Equal rights as adult individuals • Independence and precious choice • Balancing rights and risk • Emotional needs • Self-esteem • Culture and prejudice • Privacy and personal space • Confidentiality • Routines and habits • Mealtimes

How do you see a new resident who has just been admitted to the home in which you work? As she walks or is wheeled through the door on her first day, what are her thoughts about herself? Does the daughter accompanying the old lady already view her differently now she is about to become one of a group of "residents" and not just her mother?

Sadly, it is all too possible that the resident and her relatives will have been conditioned to think that on entering a home not only will her life be completely changed but that she will no longer have the individual rights and freedom of choice which she has previously taken for granted. She will no longer be her own person. What is your view?

Will you, as a care assistant, treat the resident differently from an old person you might find next to you in the supermarket queue? Of course, the person is in the home because she needs personal care of some sort, and it is your job to give this help. But if you behave towards her differently from the way you would act towards an old person outside the home, you may be "discriminating"

against her just because she is in a home.

If, on the other hand, you get to know her as an individual and try to understand whatever she wants you to know of her background and previous lifestyle, you will build up a relationship of mutual respect. You will then be able to give her the care she needs without diminishing or belittling her.

Equal rights

It is all too easy unwittingly to categorise residents, and as a result to discriminate against them. How often, if someone is in a wheelchair, but mentally alert, is she spoken about instead of to, as if she were incapable of speaking for herself?

Residents who are deaf, or with a poor memory, or who have messy eating habits, or who have difficulty communicating, or who look different, have as much right as "easier" or more attractive residents to be approached with sensitivity and respect. Otherwise they are being stigmatised and treated differently just because of some particular characteristic.

The background and interests of some residents may be very different from your own. Staff who are working hard to provide stimulation and activities for residents may subconsciously resent the fact that a particular person has solitary tastes and chooses to spend much time in her own room rather than take part in, for example, bingo sessions. Subtle pressure to conform, however kindly meant, cannot be justified.

Don't patronise

Everyone has a right to be treated with dignity as an independent adult. Just because someone needs help with certain tasks of daily living this is not a reason for presuming to treat them like a child. "That's a good girl" is an insulting way to speak to an elderly person, even if she is more than a little confused from time to time. To have a friendly approach and manner is of course a good thing, but you should beware of letting this degenerate into a patronising over-familiarity.

In most homes the use of first names among both staff and residents is common practice, but some older people will not have been used to being addressed by their first names by younger people. Each member of staff should therefore wait for a personal invitation to abandon using "Mr" or "Mrs". The aim must be to establish in the home relationships of mutual respect. (A good head of home will be as concerned to deal with incidents of residents treating members of staff rudely or inappropriately as he or she will be to ensure that staff always speak and act towards residents in a proper manner).

Precious choice

Becoming a resident in an old people's home is usually one of the most significant milestones in that person's life. It marks a huge decision; to give up her own home – perhaps the house in which she has lived for sixty years or more – and to begin living in a house which is home for possibly also twenty or thirty other elderly people.

The freedom we all have to live our life in the way we choose, and just to "be ourselves" is very precious to us. Must this freedom be a thing of the past for the elderly person who comes to live in a home? You might think so, to hear what some well-meaning people say.

They talk in terms of residents "being looked after", of being "cared for", of having no responsibility, or never being alone – or lonely – again. Small wonder, then, if the new resident feels as if everything that made up her old life has now finished, and everything about her new life will be decided for her. So, questions asked about life in the home, are very frequently phrased in terms of "Will I be able to...?" or "Will she be allowed to...?" or even "What is the rule about...?"

It's their life

It is vitally important, therefore, that as soon as a resident comes in, and even before, everyone concerned tries to reinforce the idea that as far as possible, the aim will be to enable her to continue to live her life in the way she chooses, but with the positive addition of the particular forms of help that she as an individual needs, whether this be help with washing and dressing, assistance with mobility or with maintaining continence or with preparation of meals.

Encouraging choice

Think about the number of choices we all make during the course of a day. What time to get up, whether to bath or shower, what clothes to put on, what to have for breakfast, whom to talk to during our tea break, whether to drink tea or coffee, to eat a biscuit or not, which newspapers or magazines to read, which TV channel to watch, how to spend our spare time and with whom... We could go on and on, there are so many different opportunities for choice. We take them all for granted.

It is a useful exercise to make a list of all the choices you can think of that you make every day. Then go through the list, ticking off those that residents also are able to make for themselves. Now think about those you have not ticked, and ask yourself why residents don't make these choices. Is it that they won't choose, or that they are not allowed or encouraged to do so?

Do staff help residents get up or go to bed, or have a bath at times that suit the work routine? Is there very little real menu choice available? Has anyone ever taken the trouble to find out what are residents' favourite meals? Did someone once ask the person if they wanted tea or coffee and then assume that they would always want the same? One lady, in her own home, regularly ate Weetabix for breakfast. However, it was not on offer in the home, and no one asked her what she normally had. As she was a rather timid person, she uncomplainingly ate the cereal that was on offer.

Many residents feel that they do not want to put staff to any trouble, and so it can be quite hard to find out what they would really like. Talking with a relative may help, or if there is no near relative, it may be a good idea to try and find someone who would act as an "advocate" for the resident. That is someone independent who will act for the person, and speak for them to ensure that their wishes are made known. This will be particularly necessary for people who because of mental incapacity may not be able to speak for themselves.

For most residents, a variety of methods can be used, including residents' meet-ings or committees, to ensure that they have a full say in decisions that affect them.

Balancing rights and risk

Sometimes of course, one person's choice may conflict with other people's rights or wishes. An elderly person in the home has the right to choose to smoke, but other residents have the right to be protected against fire risk (see chapter 11).

A resident may choose not to bath regularly, and her bodily odour may offend other residents. This situation requires care staff to find a way round the problem which will be acceptable to all concerned. Offering help at a chosen time of day or night, encouragement to use attractive toiletries or new underwear, or helping with an all over wash instead of a bath or shower may be possible answers.

How far does a resident with diabetes have the right to choose to eat the "wrong" foods? Should a frail resident be allowed to go out for a walk on a bitterly cold day, especially if she is inadequately clothed? These are examples of the everyday decisions you will be called upon to make.

If elderly people with failing eyesight and shaky hands choose to help with washing and drying dishes some breakages are inevitable. The importance to the person, however, of feeling wanted and useful, may far outweigh the disadvantage of the cost of replacement dishes!

There may be a genuine fear of danger to the elderly person or to someone else. Proper precautions need to be taken and appropriate provision made, for example by making available attractive diabetic foods, by removing obvious sources of danger, by having equipment at the right height, by installing non-slip surfaces etc.

Tackling this sort of problem is part of

what being a care worker is all about. But solutions must never depend on ignoring a resident's right to choose and to be treated with respect. It is essential that residents have real opportunities to continue to make their own choices about the way they want to spend their time and otherwise live their lives.

Situations will occur where there is conflict between the care assistant's professional responsibility and the resident's rights, and you may be fearful about the consequences. Staff have a right to receive good training and support. If an accident or illness does unfortunately occur as a result of a resident's own chosen action, then provided staff have acted in a responsible manner and followed relevant guidelines, they should not be held to blame. There are no easy answers, but you must always remember that you are caring for the person in what is their home, and that they do have the right to control their own lives.

Independence

All residents should be enabled and encouraged to remain as self-sufficient as possible, even if they can only do small things for themselves. This can be a means of helping them come to terms with the humiliation and embarrassment they may feel, especially if they need help with personal bodily functions.

Staff are sometimes heard to say that a particular resident has become more frail, and now needs "total" care. What does this mean? Someone who is completely paralysed and in a coma may need total care. But the most frail elderly person will be able to do some things for herself, whether it be, for example, choosing which dress she wants to put on, turning over the pages of a book of pictures, straightening the cover on her bed after it has been made for her, taking a cake from an offered plate of cakes.

The approach needs to be to look for things that a person can do, and to build any necessary help around her capabilities rather than concentrating exclusively on her disabilities. Assessment always needs to be on an individual basis, and it is unhelpful to fit residents into broad categories of "independent" or "needing full care".

If a resident is unable to wash herself all over but can manage to wash her hands and face provided the soap and flannel are handed to her, encouraging her to do this makes an important contribution to her dignity and self worth. The fact that it would be quicker for the care assistant to do the task for her is quite beside the point.

If someone is too shaky to pour a cup of tea out for herself, but is able to put the sugar in the cup and stir the tea (even if some goes in the saucer!) then it is important that she is encouraged (not just allowed) to do so. In other words, it is as important not to do for someone what they are able to do for themselves, as it is to help someone with a task that is clearly beyond them.

Emotional needs

Of course, residents in a home will, like any cross section of people, include those who will decide not to exert themselves at all when "the staff are paid to do it for me", as well as those who will struggle indefinitely before asking for help. But getting to know the residents as individuals and adjusting one's intervention accordingly, is part of what the professional task of working in a residential or nursing home is all about.

Fundamental to this is understanding something about the resident's background and emotional needs which are a part and parcel of her behaviour and atti-

Don't generalise: each older person is a unique individual.

tudes towards staff. For every resident is an individual, and has a right to be treated as such.

Indeed one of the satisfactions of working in a residential home can lie in establishing real relationships with a number of elderly people who are all different and who have a wealth of experience of life by which staff and fellow residents can be enriched.

Individuality and self-esteem

The danger is to try and make everyone fit into the same "mould", and so lose out on the potential of the variety among the residents. Encouraging residents to talk about some of their past life experiences may help them establish themselves as individuals in the group, as well as being very illuminating for the staff whose own experiences may be so different.

Each of us needs to be valued as an individual. The beliefs and practices that are important to us personally may be very different from those that are valued by our neighbour. Staff who make it evident that they accept and respect a resident's particular beliefs and values, can contribute to that resident's self esteem.

This can be done through apparently trivial matters such as a going to bed ritual (the warm drink, a special order for undressing and washing), different clothes for Sundays, reading a particular newspaper, Saturday night being a night for entertainment. More fundamental beliefs and customs relate to religious worship, and practices surrounding terminal illness or after someone has died. By making it possible for residents to continue to follow established patterns of behaviour in these matters, staff can help to preserve each person's own identity.

Culture and prejudice

People whose cultural background is different from our own have an equal right and need with us, to be valued as individuals. Staff may have to remind themelves that cultural background is a very significant part of a person's self esteem and sense of individuality.

It is important, then, to encourage them to continue with habits and preferences that are important to them. Learning about particular ways in which the customs and perceptions of other cultures differ from our own can help. The residents themselves, if they can be encouraged to talk about their background experiences, will be a natural source of such information (see also chapter 5).

We need to be aware that we are almost bound to have unconscious prejudices derived from our own upbringing and must therefore actively guard against stereotyping, whether on grounds of religion, skin colour, habits, dress, age, sex or anything else. Try to examine the patterns of events and activities that have become standard practice in the home in which you work, and decide for yourself to what extent these are determined by the expectations and background of staff rather than residents. We can often ignore the prejudice behind familiar behaviour just because it is familiar.

Privacy

For most of us, only a very small part of our lives is open to being observed by other people. We mix with others at work, out shopping, at church or club, in the doctor's waiting room or on social occasions. The people we meet are many and various, but usually it is we who decide how much they know about us. And when we arrive home from work, how thankfully we shut our own front door. We can then just be ourselves, and totally relax, either on our own or with our close family. When we do have visitors to our home, we ourselves decide which parts of the house we let them see, and which we keep private.

These freedoms are largely denied to residents in homes. Another useful exercise is to note what proportion of the day a resident can choose whether they want to be alone or with other people.

The transition from living on one's own or with just one or two people, to living in a building where there are maybe twenty, thirty or more other residents and as many staff, coming and going, can be very difficult. It can mean having to carry out many of the activities of daily living effectively in public. Other people necessarily invade residents' privacy even in the bedroom and the bathroom.

For a very "private" sort of person, the thought of eating her meals regularly in a large dining room, and of having to share a table with strangers, can be quite terrifying. Knowing that everyone in a large lounge is watching and listening when one's visitors arrive, or when the doctor calls, may be another source of embarrassment for some. For many elderly people, the most feared aspect of residential care may be the prospect of someone seeing them undressed while helping them to have a bath.

The communal aspect of a residential home can of course be very stimulating to some people and the fact that there is always someone around to talk to may be very attractive to others. But it is essential that staff recognise the need to preserve residents' rights to privacy at all costs.

Personal space

The majority of residents will have their own rooms. For someone living in a community, this, their only "private" space becomes all important. Even a small room, or even a part of a shared room, can be personalised by pictures, photographs, ornaments.

If there is not room for a lot of furniture, one favourite armchair, and a shabby but well-loved cushion, can make the room feel immediately more like home. Having a second comfortable chair can encourage the resident to think of her room as a place where she can entertain a friend, whether someone from inside the home or from outside. To rearrange furniture so that the room can truly be used as a bedsitting room, that is somewhere to live as well as just somewhere to sleep, may also make a lot of difference.

Above all, the resident must be able to feel that it is her own room and that her privacy in it will at all times be respected. A very timid resident suffered agonies during her first few days in a home, since she had not realised that she could slip the catch on the inside of her door to ensure that no one would walk in unexpectedly, while she was undressing. Every resident should have the confidence of knowing that she can secure the door from inside (a master key will always be available in a case of emergency), and that in any case, no one will enter her room without knocking and waiting for an invitation to come in!

Of course some residents are deaf, and will want to give permission to known people to come straight in. But to deny all residents privacy in their rooms because some are deaf is unacceptable. Each resident should be provided with a key for her room and not made to feel a nuisance if she decides to use it – or if she sometimes loses it!

Staff who clean residents' rooms have a particular part to play in ensuring that rooms are regarded as private, by respecting residents' patterns of life when choosing times of day for cleaning. Staff have their own work to get through, but to make a mutual agreement with a resident about a convenient time for the room to be cleaned is to treat that resident with equality and as an individual.

An interest in and respect for the resident's possessions, shown by the person doing her cleaning or washing can do much to affirm the resident's worth as an individual.

In one home, several different colours were available in the bed linen used. A particular resident had a great dislike of the colour yellow. She never failed to express her appreciation of the fact that a new member of staff had discovered this and subsequently ensured that when she was on duty the lady's bed was never made up with yellow sheets. A very small thing, but a recognition to that lady that she mattered as an individual, and that she was not just "one of the residents".

Confidentiality

Confidentiality in handling personal information about residents is essential. You will inevitably learn a great deal about the elderly people for whom you care, and it is vital that this information is handled sensitively and professionally. You may know that a resident has just been diagnosed as having cancer. Someone outside the home, aware that the resident is unwell, asks after her. If you pass on the diagnosis, you have no control over further gossiping, and a relative who heard the news this way would rightly feel that confidentiality had been breached.

Family relationships can be very complicated, and you probably know only part of the story. You may feel very aggrieved on behalf of a resident whom you consider is being neglected by her son, but you have no right to pass on comments or information about visits or lack of them to any other person.

Of course there is a need for information about residents, often of a very personal nature, to be shared between care staff, either at verbal handovers, or in written report form. It is vital though that care should be taken to record factual information, and not opinions which may be coloured by personal likes or dislikes, or by the frustrations of a trying shift. It is good practice regularly to review the purpose of information sharing and to ensure that continuity of high quality care is the objective. It is all too easy for handover meetings to become cosy gossip exchanging sessions.

Information about residents of a confidential nature should never be passed on to other residents or their visitors, and should never be discussed outside the home. The village shop or pub should not be a place where a relative can overhear her mother being discussed. If you are on a college course, case studies may form part of your discussions. Here too you should be aware of the issue of confidentiality. Your tutors will be able to guide you.

Dilemmas

Sometimes a care assistant will be faced with a conflict. A resident may pass on some information "in confidence". For example that she is keeping a large amount of money under her mattress, because she doesn't trust banks; or that she has a lump in her breast but doesn't want to tell the doctor or her daughter; or that another member of staff is abusing her. All these are clearly extremely serious situations about which action has to be taken.

Sometimes the dilemma can be forestalled when a resident is obviously about to talk to you confidentially, by your making it clear that it may be something you will have to pass on to your manager. What you must not do is promise to keep a confidence and then break that promise. If you feel that you have a duty

to pass the information on, you should always tell the resident what you are going to do.

Living to the full

Residential and nursing homes should not be places where people are waiting to die! They should be places where people are enabled to live their lives to the full despite the limitations which frailty or weakness may place upon them. And this is the rewarding role that staff can play – to encourage and make possible a positive approach to life.

Staff can sometimes get so anxious about caring for the residents and about protecting them from potentially risky activities that they are in danger of making it almost impossible for the elderly people to keep hold of the very things that for them make life worth living.

Home from home

A "home" can never be exactly the same as the resident's own previous home. But it can become, for an individual, "my home". An old lady, who had been most reluctant to enter the home in which she had been a resident for several months, had to be admitted to hospital after a heart attack.

After her return to the home, she recounted that while she was recovering in hospital, she found herself "longing to go home", and added that before she became a resident, she would never have imagined that she would "ever say that about this sort of place". It was clearly not just a natural reaction to being in hospital. She genuinely felt that this was her home.

What is it that will make "a home" into "my home" for an individual elderly person? Much will depend on the extent to which the principles which we have already discussed are put into practice. It is likely to be achieved

• if the staff ensure that the resident's needs for assistance are met, but also that she is encouraged and supported in continuing to do for herself everything that she is able to do

• if each resident is accorded dignity as an independent adult person, and if the relationships staff have with her are characterised by friendly respect and equality; if her right to privacy as and when she chooses, is ungrudgingly preserved

• if she is treated always as an autonomous individual, with the right to choose for herself how to live her life, subject only to the inevitable constraints of living within a community

• if she is given every opportunity to lead as fulfilling a life as possible and encouraged to be outward rather than inward looking.

Routines and habits

Getting up and going to bed can be crucial times in the life of a home. People tend to have very individual and sometimes very firmly set habits relating to these activities. Fortunately these different preferences can be more easily accommodated than some other aspects of daily life in the home. A flexible breakfast time together with the opportunity and encouragement to get one's own breakfast for all those able to do so, ought to be able to be achieved in most homes.

Few elderly people want more than a simple breakfast, which makes it quite possible to cater, for example, for the one man in a particular home who likes his bacon and eggs every morning. It seems hard to ask someone who has had a cooked breakfast for the last eighty odd years to change his habits at the age of ninety-one because he has come to live in an old people's home.

Certainly there ought to be no restrictions at all about times of rising or of going to bed. The fact that there are staff on duty 24 hours a day ought to make this not a problem, but it will only happen if routines of staff work are considered to be secondary to residents' chosen ways of organising their lives and not the other way round.

The significance of this is seen in the way staff give help to residents with bathing – a task with which most residents will need some assistance. Privacy and dignity can be maintained by keeping doors shut; by the same care assistant being involved regularly whenever possible; by staff not talking to one another over the resident's head if it is necessary for more than one to be present. Giving only what assistance is actually needed – and for some this will just be seeing them safely in and out of the bath – and encouraging them to do the rest for themselves in privacy will be a valuable contribution to maintaining their independence.

Respecting personal preferences as to how often to have a bath and whether to take it in the morning or just before going to bed demonstrates a recognition of that person as a unique individual. Of course, demands upon staff time may determine how far resident choice can be completely catered for, in relation to those who need help with bathing as well as with getting up or going to bed, but a "negotiation" between resident and staff on the arrangements implies a healthy mutual respect.

It is good, too, to see bath time not just as a chore, but as a perfect opportunity for getting to know one another, which often comes more easily in the intimate setting of the bathroom. It can also serve to reassure the resident that she matters to you as a person.

Meals and choice

Food can loom large in any residential home, and is often a focus for complaints! Sometimes, it would appear, because residents have too little otherwise to occupy their thoughts; sometimes because complaining about food may be "acceptable", whereas complaining about what are the "real" causes of discontent, (perhaps a feeling that residents' views are not being sufficiently considered in decisions about the running of the home) is thought to be too threatening.

Thus, as with a small child and its mother, complaining about food can be a weapon used by residents against staff who can take it as a personal insult to have their best efforts constantly criticised! Sometimes, therefore, criticisms need to be taken lightheartedly, or attention given to other apparently unrelated aspects of life in the home. However, food is important to most people, and it can be one of the more difficult areas in which to avoid an institutional approach. The aim should be to arrange for each resident to be able to choose, as far as is possible within the constraints of communal living, when they eat, what they eat, where they eat, and with whom they eat!

You may immediately say, that this is impossible. Perhaps the most helpful way to approach the subject is to think about your own experience in your own home. In any family, certain patterns become established about times of meals, type of food served, and the occasions when people eat together or separately. These patterns will almost certainly have been set by mutual agreement as a result of the personal preferences and commitments of different members of the family, with compromises where the choices of some members conflict with one another. This is what should be aimed at

in a residential home.

Special dietary needs will, it is hoped, certainly be catered for, but over and above this as much choice as possible should be built in to meal arrangements.

Getting to know likes and dislikes and what for an individual resident makes a "special" meal, is another way of treating someone as an individual. Birthdays are obvious times to mark with chosen meals. It is good, too, if the special days which are celebrated in families, are marked in some way. One home had a very successful Pancake party on Shrove Tuesday, complete with tossing the pancake!

Activities and outings

The whole area of activities for residents can become a very vexed one, with staff complaining that residents don't want to do anything, and residents refusing offered outings, while spending much time asleep apparently out of boredom. The issues are complex, but some guidelines could be considered.

Every resident has a right to choose whether to participate or not in any particular activity. However there will undoubtedly be some who, because of failing eyesight or arthritis, for example, are no longer able to pursue hobbies they previously enjoyed. Some of these may positively welcome the opportunity to take part in activities which are only possible because they are part of a group. Sitting down Keep Fit classes are one example. Chapter 7 gives detailed ideas for encouraging activities and outings.

As much "normality" as possible should be the aim. If an outing to the theatre is being arranged, don't assume that of course it will be the matinee. It will probably be much more of an excitement to go to the evening performance and arrive home late in the dark! It is too easy for staff to assume that they know what is good for residents instead of really asking them what they would like.

Whose home is it?

Perhaps the crucial question to ask is always "Whose home is it?" Most residents will have previously been used to running their own homes and there are many ways in which they can be involved in making decisions about the way in which the home in which they are now living is organised.

Each home will need to discover for itself the best way of finding out residents' opinions on relevant issues. Residents' meetings will be successful in some cases; in others a more individual approach will be needed.

What is important is that staff do not act as if they have the right to decide on matters which affect all residents and as if any consultation is a privilege. If each resident is truly treated with dignity and respect as an independent, adult individual, there is a very good chance that she will soon come to feel that the "Home" is her home.

Points to remember

1. Each resident is a unique individual. Don't treat a person differently just because she is old or has some particular handicap.

2. We often don't see the prejudice that lies behind familiar routines.

3. Encourage residents to make as many choices as possible for themselves. Some may need an advocate to speak for them.

4. Don't treat residents like children, or patronise them, however dependent they are.

5. Look for the things that people can do for themselves, and build your help around this.

6. Being independent may involve some risk to the resident. Your duty is to act responsibly but not to overprotect.

7. Each person needs to be valued for themselves. Find out about the different cultural backgrounds of residents, and learn to respect these.

8. Residents have a right to privacy and personal space.

9. Confidentiality is essential in dealing with information about residents.

NVQ Level 2 Core Units
O Promote equality for all individuals.
(This chapter relates to and integrates with all other units.)

CHAPTER 5

Multicultural care needs

Mansour Jumaa

• Food and diet • Practical care • Spiritual care • Dying and death
• Religious practices at death • Respect for individuals

People from Black and minority ethnic groups need the same respect, friendly and individually focused care as any other resident. They may also have special care needs which stem from their cultural or religious background. Knowledge of these areas will help you give better, more individual care – provided that you remember that everyone is different, and it would be as wrong to lump together all Muslims (for example) as the same, as to ignore their special needs altogether.

You should try to find out as much as possible about an individual's habits and preferences from them, their family and/or friends, and you may well need help from them or a representative of their community if there are language or communication problems.

I hope this chapter will raise your awareness of differences between your own beliefs, practices and expectations, and those of your residents from different cultural backgrounds. It focuses on the following areas:

- Food and diets
- Spiritual care
- Practical care
- Dying and death

Food and diet

Food and diet needs of people from other cultures are usually but not always dictated by their religious beliefs and practices.

Muslim people are not allowed to eat pork. All meat must be slaughtered according to the Halal ritual. This ritual ensures that the blood of the meat is drained. Devout Muslims may want to fast (no intake of food or drink between sunrise and sunset) during the month of Ramadan. Those who are sick are not compelled to fast. Muslims are also forbidden to eat shellfish and eels, but may eat fish that have fins and scales.

Jewish people also are not allowed to eat any pig products. They may eat only animals that have been ritually slaughtered in the Jewish tradition (Kosher). Meat and milk dishes are never allowed to be mixed within the same meal. In fact Jews will be offended if offered pig meat in any form.

Like the **Rastafarians**, many **Buddhist** people are vegetarians. Alcohol is strictly prohibited for Rastafarians, and some follow strict dietary restrictions similar to Jews. Many **Hindu** people do not eat meat and are forbidden to kill any animal, especially the cow. Hindus who are vegetarians cannot eat off a plate on which meat has previously being served.

Most **Sikh** women are vegetarians, and may also exclude egg and fish from their diet. Those (very few) who eat meat will not eat beef. So it is important to explain to a resident what a particular dish – eg "hotpot" – contains.

Ensuring that residents from different cultural backgrounds have access to appropriate diets will help to maintain the sense of cultural identity which is vital to their self-esteem.

Practical care

Knowledge will enable you to be sensitive to specific health beliefs and practices. For example, how would you, a female care worker, interpret the refusal of an **Orthodox Jew** to shake hands with you? You are a care worker and female. The explanation may be that Orthodox Jews may not have any physical contact with women in case they are currently menstruating. Even a husband and wife may not be able to pass an object directly from one to another without first putting it down.

Hindu, Sikh, and **Muslim** women are likely to have a strong preference to be seen or treated by a female care worker. Other individuals, especially elderly people, may also not allow someone of the opposite sex to see them undressed.

Afro Caribbean people have specific skin and hair care requirements, requiring hair gels and oils in order to prevent their hair becoming matted and their skin dry and sore. Many **Asian** women always cover their hair and their legs. **Sikh** men always wear turbans and these are not removed.

Washing and bathing

We all know that hygiene and cleanliness are essential in maintaining health. Yet experience suggests that many health care workers always want to impose their own principles of hygiene and cleanliness. It is crucial for effective care to accept that people from different cultural backgrounds also have different but equally valid, and sometimes better, principles of hygiene.

For example, many **Asian** people do not like to bathe because they see this as sitting in dirty water; they prefer to rinse themselves with clean water.

For religious, personal, and or moral reasons, hygiene may be neglected or actively encouraged; rituals of washing and purification may be carried out on a regular basis, as in the case of devout **Muslims**; and bathing arrangements may be private or communal. Unless you have evidence to show how these practices could be harmful, you should sensitively support them.

Spiritual care

Do not assume that all spiritual care has to be dictated by religion. Strong personal beliefs that the individual finds comforting may form the basis of their spiritual wellbeing. Nevertheless, the spiritual care needed by most people from different racial backgrounds is dictated by their religious beliefs.

Worship and prayer

Worship and prayer play a vital part in the life of religious people of all faiths. Each person will have their own specific prayer and worship needs. Devout **Muslims**, for example, will want to pray undisturbed five times a day at special prayer times from early morning to late evening.

All staff must be aware of a person's

religious requirements, and must accept that this aspect of their life is very important to their wellbeing.

Some **Sikhs** chose to "take Amrit" (a kind of confirmation) and are therefore bound to observe special rules, for example the wearing of the "Five Ks": Kesh – uncut hair; Kangha – the wooden comb; Kara – iron wrist band; Kirpan – a short sword; and Kach – short trousers/breeches. These symbols should not be disturbed nor laughed at.

Pain

Pain may be private (not visible to others) or public. Pain can also serve many purposes: social, physiological, psychological and spiritual. The spiritual aspect of pain differs among different cultural and racial groups. This means that they may respond to pain in ways we don't expect. We may, for example, assume that painkilling drugs are working, when in fact the person is uncomplaining because they feel they should have to suffer.

Dying and death

People from different racial backgrounds have religious practices which must be followed for the care of the dying and the preparation of the dead.

A dying **Muslim** resident may wish to sit or lie facing towards Mecca. He or she will also appreciate recitation of Prayers from the Holy Koran by another Muslim. Dying **Jews** may appreciate hearing special psalms, such as Psalm 23, and the special prayer (the Sherma). A dying **Sikh** may receive comfort from reciting hymns from Guru Grant Sahab, the Sikh Holybook. Similarly, hymns and readings from Bhagavad Gita, one of the Hindu Holybooks, may be a source of comfort to a devout **Hindu** who is dying. Some

may request to lie on the floor – a symbolic gesture of closeness to Mother Earth.

After death

If the resident dies, certain practices must be carried out, some of which are listed below. Through discussion with relatives staff should know how to contact a local religious leader if this is desired.

Religious practices at death

ISLAM

No part of the body must be cut out, harmed or donated to anyone else. Devout Muslims will not agree to organ transplants. Non-Muslims must NOT touch the body. Always wear disposable gloves. Do not wash the body, nor cut hair or nails. Seek more details from the qualified registered practitioner. Funeral is preferred within 24 hours. Always buried, never cremated, with the head facing Mecca.

HINDUISM

If permission was previously sought, no religious objections to organ transplantation. Non-Hindus must NOT touch the body. Do not remove jewellery, sacred threads or other religious objects. Wrap in a plain sheet without religious emblem. Relatives will wash the body. Adult Hindus are cremated. Infants and children may be buried. Funeral must take place as soon as possible.

JUDAISM

No objection in principle to organ transplant, provided no organ is removed until death is definitely established. Body to be handled as little as possible by others. Burial, preferably within 24 hours of death; only delayed for the Sabbath. Orthodox Jews are always buried.

BUDDHISM

No objection to blood transfusion or organ transplant. Ritualistic requirements almost nil. Very important that you inform a Buddhist minister or monk of the same school of Buddhism as the deceased, as soon as possible. Body should be disposed of between three to seven days. Most prefer cremation.

SIKHISM

No objections to organ transplant. Non-Sikhs are allowed to tend the body, and perform the normal last offices, if the family wishes. However, in Sikh tradition the family is responsible for all ceremonies and rites connected with death, so if they are available, consult them. Do NOT trim hair or beard. Sikhs are always cremated, except still-births and new born babies who may be buried. Cremation should take place within 24 hours.

Respect for individuals

As always, remember that every resident is an individual: delivering stereotyped care because they are from a certain culture would be as bad as ignoring their cultural needs altogether. One of the most important things to remember is that each patient will follow their religion to different degrees. Each patient will still have their own personal needs, and will have their own way of living their faith.

Your role in providing care is the same as for any other patient, with a special regard for any specific needs. You must not judge patients because of their beliefs or customs, and must always respect those beliefs and traditions.

You also need to understand that elderly people from the Black and ethnic minority groups expect a great deal of respect from the younger generations. If you bear this in mind you will be able to form an effective working relationship with them.

Points to remember

1. People from different cultural backgrounds may have special care needs, **but** don't assume that an individual will follow all the traditional customs and practices of their ethnic or cultural community.
2. Respect and don't discourage traditional beliefs and practices unless they have been proved to be harmful.
3. Be aware of how your own cultural values may prejudice you.
4. Try to work with individuals to fulfill their spiritual needs in a positive way.
5. When caring for a dying person, ensure that you are familiar with any special preparation, and cultural ceremonies, relevant to their or their family's wishes.
6. Do not be afraid to raise the awareness of other care staff who may not know what an individual has requested.

Resources
Mares, P. Henley, A. & Baxter, C. (1984) *Healthcare in a Multiracial Britain.*

Squires, A. J. (Ed) (1991) *Multicultural Health Care and Rehabilitation of Older People.*

Pami Bal. *Health Needs of a Multi-Racial Population.* £4.99. Liverpool Health Authority Community and Priority Services Unit, Sefton General Hospital, Smithdown Road, Liverpool, L15 2HE.

Collins, D. Tank, M. Basith, A. (1993) *Concise Guide to Customs of Minority Ethnic Religions.* Arena Aldershot.

NVQ Levels 2 & 3 Core Units
O Promote equality for all individuals.
U4 Contribute to the health, safety and security of individuals and their environment.
Level 2 Core Unit
W2 Contribute to the ongoing support of clients and others significant to them.
Level 2 Direct Care
Z9 Enable clients to maintain their personal hygiene and appearance.
Z10 Enable clients to eat and drink.
Z11 Enable clients to access and use toilet facilities.

CHAPTER 6

Talking and listening

Jane Maxim and Karen Bryan

*• Listening is the most important part of good communication
with elderly people • Using your eyes as well as your ears • Specific language and
speech difficulties • Speech and language therapy*

What is communication? What can make communication difficult for an older person? What can be done to make communication easier?

These questions all use the term communication. It is often said that someone is a good communicator when they can talk well and interest their listener. But there are two sides to good communication: being able to make the meaning clear **and** being able to listen and understand what is being said.

In working with elderly people it is often listening which is by far the most important part of good communication. Listening can be done well or badly: think of how annoying it can be when someone does not appear to be listening to what you are saying. To be a good listener it is important that your conversational partner can see that you are attending.

For most people, good communication is a very important part of their lives. For many elderly people it is particularly important because they have limited mobility and are restricted in their activities. For example, the frail elderly person, the person with arthritis, the person who has difficulty walking

after a stroke – talking and listening are vital ingredients in their everyday lives.

How can people be good communicators and good listeners?

Of course good communication does not mean just speaking clearly. It means using an appropriate tone of voice, making eye contact with the listener, perhaps using gesture to emphasise a particular point, perhaps altering body position to show someone that you are talking to them rather than someone else. In other words most people, including elderly people, listen with their eyes as well as their ears.

Some elderly people have hearing difficulties or cannot see very well. Communicating with them requires the same set of good communication skills but with a different emphasis.

An elderly person with hearing diffi-

> **Is the elderly person**
> • wearing cleaned glasses?
> • wearing a hearing aid in good working order?
> • wearing dentures that fit well?

culties will be much more reliant on their eyes when listening. They will only know when someone is speaking to them because that person is facing them. They may be able to lip read and so need to be able to see the person's face well, in good light. Also, they need to see normal speech to be able to lip read. This comment may seem strange but when someone is shouting they distort their normal speech. Not only is lip reading then more difficult but, if the person listening can hear something, it is more difficult to understand and it can even be painful to the ears (see chapter 23).

In much the same way the elderly person who has poor sight needs alerting to the fact that someone is talking to *them*, rather than anyone else. It often helps to call their name or to touch their arm so that they are alerted and ready to listen.

But even someone who cannot see is helped by the same good communication skills. Tone of voice becomes very important but, because they are relying on their ears, it is also important to face them so that your speech can be heard clearly.

• **Be sensitive to the different ways people speak.**

• **Be aware of how you are speaking yourself.**

• **Don't jump to hasty assumptions about people just because of the way they sound.**

Do elderly people speak and understand in a different way from younger people?

The answer to this question is, probably not. Some research has been carried

out which shows that elderly people hesitate and pause more when they speak. Elderly people themselves say that they sometimes find it difficult to remember a particular word, often a name. But everyone has this same difficulty from time to time.

Sometimes elderly people do not understand what is being said to them, but they usually have no difficulty when something is repeated. Part of this difficulty may be hearing loss, but part of it is due to psychomotor slowing. Psychomotor slowing is the slowing down of thought and the following action. Elderly people may be somewhat slower at understanding what is said to them than younger people.

One of the few changes which definitely does occur with age is a change in voice quality. In elderly men the voice often becomes higher and in elderly women it sometimes becomes lower.

Of course elderly people do have difficulty communicating at times. Illness, fatigue and anxiety all make talking and understanding more difficult for an elderly person. An elderly person with bronchitis, for example, or in pain with arthritis may find communicating more difficult temporarily.

Do people speak differently to an elderly person?

Yes, they can do. Most people adopt different tones of voice depending on who they are talking to. People may sound very different when they are speaking on the telephone.

People often speak very differently to small babies and dogs. They make their voice higher, they speak more slowly and their voice often has a different rhythm. Researchers call this "motherese" because mothers of small children use it a great deal. Some research has shown that people use the same sort of voice when talking to elderly people.

This is not a good idea. It may be very irritating to some elderly people. To make sure that you are not using motherese, make a tape recording of yourself and your colleagues when you are talking to elderly people, and then listen.

What helps good communication in a care home?

It is very easy for communication to go wrong between the care worker and resident in a home, but it is also quite easy to put it right. One of the delicate balances in looking after someone is the relationship between the resident's needs and the care worker's time and interest. Good communication needs time and a genuine interest between the people having the conversation.

It is quite easy to have low expectations about how elderly people communicate. It is also quite easy to forget that they may have a great deal to contribute to a conversation. As well as asking the elderly person how they are, encourage them to ask how you are. Ask for their opinions about the weather, politics, sport, the newspaper or television and give them yours.

This is real communication and it is quite unlike the passive communication which sometimes can happen. Real communication includes the kind of teasing and telling jokes which is natural between friends.

Most human beings like change. Change stimulates conversation. Going for a walk, meeting a new person or old friend or changing activities can all start a conversation.

What about television? Television can be an excellent activity but it needs to be watched actively. It is much better to turn on the television for a particular programme and then turn it off at the end. Television requires concentration and, if it is left on all day, it becomes just another noise. It is easier to listen to music, but make sure it is appropriate for that age group.

Language barriers

Most people have experienced difficulty in communicating while on holiday in another country. A simple task such as buying a railway ticket can become almost impossible when two people do not speak, understand, read or write the same language.

There are many people in Britain who live within communities where little or in some cases no English is spoken. In order to make communication easier:

• watch the person's facial expression and gestures as these may convey some of the meaning

• try to anticipate their needs, for example by looking around their bed and on their locker to see if anything is wrong

• speak to the person in a normal voice at a normal speed, but use short sentences and attempt to convey only the important points

• use gestures as you speak, for example "Do you want a drink?" can be accompanied by a mime of drinking

• try to find out about the person from their family or friends, who may be able to help by writing down some key words for you with a translation, and can tell you a little about the person, the way they are feeling and any particular dislikes they may have.

Communication problems

Imagine how you might feel when first coming to live in a care home: unsure about what is happening, worrying

• Communication difficulty leads to immense frustration.

• It often gains the person the label of being "difficult"

• Communication difficulty can also affect relationships with other people, including family and friends, and can lead to social isolation.

about what will happen next, perhaps feeling ill, uncomfortable, or in pain. All these factors are bound to affect the way a person communicates with others.

Some people may react by being over-cheerful and trying to convince everyone else that they are not at all worried; others may become very quiet and withdrawn; others may be abstracted and so appearing to not really know what is happening; others may be very forceful and angry, perhaps about trivial things. Therefore it is important to think about why a person may speak to you in a way that you don't expect.

Anxiety and embarrassment

Anxiety or worry can obviously cause a person to react in an unexpected way. Embarrassment can also lead to this. A previously independent person may be very embarrassed by needing help with, for example, toileting.

It is important that although *you* have become used to the home's routines, you do not forget that these can be strange or even seem degrading to some people. It is therefore important to explain what is being done and why, and to understand the reasons why someone might be unco-operative or even get angry with you.

Anger and abuse

A resident who is angry may even show this by shouting at you, possibly by verbal abuse such as swearing and especially if he or she has difficulty in talking, by trying to push you away or even throwing something towards you.

Remember to remain calm and try to understand what is happening. Often the person has been gradually becoming more frustrated, perhaps by their restricted mobility, or maybe they are really upset because their family have not yet visited. Or perhaps they have just

Coping with anger:

• accept that the person is expressing strong feelings and do not try to contradict or belittle these feelings

• give the person a chance to discuss how they are feeling and what is really upsetting them so that you can try to understand the situation

• speak calmly and gently and offer reassurance once the outburst is over

been told bad news about their medical condition.

Some residents may also have specific difficulties in communicating (described in the following sections of this chapter). It is important to consider the impact on a person of not being able to communicate normally. It will lead to:

• difficulty in expressing immediate wants, for example to go to the toilet

• difficulty in expressing feelings such as sadness, anger

• difficulty in expressing needs, for example to see a particular member of their family.

Stroke

A resident may have been admitted to the home following a recent stroke, or they may be have some disability from a stroke in the past, including communication difficulties.

Dysphasia

Stroke can damage certain areas of the brain, which causes an adult to have an acquired language disorder called dysphasia. In dysphasia the ability to understand and express meaning through words is disrupted. This may affect speech, reading and writing.

The exact effect of a stroke on speech and language will vary from one individual to another depending upon their injury, their previous education, work and experiences, their personality and their present communication needs relating to their environment.

Dysphasic adults may have non-fluent speech: they have difficulty producing sentences or even words in severe cases. For example, they might say "doctor" where "I would like to see the doctor" might be expected, or "wu" for water.

Sometimes errors are made. These may involve changing sounds – "ted" for "bed" – or use of an incorrect word –"boy" for "girl". Other dysphasic people may have fluent speech but difficulty in finding the right words. For example:

"That's a, oh a, you know, tea, tea, drink it, no *cup*".

In other cases, although speech is fluent, it is not correctly structured so that little meaning is expressed.

A person's understanding of language can also be disrupted by dysphasia but not necessarily in the same way as their expressive speech. Reading and writing are usually affected in the same way as speech, but occasionally someone is able to write down what they cannot say.

Where possible a speech and language therapist can be asked to give details of a dysphasic person's speech and language abilities and to give specific advice on the most effective ways of achieving communication. Staff and carers can also observe a dysphasic person, noting the difficulties that they are having with communication and what helps them with this.

The following general guidelines are helpful to remember when speaking to a dysphasic person:

• Slow down.

• Remove distractions (eg TV).

• Break any speech into stages. For example :

"It's getting cold, isn't it?"
"Are you cold?"
"Do you want a blanket?"

• Try to understand the person. Asking questions which only need a yes/no answer may help to give you clues. For example "Is it sore?"

• Maintain contact with the person while they struggle to speak: look towards them, look interested and wait patiently.

• Give them time to speak.

• Commiserate with them if they become upset or frustrated.

• The person is not stupid; speaking loudly and slowly does not help. Use normal voice and expression.

• Ask the person's opinion.

• Use gesture – "Would you like a cup of coffee?" – point to the coffee pot while asking.

• Speaking and understanding may be a great effort. Do not expect a dysphasic person to talk for too long, and be alert to signs of fatigue.

Dysarthria

Problems with physically producing the sounds of speech can also occur after stroke and some other diseases such as Parkinson's disease, multiple sclerosis, and motor neurone disease.

This is called dysarthria and refers to a difficulty in speech production with no problems in understanding, reading or writing (unless another physical problem, such as arthritic fingers, affects these).

The main forms of dysarthria are:

Flaccid dysarthria: Here the muscles are weak and floppy. The person may have a very quiet voice making them difficult to hear, and their speech may sound unclear.

Spastic dysarthria: Here the muscles are very stiff, making movement difficult. Speech is therefore jerky with sudden changes in loudness.

Parkinsonian dysarthria: Here the muscles are stiff and unco-ordinated. This causes the person's speech to speed up, and the speech is often difficult to hear at the end of a sentence.

A person with dysarthria can understand language fully and has no problem in thinking what to say or in formulating a response in his head, but has a physical difficulty in speaking the words because the speech muscles are not working normally.

> **Dysphasia is a language disorder which may affect understanding, speaking, reading and writing.**
>
> **Dysarthria is a speech disorder caused by poor muscle movement or poor muscle coordination.**

In some cases very little speech can be achieved, or the speech is unintelligible. However, it is often the case that people in everyday contact with a dysarthric speaker can "tune in" to their speech and understand them well. Some dysarthric people are able to use writing or a communication aid such as a pointing chart or an electronic device, to add to or replace their speech.

Confusion

Confusion arises due to alteration in a person's mental state. This alteration is often variable; the person may be disorientated in time and place (perhaps insisting that he is in another place) and may fail to recognise familiar faces or surroundings.

He or she may say a mixture of quite sensible and very odd things or take offence through failing to understand what has been said. Confusion is commonly associated with illness such as urinary tract infection, changes in medication and life events such as entering a residential home.

When communicating with a confused person, it is helpful to provide information about the here and now, to assist in orientating the person to the present. It is advisable to confine speech to the essentials that need to be understood. Understanding will be helped by clear informative speech produced in short sentences, allowing time between sentences for the meaning to be absorbed.

Repetition may be needed to clarify the meaning. Normal voice and expression should be used and it is helpful to face the listener since understanding is aided by the additional information gained from the speaker's facial expression and gestures.

Particular effort to help re-orientation

Communicating with a person suffering from dementia may be difficult, but it is important to encourage them to talk, discuss and remember.

becomes rambling and fragmented. Here is an example from an eighty-two year old lady with a two-year history of dementia, describing a picture of a busy high street. She has been widowed for twenty years:

"Two ladies, baker, somebody leading a little baby. I had a little baby. I don't see much of my husband now. She turned around and looked at me. Supermarket".

Understanding becomes gradually more difficult and there may be problems with reading and writing.

is needed when confusion recedes. The person will need to be reassured about where he is and what is happening to him. Discussion of this and daily activities and pastimes will be beneficial.

Dementia

Unfortunately, a minority of elderly people suffer from **dementia**, a condition resulting in progressive loss of memory, slowing of activity and difficulty with the tasks of everyday life (see chapter 24). Communication is also affected in dementia.

As the disease progresses, communication is affected by memory loss, and the ability to name people and objects is gradually reduced. The fluency of speech increases so that speech

In the later stages of dementia, speech reduces until the person only speaks occasional words. Some people also produce echo-speech, repeating what has been said to them. By this stage the person has severe problems with understanding and is probably only able to understand a few conversational points. Reading and writing become impossible.

It is obviously difficult to communicate with a person suffering from advanced dementia. However, the early and middle stages can last for many years, and during this time effective communication can be achieved.

There are five basic points to consider to assist communication with someone who is suffering from dementia:

1. Do not assume that any aspects of meaning which are not specified will be understood. For example, you may talk about the next meal and be very well aware that this must be breakfast because it is 7am and the elderly person is just getting up. But you must make this clear, by using the word "breakfast".

2. Be very direct – cut out any unnecessary details.

3. Keep the content direct. For example, the remark "I imagine it's rather like flying" would be very difficult for a dementia sufferer to understand.

4. Do not assume that the person remembers; he or she is likely not to, even though what you refer to may be a daily event.

5. Try to give additional facial and gestural clues to assist understanding.

Speech and language therapy

Speech and language therapists (formerly called speech therapists) provide a service to people with communication impairments or swallowing disorders. Anyone who has difficulty understanding, whose speech is not clear, or who has reading or writing problems may benefit from this service. Speech and language therapists will assess someone referred to them, give advice to staff, other carers and family and, where appropriate and possible, they will treat the problem.

Sometimes people are not referred for therapy if they have no speech, but speech and language therapists also help the speechless, sometimes by providing a communication aid for the patient. On the other hand, sometimes after a stroke, a person may be speaking quite well but have difficulties reading or writing which the therapist may also be able to help.

If you think someone has a communication problem or swallowing disorder, you can ask for them to be referred for speech and language therapy at your local hospital.

Points to remember

Being a good communicator involves much more than just hearing accurately and speaking clearly. It involves establishing a rapport with the person by making them feel that you are really listening. So:

1. Establish appropriate posture and position, such as facing someone and perhaps sitting or kneeling to be at their level.

2. Look at the person and establish eye contact.

3. Show that you are interested by listening carefully, nodding appropriately, and responding to what the person says.

4. Use a gesture such as touching their arm for reassurance, where appropriate.

5. Speak in a way that makes the person feel that what they want or are asking about is considered important.

6. Encourage people to talk about themselves, but also about more neutral topics such as the weather, or what has been happening on the news, or in their family.

7. Maintain politeness and do not invade a person's privacy. Remember that people may have different views from you on what is an appropriate topic for conversation.

NVQ Level 2 & 3 Core Units
O Promote equality for all individuals.
Z1 Contribute to the protection of individuals from abuse.
Level 3 Core Units
Z4 Promote communication with clients where there are communication difficulties.
Z8 Support clients when they are distressed.

CHAPTER 7

Interests and activities

Margaret Cheetham

• Apathy – "the enemy within" • Encouraging residents' interests
• Communication • The right to opt out • Group activities and outings
• Fund-raising and social events in the home • Everyday activities
• Education and discussions • A sense of purpose

If a home does not deliberately set out to provide opportunities – social, cultural, educational, group or individual, both inside and outside the home, the residents will quickly deteriorate mentally, and therefore physically, to a state of apathy. They may well become inward looking and find ailments, real or imaginary, to occupy their time. Their state of health takes on an unnatural significance in their lives. Apathy is the "enemy within" homes for elderly people, and we who work in these homes must continually fight against it.

All residents, whatever their state of health, need to fill their days usefully and purposefully. Some may require little or no assistance from care assistants in order to do this, but many will need encouragement and even physical help in order to carry out particular activities. Care assistants therefore need to have a good working knowledge of the residents in their care, including knowledge of their physical and mental problems.

It is very helpful also if, on admission, a resident is asked for details of her life and what hobbies and interests she has

had. The information can be attached to her file and it may be possible then or at a later stage to introduce her to another resident with the same interest, to form the basis of a new friendship. One of the main objects of organising activities is to bring people together and ease their loneliness.

Communicate

Especially in a large home, such as the one I worked in, communications are vital to the smooth running of the establishment. In the context of organising activities good communications are also essential, so that everyone knows what is going on and where. The home has a large notice board on which notices of external events as well as those within the home are pinned.

Local theatre productions, fund-raising events in the area, holiday post cards from staff and residents – all these are alongside a weekly diary of events and activities in the home. The residents have become accustomed over the years to studying the notice board each day for

Residents study this noticeboard every day.

criticisms and compliments which are handed out by the residents at these meetings, ideas are put forward for new activities and arrangements are made for parties, fund-raising events, and so on.

Opting out, or in...

It is important to point out that in every group of residents there will be a few non-participants. It is every resident's right to opt out, if she so wishes, of any organised activity without being made to feel an outcast of the community. As staff we have a duty to provide opportunities for enjoyment and creativity, and encourage residents who show any interest, however small, but certainly not put pressure on them in any way.

We have to accept, reluctantly perhaps, that there are those who wish to keep out of social activities and have no intention of doing anything whatsoever. There are others, however, who whilst saying they are loners because they do not wish to commit themselves, or through lack of confidence, can with help be drawn into a group and encouraged to join in. For example, by suggesting that they just watch an activity such as Keep Fit or singing, or make up the numbers at a card game to assist the others, they may find themselves irresistibly drawn into the group. By such devious means reticent residents may find enjoyment in pastimes that normally they would not have attempted.

Activities may be categorised in different ways – individual or group, indoor and outdoor, social and educational, physical and mental. Many activities fall into more than one of these categories. I would also suggest another way of classifying activities – into those which are organised by the staff for the residents, and those which the residents organise for themselves or which improve the

any additions or alterations. It is helpful to residents with poor sight if the notices are written in black marker pen on white paper for clarity.

Another interesting and useful way we have of keeping everyone informed of future and recent past events is by the monthly production of a newsletter. This is compiled, edited, and produced by the residents and circulated to all the residents and staff free of charge. Additional copies can be purchased to send to friends and relations. The newsletter contains detailed accounts from individual residents of all happenings and developments inside the home, as well as reports on outings in the minibus, visits to the theatre, and family affairs. In most editions there is a crossword with a prize awarded for the first correct entry.

A third way by which residents may communicate with administration, staff, and other residents, is by holding regular residents' meetings. As well as the quality of their own lives and those of their fellow residents.

The following activities are organised in the home, some weekly, some at less frequent intervals, but regularly:

Keep Fit

As well as being a popular group activity this also is beneficial to health. Residents who suffer from conditions such as arthritis, and come to Keep Fit, tend to complain less than those who do not take any kind of regular exercise. They maintain that the exercise helps to reduce joint stiffness, keeps them mobile, improves circulation, and gives them a feeling of wellbeing. These sessions are combined with techniques in relaxation which help reduce tension and stress.

Occasionally other physical activities are incorporated into the more formal Keep Fit. There can be a great deal of movement involved in the throwing and catching of a large ball or bean bag, or kicking a football round a group. Keep Fit is very enjoyable, especially when the exercises are performed in time to music with a group leader who has the necessary enthusiasm and personality to encourage those taking part.

There are other pastimes which are physically beneficial to residents as well as giving pleasure and companionship. Snooker, darts, indoor and outdoor bowls, putting and croquet, are all games which improve fitness while socialising. Our garden is very large and residents who lack confidence to go further afield enjoy walking in the grounds with staff on fine days.

Handicrafts

Weekly handicraft sessions are run by an outside volunteer and are very popular.

Residents bring their own knitting, sewing, or whatever they are working on, or if there is a fund-raising event coming up they work together as a team to make items to sell on their stall. These afternoons are as popular for the social opportunity they provide as they are useful. A tea trolley is provided midway through the afternoon from which the residents serve each other.

Fund-raising

Each year there are at least three fund-raising events for the residents' Amenities Fund which provides the "extras" for the residents – large print books for the library, garden furniture, Christmas decorations etc. The residents help a great deal before and during these Coffee Mornings or Christmas Fairs or Garden Parties. They donate items for the stalls, design publicity posters, man the stalls, sell raffle tickets and encourage many of their friends and relations to attend. Normally a large number of people from the area attend, and again these events are very much a social occasion with the home as part of the wider community.

We should never forget that the home is part of the community and ought to make efforts to be involved in outside affairs, by fund-raising for example. In recent years this home has been involved in raising funds for two local churches, the hospice, and equipment for the hospital, as well as supporting efforts by individuals such as helping to fund participation by a young woman in Operation Raleigh.

Social events

Purely social events – parties – play an important part in the life of any home. They are another link with the outside world and give residents the opportunity they would otherwise miss of dressing in their best clothes and acting as hosts and hostesses to their guests. Parties are occasions when staff, residents, and outside people can socialise together and get to know each other better.

Play reading

This may appeal to some residents who can read and hear well. They can have a great deal of fun choosing and rehearsing plays. We find that the most popular plays are comedies and these are eventually performed for the rest of the residents.

Outings

There is another way of keeping in touch with the outside world. After a winter of intensive fund-raising the home was able to buy its own minibus, adapted for disabled residents by the addition of a folding step at the side and a ramp for wheelchairs at the back. Having the bus has added another dimension to the lives of the residents who now enjoy regular outings such as twice weekly shopping trips to town and on fine days trips to the countryside. These runs out of town usually include a stop at a cafe or perhaps for a picnic in the summer.

Twice a year the bus is used for taking residents away on country or seaside holidays. Outings provide residents with something new to talk about as well as a complete change of scene. Some have not been able to go out at all before coming to the home and are a little afraid of venturing into the outside world again, so frequent short trips may be necessary to restore their confidence. As well as catering for all tastes, outings should include visits to new developments and buildings in the area to help keep residents abreast of what is going on in their town.

Shopping

Even though the regular visits to town mean that a number of residents can choose what they want to buy, some housebound residents would have to depend on the choice of others for their shopping if it were not for the fact that local shops are willing to visit the home. Exercising choice, and making a decision about what to buy is something most of us take for granted; it is important that the element of choice is maintained in the lives of all residents.

Particularly around Christmas time we have found several shops prepared to come on the same afternoon with a range of their goods to put on display, to form a mini-market in one of the larger lounges. Cosmetics and toiletries, jewellery, leather goods and stationery are placed on tables all round the room to give residents plenty of choice when buying gifts for loved ones, or simply treating themselves to something.

Several clothing firms, some who specialise in clothes for elderly and/or disabled people, visit during the year with the changing seasons and show appropriate clothes for the coming season.

Education

Continuing education for residents may mean they widen their knowledge by attending activities outside the home, and they should be encouraged to keep up with their attendance of any societies or courses that they were involved in before coming to the home. For many though this will not be possible, so the provision of informal educational and cultural opportunities within the home helps to keep up existing interests and possibly develop new ones.

We offered the local University of the Third Age (U3A) branch facilities at the home for meetings some years ago, and it has been mutually beneficial to residents and members of the outside community alike. Courses held at the home have included music appreciation, painting, dressmaking, and local history.

The U3A is run by and for retired people, with tutors taken from among the membership. Any person who has a particular skill or is knowledgeable about a subject and is willing to pass on this knowledge to a small group is a "tutor". So it is that one of our residents who has always been a skilled soft toy maker is now a tutor and holds her small class in the home each week. The emphasis here as with other activities is the social side. Each afternoon session provides a good reason for coming together with people of similar interests.

Religion

Religion can play an increasingly important part in the lives of older people and each person's spiritual requirements should be accommodated as far as possible. Those who are able and who like to attend church are taken by car or minibus each Sunday.

Holy Communion is also brought to the home once a month and one of the lounges is temporarily converted to a chapel for the occasion. In addition once a month a service is taken by a local minister, and the Gideons also hold a monthly meeting in the home.

Reminiscence

Many old people have no difficulty at all in remembering the distant past, but find remembering what they did yester-day very difficult indeed. Apart from being very frustrating this can be demoralising and add to a feeling of worthlessness. Holding a small group where they are encouraged to remember the past can help them: they can contribute something worthwhile again, and others can learn from them.

In order to get a discussion started there are aids in the form of slides or photographs of days gone by, or old fashioned household objects. Care assistants, especially the younger ones, find that they can learn a lot from residents about their youth and the times they lived in.

Discussions

Initiating and sustaining a discussion is one of the hardest exercises to undertake, but if it can be done successfully it is very rewarding. Apart from reminiscence discussions we have found it difficult, partly because residents are unwilling or unable to advance beyond their own set ideas. We have had some limited success using television programmes as a basis for discussion. Programmes which are designed especially to interest elderly people are recorded and later watched by a group of residents, who enjoy discussing what they have seen together.

Passive entertainment

Watching television occupies much of residents' time; it may be classed as passive entertainment. Passive entertainments are those in which the residents do not take an active part but nevertheless provide them with a new experience to think and talk about.

In this category of organised activity in the home, there are weekly slide shows or talks by invited speakers on different parts of the world or local familiar places. At the end of these sessions residents may take a more active part by asking questions if they wish to.

As an alternative to slide shows or talks about travel, we have invited guests who have interesting collections or who are willing to come and talk about their hobbies, for example collecting Eskimo carvings, glass ornaments, or stamps. We also invite people who have a special art or craft they can demonstrate, such as portrait painting or flower arranging.

Concerts regularly occupy an afternoon or an evening. Soloists, music ensembles, or choirs give great pleasure, and those who come to entertain in this way come from local schools, churches, and surrounding villages. We are also very fortunate in having a resident organist and a resident pianist – both of whom live close to the home and give regular concerts to our residents.

Self-starters

All the activities mentioned so far have been arranged by the home for the residents, but there are many other activities which residents have initiated or have been encouraged by staff to take up, and have then developed themselves.

Experience shows that the happiest and most fulfilled residents are those who are actively involved in the daily life of the home, which includes helping others. We all need to feel that we are of value and worth to the community and should accept responsibility for what goes on in that community. As staff we should actively encourage independence and allow some risks to be taken towards that end.

We should also promote self-help among the residents and there should be an atmosphere in the home that welcomes initiatives and offers of practical help from residents. The activities which follow are those which are carried out by

residents in the home, and they all in some way contribute towards improving the quality of life for all residents.

Daily life

We are fortunate in having a large well-stocked library containing many large print books. (We have noticed that even residents with good sight prefer to read these.) The library is completely run by two residents who check the incoming and outgoing books, and periodically present an order for new books to replace those which they have discarded. Other residents select books and take them for residents who are unable to leave their rooms.

It is residents who tend the plants which adorn every window sill and table top in the home, and also see to it that there are fresh cut flowers placed in the entrance halls and lounges.

Other residents, on receiving the next day's menu from the cook, make up the menu board for the next day and display it in the entrance hall.

In the evening the local newspaper is read to residents who are not able to see the small print, or who simply enjoy being read to. This is done each evening by two or three residents in turn. This practice incidentally can give rise to lively comment, discussion, or reminiscence.

The home has a pond with goldfish, two budgerigars, and a golden retriever bitch. These are cared for by several residents, and as is well documented pets have a therapeutic value all of their own.

The large garden needs a great deal of attention to be kept tidy. The heavy work of grass cutting, edging, and digging, is carried out by a firm of gardeners, but there is still much to be done in growing seeds in the greenhouse, planting seedlings out, and weeding, and it is the residents who undertake this kind of work. With the recent addition of raised flower beds in part of the gardens this activity has now been opened up to more residents who may be interested.

Of the more active residents there are several who help the staff in different ways by assisting frailer residents. They may accompany residents on outings or appointments, help with wheeling chairs or just walking alongside someone to give confidence, or even assist a resident to be dressed if through arthritis or as a result of a stroke this is a problem.

Some residents organise their own small parties in one of the lounges, with no staff help. They invite friends from inside and outside the home and these events give great pleasure to residents who prefer smaller numbers of people to the larger social gatherings. Two residents alternate to provide evenings of playing records each week.

One gentleman is on hand to help any resident with an electrical or any other kind of appliance which needs repairing.

One lady makes sloe gin, and although unable to go out herself, she has regular supplies of ingredients brought to her. She enjoys providing the sloe gin as presents or for fund-raising events.

All used envelopes are kept and people from outside the home bring in theirs too. The residents cut the stamps off and these are sent to local charities.

The residents have a large collection of jigsaws and leave one out in a lounge for all to complete; they then replace it with another.

Residents organise for themselves and for others afternoons of games such as Bingo, Trivial Pursuit or Bridge – games which aid memory or concentration.

The purpose of activities

All activities, whether provided by the staff of a home or by the residents themselves, are there to help residents to remain motivated and interested in life.

With better provision in the community fewer older people in the future may be compelled to leave their homes, and residential care may be a positive choice. These people, and their relatives, will look only at homes that look beyond catering for the obvious physical comforts and give to their residents the opportunity to reach their maximum potential.

Points to remember

1. Find out about each individual's interests and skills.
2. Encourage residents to be involved in every aspect of the home's life.
3. Make links with your local community.

Resources

Exercises for Older People. A Better Care Guide from Hawker Publications, 13 Park House 140 Battersea Park Road London SW11 4NB. Tel: 071 720 2108. ISBN 1 874790 20 5.

Activities for the Frail Aged, Patricia M. Cornish. Winslow Press. Catalogues with ideas for games and activities from both Winslow Press and TFH (see Useful Addresses p207).

Older Learners, edited by Susanna Johnston and Chris Philipson, published for Help the Aged Education Dept. by Bedford Square Press, 26 Bedford Square, London WC1 3HU.

Encouraging Residents' Activities (Booklet No. 4 *Home Work*), Judith Hodgkinson, and *Staying Active,* June Armstrong, both from the Centre for Policy on Ageing, 25-31 Ironmonger Row, London EC1 University of the Third Age 1 Stockwell Green London SW9 9JF. Tel: 071 737 2541.

NVQ Levels 2 & 3 Core Units

O Promote equality for all individuals
U4 Contribute to the health, safety and security or individuals and their environment.

Level 2 Core Unit

W2 Contribute to the ongoing support of clients and others significant to them.

Level 2 Direct Care

Z6 Enable clients to maintain and improve their mobility.

CHAPTER 8

Relatives and carers

June Andrews

*• All relatives, carers or friends are different • Good reasons
why their involvement is different • They will be anxious, and you can help
• Good and bad ways of communicating • Responding to complaints
• Support groups • Death in the family*

The "relative" of your latest resident may be a husband or wife, son or daughter, nephew or niece, brother or sister, granddaughter or grandson. Or the person who is closest to them might not be a family member at all.

For example, the person who comes and takes most interest might be the man who has lived with your elderly resident for the last twenty years as her lodger. He means more to her than any of her cousins, and you may have much more contact with him than them.

Or it may be that a close friend or partner has lived with the older person for many years, and cared for them with or without help from care agencies.

Whether the person closest to the resident is a relative or not, they may have lived with and cared for them, perhaps for years. You can see it will not be easy for the carer when the older person is admitted into a home. They are bound to feel a mixture of strong emotions, including:
• relief that the exhausting burden of caring is lifted
• guilt that they could no longer cope
• anxiety that no one else will be able to give the personal care they did, attending to all the little details, likes and dislikes, that are important to the individual.

If someone is admitted for respite care the same emotions and anxieties are felt. In either case it is vital that you attend carefully to everything the relative or carer wants to tell you about how the person likes things done. Don't ever assume that you, or other staff, will know best how to care for them just because it is your job.

Individuals

The important thing to remember is that every older person is different, and their relatives are different. Some residents have a close relationship with a family member or friend who cared for them; others have lived alone for many years, and may have no relatives nearby, or even any at all that are still alive.

Think about your own family. There may be some old relatives, for example an elderly aunt, that you send a card to at Christmas, but who lives too far away to visit. On the other hand, your grandma may live in the same town as you, and be visited each day by a stream of children and adults, so she actually has to get out of the house for a bit of peace and quiet. Then there may be an uncle no one has heard of for years, and you sometimes wonder if he is still alive.

Relatives and carers:

• **are all different, so their involvement will be different.**

• **may be anxious, and you can help them by anticipating their fears, welcoming questions, finding answers and giving practical information**

• **are often adjusting to a great change, and you are very important in making that possible.**

• **are expert in individualised care if they looked after the resident at home**

• **often get support from each other.**

Remember:

• **The way you tell relatives about the care of elderly residents has a powerful effect on the way they feel.**

• **Complaints can be a good thing if they are handled sensitively.**

Different relationships

The way the relatives behave towards the home and staff, and the elderly resident, depends on what their relationships have been like in the past.

• "Mum is in a home just three miles from us so we can call round in the car every day, and if the weather is nice, she comes out with us when we go to do the shopping and buys a few bits for herself. When everyone comes to our place for a party, we either fetch her along, or take the party to her, and her friends can see what a big crowd we are and join in the fun. We've almost adopted the women at her place, and they know all of us".

• "I hadn't really spoken to my aunt since I was a child, but as I am a solicitor the family looked to me to make all the arrangements about the home and other financial details. Actually, my brother who is a nurse would have been a better choice. Anyway,

they know at the home that they can write to me if there are any problems, but I don't see the point of asking to speak to her. She doesn't know me anyway."

With each of these relatives you can see what the position was before the change of coming into a home. This explains why some relatives have less contact.

Listen for their anxieties

The way people react is very different, but there are a few things you can guess.

If they have experience of what a home is like they will compare you and your surroundings with that. They may have looked at a number of places before choosing yours, so at least you know that you must have some good points.

If they find other things that trouble them, you can do a lot to make them less anxious. They may not ask you directly, but if you listen very carefully to what they say, you may be able to guess their worries.

For example, a son might say, "It's a long way to the dining room from the bedroom". You might think that he was complaining, and think that it is not his problem. You might say, "Yes, and my feet are killing me by the end of the day!"

But if you listen again you will hear that what he is really saying is, "My dad can't really walk that far in the morning. Will he be all right?" Your answer could be to explain what you do to overcome the problem of the distance, by serving breakfast in bed, or having a buffet breakfast bar where people can get breakfast at any time up till lunch, no matter how slow they are at getting going in the mornings.

You are important

You can also predict that the relatives may be anxious. They may have gone through a great deal of trouble to make this arrangement and they are anxious that nothing should go wrong. When people are anxious they behave in strange ways. Have you ever been to an interview and found yourself laughing nervously at the wrong time and dropping things? Do you remember waiting for ages to see a doctor and then coming out unable to remember what he said, and with a list of unanswered questions in your head?

You might not think, if you are working as a care assistant in a residential or nursing home, that you make other people nervous, but you should consider the possibility. You are very important to relatives. What you seem to think and feel about their elderly relative can make all the difference between them feeling good or feeling bad about the whole place.

But of course it can work either way. Either the relatives hang on to your every word, and go home and worry about all that you said, or they ignore you and ask to see the person in charge.

If you are always willing to talk, they will eventually discover that you are likely to be able to help or to find out information for them. A word from you about how the resident is doing, or a quote, can make the relative feel better.

• "Janice (she's the little care assistant, who works mornings) says that whenever Dad wakes up he asks for me, and she tells him that I'll be along at the weekend. That keeps me going now. I used to get him up myself, every day, and now he doesn't even recognise me when I sit with him."

Janice is giving the daughter the thanks for all her years of care that she will never hear now from her father himself.

What kind of questions will they ask?
Relatives will often ask the kind of questions that will be answered by this book. Other questions include general information about your residential home that you can answer yourself. Some questions that they ask will seem to have no answer.

People might ask about:
• your residential home
• the care of the elderly person
• complaints
• other things that you have to make sure are passed on.

About the home

There may be a leaflet that can be given away that will help the relatives to remember some of the information about your home. If there is not, you might be a good person to design it, as the person who does most of the personal care of the resident and therefore has a lot of contact with relatives. You know the kind of questions that can be asked.

Try to fill in this information form from memory, and then ask around to find out the extra information that you need.

NAME OF HOME
FULL POSTAL ADDRESS INCLUDING POST CODE
TELEPHONE NUMBER AND CODE
NAME OF THE PERSON IN CHARGE AND THEIR QUALIFICATIONS
LOCATION: How to get there (maps, and details of public transport might help, and approximate cost of a taxi if necessary).
VISITING: The details of restrictions (if any) or an encouragement to open visiting. Where the visits may take place: in the resident's room, or a private sitting room. Access to the gardens or patio. Whether visitors may take meals by arrangement or make tea.
PERSONAL POSSESSIONS: Can residents bring their own furniture? What security is required? What about insurance, televisions, radios etc. What can be done about labelling, storing and cleaning personal clothing? Can rooms be locked, and is there a lockable cupboard for the resident to keep their private things in?
TIMETABLES: Including details of regular

social and recreational activities and outings, times of meals and arrangements to be made for outings, eg packed lunches. Details of local church services.

OTHER: For example who provides any necessary medical cover. Where to get information about fees and pensions and other money matters is also important.

Not least, how to make a complaint.

Ways of telling

When it comes to the care of the elderly person, there are good and bad ways of communicating with relatives:

• "In the morning we get them up and wash them and toilet them. Then we feed them and toilet them again. They get three meals and a cup of tea between and we change them when they're wet. The TV is on for them to watch all the time, and we get them ready for bed after supper. The night staff are supposed to do them twice in the night to see if they are wet, or anything. Basically that's it."

• "Hello... How is who?... Wait a minute... Oh, you mean the one who came yesterday in room one?... I've just done that room. She's a bit aggressive, isn't she? Don't worry, we'll take care of that."

Why wouldn't you want to be a resident in that home? Frankly, I don't think you'd even want to work there. What is wrong?

But if you were to visit the home that has been described in this way, it might not be as bad as it sounds. You might find, in the early morning, that some residents are still in bed, some are up and some are quietly getting themselves ready for the day. Of those who need assistance, some are being helped to get washed or to eat and drink, and some are resting quietly.

The atmosphere is calm, but there is a lot of conversation, some laughter, and people listening to each other. People who need help to use the toilet are being

helped discreetly. What is the difference?

It is the same place described differently. When relatives ask about the care provided, remember that the way you tell them can influence how much confidence they have in your capacity to care. You can show in your answer that you regard each person as special. When you ring up about your elderly relative late at night it would be better to hear:

• "Hello, Janice Jones speaking. Can I help you?... You want to know about your grandmother who has just come to us. Can you hold on a minute?... Yes, I can tell you I have just been in to help her settle for the night in her room. It takes a little time to get used to a new place, as I'm sure you know, but you can be certain that we will do everything we can to make her comfortable. Can I give her a message from you...?"

Complaints

The same applies to complaints; there are good and bad ways of handling them. When relatives complain they usually want at least one of three things:

• to get an explanation and an apology
• to get some recompense
• to draw attention to the fact that they are paying attention.

Sometimes the first can be done quite easily:

"This is the third time I have visited and found that my mother does not have her dentures. What kind of place is this?"

It oils the wheels to start by saying that you are sorry that they have been upset in this way, and give an immediate explanation. For example:

– she keeps removing them because they hurt, and she is waiting for a dental appointment for some new ones;
– she keeps leaving them in the toilet when she goes to rinse them after meals,

and other residents pick them up (but you have had them marked and you are attempting to keep track of them).

You always have to tell the truth, but a good response includes the reason for the problem, and an indication of what is being done about it. This will often be enough to satisfy the person, but it is wise to let other staff know that the problem exists, especially the person in charge.

The question of recompense rests with the manager of the home, and the owners and insurers. Often people only go on to demand satisfaction if the first stage of apology and explanation is handled badly.

The third item, drawing attention to the fact that they are paying attention, is one which staff often quote to each other. "His niece was always in here going on about the food and his clothes and the way we cut his hair. Every little thing and she'd be running to the office. You can tell that she felt guilty about putting him here in the first place".

Some wise person has said that a lot of the anger expressed to staff by relatives is a result of the guilt feelings that they have. They get over their guilt by letting you know that you are being closely watched.

It is true that when you know that you have done something wrong you may take it out on someone else. It is a short step from slamming the door or shouting at the kids, to picking on a care assistant.

Unfortunately, some staff think guilt is the only explanation for dissatisfaction. Instead of examining what they do in the light of the complaint, they accuse the relative of feeling guilty, and dismiss the complaint without thinking.

Complaints are a good thing. They give you a chance to improve care. Maybe it takes someone's niece to have the courage to say that unless the cook takes a long holiday you'll all die of malnutrition. Relatives' views are valuable and their knowledge may be put to good use.

Complaints also give you the chance to justify the care that you give:
• "I understand that you don't like me calling your mother by her first name, but I have asked her on more than one occasion, and that is what she tells me she prefers."

Give people confidence when you answer their questions. This means:
• Listen very carefully to what they are saying.
• Give an answer if you can.
• Don't be afraid to say you don't know.
• Make sure that they know that you will find someone who can give an answer.
• Make sure that the person in charge knows what kind of thing the relatives are concerned about.

Involvement

Some people want to get very involved in what is happening and some keep well out of the way. How do you feel about this? You might feel that the relative who stays away has dumped the resident, and doesn't care. But that may be wrong.

• "I don't go to see mum in the home. Well, the nurses all seem to know what they are doing and I only get in the way. I feel silly just sitting there – she doesn't know me any more. Do you think I'll end up like her?"

As a care assistant you know that older people with dementia appreciate company, even if they do not seem to know who it is. You can tell the relative this, and make sure that they do not feel in the way, as you get on with your jobs.

It is easy to forget, as you do this work every day, that contact with illness or disability (especially dementia) makes many people very anxious. And they do worry about whether a disease runs in the family.

If you realise that they are possibly afraid, you can do the kind of thing that helps in an ordinary way. Let them get involved in activities, make them feel wanted, listen to what they say and make sure that they can get to talk to the person in charge if they need to. Relatives and friends can get involved in many different ways, from helping to serve teas to providing a light entertainment, for example.

• "When our Sarah got married, dad brought the video and slides to show gran at the home. Some of the other ladies showed more interest than gran did, and he goes back once a month now to show his old holiday slides and pictures of us!"

Other relatives seem to show too much interest. Always diving into drawers, turning up at awkward moments and asking questions. But if someone has been taking care of her father at home for years, it can leave a great gap when he goes into a home. She is not feeling guilty, she is feeling lonely, and a bit at a loose end.

So welcome all the attention! If you are abrupt and avoid questions, they will multiply and come back in greater force. If you answer fully and pay a lot of attention to the person asking, you may find that they are satisfied and turn their attention elsewhere.

Suggest helpful things that the person might do. The really lonely person will love it. The interfering person may back off a little, or even better, find a good channel for their energies.

Support groups

When you are going though a difficult period, it often helps to meet with and speak to someone else with the same problem. There are practical as well as emotional problems associated with moving someone into care, and the help and advice that relatives can give each other is invaluable. They may meet by chance during visiting, but sometimes they form a

SEA VIEW REST HOME FRIENDS GROUP
MEETING 7PM LAST THURSDAY OF THE MONTH
Guest Speaker, Mr Bond from the College of Nursing on the subject of
Aromatherapy and Massage
Everyone welcome

Dear Friend,
We are a group of people who are united by having a relative or friend living at Sea View Rest Home. We meet on the last Thursday of every month and have a short talk on subjects related to some of the problems of having a relative or friend in a home. The tea and conversation afterwards usually lead to the next month's topic. We often ask a member of staff to attend. We have started a car sharing scheme for visiting and are planning a bus trip in the summer. We would be delighted if you would like to come and share both troubles and laughter.
Betty Smith (Chair)

support group. Often a member of staff will get it started in the first place, but then the relatives take it over and run it themselves. They may advertise on a notice board in the home, or by a letter to each new relative (see above).

Apart from emotional support, the relatives group can do practical things to help each other and the residents. They are also a great help at the time of a death.

Death in the family

When one of your residents dies you will have a mixture of feelings to deal with. You may feel sorrow and loss, but also happy that you were able to make their last hours comfortable. You will also have to deal with the feelings of the family.

Some people may be distressed because they were not visiting at the time of death. From a practical point of view it can be difficult if the resident is ill for a long time to arrange for them to come at the right moment. The death may be sudden and unexpected, even though the person is old, so the family or friend may have the shock of a telephone call or a message, apparently out of the blue.

It is said that when an old person becomes terminally ill, and perhaps confused or unable to look after themselves,, part of their personality dies. A daughter may say, "That's not my mother talking. She must be feeling awful that we have to do so much for her and she cannot be independent." Carers will often say that it is as if they are already dead. The real person that they know and love has left, and the body left behind is just a shadow of the real person.

So when that person eventually dies, it is a second death for the family. They may say that they feel it is better that the older person is dead, or that they feel relieved, because now they can mourn, although the old person died some time before, when they became very ill.

If the relatives come to see the body before the funeral director takes over the arrangements, it helps them if you have shown respect by making the room and the body prepared. You may be asked to help the nurse wash the body and change the sheet, and you may comb and arrange their hair neatly for the last time.

With the room clean and tidy, some flowers and personal things still around, the relatives may wish to sit there alone, or with you for a few minutes, just thinking and talking about what has happened, and shedding some tears.

Helping with these last duties can be sad, but satisfying. You know you have done your best. Sometimes it is even worse if you come back after some days off and find that an old friend has gone, and there is someone else in the bed.

You can therefore understand how people may feel. They used to visit you regularly and take part in the support group. They don't just lose a relative or close friend, they may lose all the important friendships they had in the home.

This is why many homes make a point of welcoming relatives and friends back after the funeral, for as many visits as they like. The experience of bereavement is something that they can share with the support group. The other residents also may appreciate the chance to talk to them, to express their own condolences, and to continue friendships created through earlier visits.

Points to remember

As a care assistant you have a very important role to play in helping relatives and close friends cope when someone comes to live in the home where you work. The important things include:
1. Remember that everyone is different.
2. The way you describe things is very important.
3. Know what kind of questions will be asked, and how to answer them.
4. Remember how to deal with complaints.
5. Welcome involvement, and try not to judge it.

NVQ Levels 2 & 3 Core Units
O Promote equality for all individuals.
U5 Obtain, transmit and store information relating to the delivery of a care service.

Level 2 Core Units
W2 Contribute to the ongoing support of clients and others significant to them.
W3 Support clients in transition due to their care requirements.

CHAPTER 9

Mealtimes and nutrition

Sue Thomas

• Planning appetising meals • Special nutritional and fluid requirements of elderly people • Chewing and swallowing difficulties – help with feeding • Special diets

Today's Menu
Boiled chicken
or
Flaked cod in white sauce
Creamed potatoes
Boiled cauliflower
Rice pudding

You can be forgiven for feeling that this menu sounds unappetising. It lacks colour, texture or flavour. Yet it is the type of meal traditionally thought to be the ideal "geriatric diet". This chapter aims to dispel such myths and offer some practical advice on how to help your residents to a healthy diet.

Nutritional needs

The nutritional requirements of your residents will vary greatly between individuals. Nevertheless, we can make a few general observations.

Usually old people require fewer calories than younger adults, partly because the body's metabolism slows down with ageing, and partly because many old people become physically less active with advancing years. Requirements for all other nutrients, however, remain unchanged in old age. This is why elderly people benefit from a high quality diet: good food without too much "padding" from extra calories.

Fluids
Another requirement which does not alter in old age is the need for plenty of fluids. There is a danger that some old people try to cut down on drinks – through fear of incontinence, because they do not want to get up in the night or in the mistaken belief that they should cut down on fluids when taking diuretics (water tablets). Some older people may have an age-related loss of thirst sensation.

Everyone needs about one and a half litres of fluid (8-9 cups) daily – and this is especially important for elderly people living in warm centrally heated environments and during hot weather. Tea, coffee, fruit juices, milk or water should be encouraged; but a word of warning about alcohol – it actually can cause dehydration, and so is not the ideal kind of fluid.

Mealtimes
There are no strict rules about how many

meals should be eaten daily, but it would be difficult for an elderly resident to get all the nutrition he or she requires from eating only once or twice daily. Those residents with a poor appetite might benefit from five small meals daily – the extra meals made up by nourishing snacks between main meals.

Mealtimes are the highlight of the day for many of your residents and there is a lot that you can do to maintain a harmonious atmosphere in the dining room.

The residents will choose their companions at mealtimes. However, if there are one or two people with particularly offensive eating habits, a diplomatic segregation to another table might save embarrassment all round!

Try to make a note of those residents who eat slowly and serve them first to give them more time to eat. Never outface your residents with a huge plate of food; far better to give out a modest portion and then allow time to serve out seconds. Be sensitive to those with feeding difficulties and offer them a little help when you have the time. Try to ensure that food stays hot especially if people take a long time to eat.

What kind of food?

There are no special foods recommended for elderly people. However you may notice that many of your residents prefer familiar, traditional dishes to the more modern favourites such as quiches, pizzas or pasta dishes. If you are responsible for menu planning, certainly include a few "new" foods but try to give them English names. Cheese and onion flan may well be more appealing than the mysteries of Quiche Lorraine!

Another point to bear in mind is that, just as many elderly people may have impaired hearing or vision, others may have impaired taste or smell acuity, which reduces their enjoyment of food. Look out for residents who stir in three or four tea-spoons of sugar to drinks, or those who need a lot of salt, pepper or ketchup on their food, just to give it some flavour.

Rather than the bland menu described at the beginning of the chapter, your residents need meals full of flavour and aroma. A pinch of chilli powder in the savoury mince or a little curry powder added to the chicken in cream sauce might reach the most jaded taste buds.

Healthy eating?

Once in care your residents might still be choosing a less than wholesome diet. Where improvements need to be made, introduce only small changes, one at a time, waiting for each new food to be accepted or rejected before trying the next.

The generally accepted principles of healthy eating such as reduction in fat, sugar, salt and alcohol, and an increase in fibre intake need careful interpretation for your elderly residents.

Eating less saturated (animal) fats is believed to reduce the incidence of heart disease and is an essential part of healthy eating for most of the population. However, the majority of your residents are over 75 and have survived into old age despite their diet. Many will have more pressing health concerns and the main emphasis is on keeping up a healthy appetite, with minimum dietary restrictions. Reducing the fat content of their diet could even have harmful effects for the more "at risk" residents – for example – switching to skimmed milk would cut down on essential calories for underweight elderly people and reduce their vitamin A intake.

Sugar contains "empty" calories with few nutrients. A modest reduction in sugary snacks in between meals might increase your residents' appetites for the nutrient dense main meals. However, cutting down on sugar in cooking is not necessary and may reduce the enjoyment of the meal for those with loss of taste perception. Similarly, a reduction of salt in cooking would cause a loss of flavour for some of your residents, who would simply add more salt at table!

If you are caring for a resident with a high alcohol intake, concentrate on adding some nourishment to the alcohol! Encourage your resident to eat regularly and not replace meals with alcohol. Vitamin B complex tablets may be useful in combating any deficiencies caused by the drink. This approach shows understanding and still allows your resident freedom of choice.

An increase in fibre consumption will be beneficial; this is discussed further on.

At risk of malnutrition

Many old people will arrive in your home after an illness or a long period of failing to look after themselves adequately. In both circumstances their diet may well have been neglected and they could therefore be at risk of malnutrition. Signs and symptoms of poor nutrition include being underweight, low resistance to infection and slow recovery from illness.

Once in residential care, with good food and companionship, most elderly people recover their appetite and make up for their past poor nutrition. However, for a variety of reasons, some residents will continue to eat badly and may remain malnourished. It is important to identify any residents in your care who might be poorly nourished. Some of the possible risk factors to poor nutrition are listed below.

Increased nutritional requirements
Extra calories, protein and vitamins may be needed by residents convalescing from illness, surgery, fractures or pressure sores. However it is at just these times that they have little appetite and eat less than usual.

If you have a resident who seems to be eating very little:

• Keep a record of all food and drink served to the resident, noting the amount served and the plate waste. This will highlight their actual intake, and whether they require dietary supplements.

• Add extra nourishment to their meals. For example high protein soup can be made by making up packet soup with all milk or using tinned/homemade soup with one dessertspoon of milk powder whisked in. One dessertspoon of milk powder can also be whisked into a portion of milk pudding or custard.

• Offer the resident small nourishing snacks between meals. For example: finger sandwiches with tasty fillings such as ham, corned beef, egg mayonnaise, cheese and pickle or marmite; cream crackers or digestive biscuits and cheese; a small carton of fruit yogurt or fromage frais.

• Try supplementary drinks such as Complan or Build-Up available from chemist shops. These drinks can be taken hot or cold and will add extra calories, protein, vitamins and minerals to the diet. Other supplements such as Fortisip and Ensure can be prescribed in certain circumstances.

• Make a weekly or fortnightly check on their weight. The head of the home will need to inform the doctor if there is continued weight loss.

Confusion
It is common to find that new residents suffering from confusion are malnourished, simply because they have little awareness about the need to eat and may have spent weeks or months forgetting to eat or taking a badly balanced diet. This under-nutrition usually rights itself after a few weeks in residential care.

However some confused people may

continue to eat badly even in your care, either choosing a bizarre diet or eating very little. In such instances follow the advice given above for those with increased nutritional requirements. Draw your supervisor's attention to the problem because this sort of resident might benefit from a course of multivitamins from the doctor.

Drugs (medicines)

Old people are particularly at risk from nutritional problems caused by drugs. This is because they tend to need more drugs, many of which are long term. Drugs can affect nutrition in the following ways:

• Over-stimulating the appetite – which may cause obesity: for example certain drugs for psychiatric conditions or anti-anxiety drugs.

• Causing nausea and loss of appetite: for example high doses of digoxin, commonly used for heart conditions; chemotherapy drugs for cancer treatment.

• Causing malabsorption of nutrients: for example long courses of antibiotics, regular use of laxatives, long term use of anti-convulsants such as phenytoin.

Simple **care and observation** can help to prevent or minimise some of these harmful side-effects to medication:

• Always make sure that the residents take their medicines at the required times. For example, some medication must be taken with food, while other drugs should be taken between meals.

• If you notice a resident suddenly under- or over-eating, report it to your supervisor because it may be related to new medication.

• If medication regularly causes loose stools or diarrhoea, the doctor needs to be informed because this could eventually lead to malabsorption of nutrients.

Dental problems

Total lack of teeth or ill-fitting dentures can affect food choice, making the resident avoid foods such as chunks of meat or fresh fruit. Occasionally a resident may even demand pureed food because of dental problems. Ways to help include:

• Make sure that all your residents have regular dental checks. Make use of the domiciliary dental service, where local dentists will visit the home to treat residents with no additional charge for the travel.

• Encourage all residents to wear their dentures at mealtimes. Make sure that all dentures are regularly sterilised.

• Teeth problems are no excuse for requiring pureed food. Resist all such requests and encourage your residents to attempt as varied a diet as possible – helping them to soft rather than pureed foods where necessary.

Swallowing problems

Occasionally an elderly resident may experience problems with swallowing. This can be caused by a number of medical conditions including some physical obstruction in the oesophagus or the effects of a stroke. You may be able to help a resident with swallowing problems in the following ways:

• Inform your supervisor as soon as you notice a resident with swallowing difficulties. He or she may need a medical examination and a swallowing assessment from a speech and language therapist.
• If your resident has suffered from a stroke, there are ways that you can help them return to normal eating:
– make sure that the resident is sitting fully upright to eat or drink
– check that dentures are worn at mealtimes and that they fit comfortably

Meals are the highlight of the day for many residents.

– standing to feed a resident strains your back and gives them the feeling that you're in a hurry! Sit down to feed them in a position where you can maintain eye contact and communicate with each other

– offer soft food of an even moist consistency, which can be mashed with a fork

– suitable foods include mince or flaked fish in sauce (without bones); carrots, baked beans or tinned tomatoes (avoid peas and leafy vegetables). Puddings present fewer problems - smooth consistencies such as semolina, yoghurt or ice cream are all ideal

– offer small amounts of food at a time, and make sure the resident has swallowed the last mouthful before offering another

– try to maintain a calm unhurried atmosphere at mealtimes, which will encourage residents to relax and enjoy their food

– drinking may also be difficult, and a speech therapist may advise the use of commercially produced thickened drinks

– you can contact a speech and language therapist directly, without needing a doctor's referral.

Avoid boredom

Meals are the highlight of the day for many residents, but eating the same menu week in, week out, in the same surroundings can become monotonous and even the resident with the heartiest appetite

71

can tire of the cuisine. Here are some suggestions to increase residents' interest in their meals:

• If your home offers a selective menu, encourage each resident to choose for themselves, rather than staff choosing for them. This will increase the residents' pleasure in anticipating mealtimes. If your home has no selective menu, make sure there is one easily prepared alternative to the main menu, for example an omelette. This will prevent residents missing out on essential nourishment because they dislike the main dish on offer.

• Encourage them to make constructive suggestions for new recipes on the menu. Some homes have a "residents' choice" day each week where some surprising dishes are chosen!

• Make regular changes to the dining area. Different tablecloths, flowers or table decorations will make a great difference to the residents' enjoyment of their food.

• Make maximum use of events on the calendar. In addition to seasonal meals such as Christmas dinner, what about a strawberry and cream tea for Wimbledon or sausages and baked potatoes, preferably with some fireworks, for November 5th?

Nutritional deficiencies and how to prevent them

Vitamin C

Scurvy, caused by severe vitamin C deficiency, is rare nowadays. But a milder form of deficiency is common among elderly people, including those in residential care.

Vitamin C deficiency is caused chiefly by lack of citrus fruits and fruit juices in the diet and by the overcooking of vegetables, which destroys much of the vitamin. Symptoms of mild vitamin C deficiency are vague, but can include a reduced resistance to infection, poor wound healing,

general apathy and even depression.

Any one of the suggestions below included daily in a resident's diet will ensure that they take sufficient vitamin C:

• A glass of natural orange or grapefruit juice
• One glass of cold Ribena or fortified blackcurrant cordial
• One orange or two tangerines/satsumas (much easier to peel for arthritic hands).

If you are involved in either menu-planning or cooking in your home there are a few golden rules to remember which will boost the vitamin C content of meals:

• Always prepare potatoes and green vegetables just before they are cooked. If they are prepared and soaked in advance, a lot of the vitamin C is destroyed.
• Add the vegetables to a small amount of boiling water, cover and cook for as short a time as possible. If residents complain that the vegetables are "undercooked", you may have to compromise by cooking for a longer time initially and then slowly reduce their cooking times over a few weeks, gradually acclimatising the residents to more crunchy vegetables!
• Never add bicarbonate of soda to the greens because this destroys the vitamin C.
• Salads do not tend to be a popular choice among elderly residents, but many enjoy raw tomato. Served as an accompaniment to suppertime dishes such as macaroni cheese, raw tomatoes will boost their vitamin C intake. A wedge of fresh lemon served with fried fish will add both vitamin C and flavour to the meal.

Vitamin D

In the UK most of our vitamin D is obtained from the action of sunlight on the skin during the summer months, with just a little of the vitamin coming from food. Many old people who are housebound or have inadequate exposure to sunlight are at risk from vitamin D deficiency. This causes osteomalacia (adult rickets) – symptoms include muscle weakness, bone pain and an increased susceptibility to falls and fractures.

The most important way to protect your residents from vitamin D deficiency is to encourage them out into the sunshine, which is often easier said than done! Some of the suggestions listed below may prove useful:

• Serve tea in the garden on sunny summer afternoons – it might encourage even the most reluctant residents out.

• Direct sunlight is not essential for making vitamin D – a seat under the dapple of a tree will allow some ultra-violet rays to reach your residents.

• If you have residents who are unable to go into the garden, a seat on a verandah or in a shaft of sunlight by an open window would be helpful.

Dietary sources of vitamin D are useful, particularly in the winter months when body stores of vitamin D may be running low. Foods containing vitamin D include:

• Oily fish such as mackerel, herring, pilchards and sardines. These tend to be popular with older people and dishes such as sardines on toast might be a useful suppertime dish.

• Liver

• Eggs

• Evaporated milk – served with fruit or used in custards and puddings as an alternative to ordinary milk.

• Ovaltine

• Margarine – but a word of warning - not all catering packs of margarine are fortified with extra vitamin D. Check that yours is a fortified brand.

Diet alone, in the absence of sunlight, cannot provide adequate vitamin D. The Department of Health recommends that completely housebound elderly people be given vitamin D supplements, either as bi-annual injections or as a daily dose of 10mg. A simple way of achieving the latter would be to use cod liver oil capsules. However, you must be careful not to exceed the recommended dose, as high levels of vitamin D can be dangerous.

Fibre
Elderly people are particularly prone to constipation and it is usually caused by a combination of factors including insufficient fluids, side effects of medication, immobility and lack of dietary fibre.

Offer your residents plenty of fibre as food, rather than resorting to sprinkling natural bran on their breakfast cereal or porridge, because bran is fairly unpalatable and can affect the absorption of certain nutrients from the diet.

New residents must be introduced to a high fibre diet gradually, because too much fibre given to someone unused to it, can initially cause stomach pain and flatulence. They will also need to drink more fluid.

Easy ways to incorporate more fibre into the menu include:

• Regular use of wholemeal bread. Offer residents who dislike this a high fibre white bread.

• Offer a choice of higher fibre breakfast cereals such as Weetabix, porridge, shredded wheat, bran flakes.

• In cakes, biscuits and pastries, 25% wholemeal/75% white flour seems to be considered palatable by most elderly people. Fruit crumbles are delicious when made using all wholemeal flour mixed with a little brown sugar and a handful of porridge oats.

• Serve plenty of vegetables, jacket potatoes and fruit. A fruit salad, even one using some tinned and some fresh fruit, is a good way of increasing dietary fibre as well as giving extra vitamin C.

• If your residents are adventurous with

their food, try them with wholegrain rice and wholemeal pasta which will boost their fibre intake.

Special diets

New residents requiring special diets can cause consternation to cook and care staff alike. There are some basic rules to help you sort out a suitable diet for each resident:

• Find out who prescribed the diet, for what medical condition and how long ago.

• If the diet seems old, check with the doctor that it is still required.

• If the resident has no diet sheet or a very old one (more than five years old), ask the doctor to refer the resident to your local hospital or community dietitian for a reassessment of the diet.

The following guidelines might help you deal confidently with two of the most commonly prescribed diets.

Reducing diets

It is difficult for an elderly person to lose weight because, as mentioned earlier in the chapter, calorie requirements drop with ageing. Even when an elderly person follows their diet strictly, weight loss will be slow.

Points to remember when helping a resident to lose weight:

• Only encourage them to diet if there is a good reason – for example weight loss required before an operation, or because obesity hinders mobility.

• Plan short-term diets, eg 6-8 weeks, rather than placing a resident on a long-term diet, with no end in sight. This should give them far more motivation to stick to the diet.

• The diet should be gentle: replace sugar in beverages with artificial sweeters, cut out cakes, biscuits, sweets and chocolate; provide fresh fruit as an alternative to fat-

tening puddings; allow starchy foods such as bread and potato (except chips) in normal amounts. If a stricter diet is felt to be necessary, ask the doctor to refer the resident to a dietitian.

Diabetic diets

The dietary treatment of diabetes has undergone radical changes in the past fifteen years. This has caused confusion for many elderly diabetics who are used to their old, strict diets. It has also been the source of many problems for cooks and care staff.

Most elderly diabetics are controlled with a diabetic diet alone or diet plus diabetic tablets. A simple "low sugar" diet is all that is required for most of this group. If in doubt, check with the doctor.

Low sugar diet

Foods allowed freely:

Meat, fish, cheese, eggs
Vegetables and salads
Tea, coffee, Bovril, diabetic and sugar-free drinks,
Herbs, spices, pepper
Artificial sweeteners,
eg Hermesetas, Canderel.

Foods allowed in normal amounts:

Bread (preferably wholemeal)
Potatoes
Rice and pasta (preferably wholegrain)
Breakfast cereals (preferably high fibre variety)
Fresh fruit, fruit tinned in water, unsweetened fruit juices
Plain biscuits
Milk and milk puddings (using artificial sweeteners), ice cream, yogurt
Bedtime drinks,
eg cocoa, Ovaltine, Horlicks
Salt.

Foods to avoid:

Sugar and glucose
Ordinary jam and marmalade, honey
Sweets and chocolate

Sweet biscuits and cakes
Lucozade, lemonade, ordinary squash and other sweetened drinks
Fruit tinned in syrup
Condensed milk.

Diabetics who require insulin injections need a carefully controlled diet and should be advised by a dietitian. In an emergency, if you have an insulin-dependent diabetic admitted to your care, make sure that they eat regularly, give them a "sugar-free" diet and, very important, give them a snack such as a milky drink and two biscuits mid-morning, mid-afternoon and at bedtime. Contact a dietitian as soon as possible.

Gone are the days when the diabetic had to miss out on all food treats. There are even tasty biscuit and cake recipes, including birthday and Christmas cakes, available from the British Diabetic Association (address below).

Points to remember

1. Find out clients' preferences (personal and cultural) and make sure they can choose what they want to eat.
2. Consider ways of making mealtimes varied and "exciting".
3. Consider a sherry before dinner – a good appetiser.
4. Help residents on special diets to feel normal by keeping their meals similar to those of other residents.
5. Dental health is really important.
6. Work closely with the cook.
7. Giving a resident a cup of tea just the way they like it (or better still enabling them to serve themself) helps to show the resident you know about their needs. It helps them to feel valued and cared for.

Resources
British Diabetic Association, 10 Queen Anne Street, London W1M 0BD. 071 323 1531

Further reading
Eating through the 90s. A handbook for those concerned with providing meals for elderly people. Produced by the Nutrition Advisory Group for the Elderly (British Dietetic Association). From Elizabeth Haughton, Dept. Nutrition and Dietetics, Gloucestershire Royal Hospital, Great Western Road, Gloucester GL1 3NN

NVQ Level 2 & 3 Core Units
O Promote equality for all individuals
U4 Contribute to the health, safety and security of individuals and their environment.
U5 Obtain, transmit and store information relating to the delivery of a care service.

Level 2 Direct care
Z10 Enable clients to eat and drink
Z19 Enable clients to achieve physical comfort.
Z11 Enable clients to access and use toilet facilities.

CHAPTER 10

Health promotion

Judith Roberts

• What is health promotion? • What does it mean to be healthy? • What affects health – personal, social and emotional factors • How to take action

Most elderly people who live in a nursing or residential home are there because it is seen as a positive step that should enable them to enjoy a better quality of life, though they may have specific nursing or social needs.

Living in residential care should not be injurious to health: the resident's health should be promoted, maintained, and if possible improved, through good nursing and care.

Health promotion is relevant for any group of people, or individuals, whatever their age or existing condition. It applies to the residents in your establishment, their relatives and visitors, the environment and you the staff.

What is health promotion?

Health promotion is the actions taken to encourage or help people to maintain or improve their health and wellbeing. Generally with elderly residents the aims of health promotion are:

• to preserve their quality of life, by preventing illness and disability as far as possible, or to enable the person to cope with any ill health or disability as effectively as possible
• to maintain their independence and self-esteem

• to support and preserve their relationships with relatives and friends.

Being healthy

But first, what does it mean to be healthy? To describe what being "healthy" is all about is rather difficult. Like beauty, health is in the eye of the beholder; it means different things to different people.

For one person it may mean not taking medications or drugs. But does that mean that an insulin-controlled diabetic who is fit and active is unhealthy? For another person it might mean going for a jog every day. Does that mean the person who has mastered how to walk again following a stroke, is unhealthy?

Being healthy has been described in various ways, but perhaps at its simplest it means "being able to achieve one's full potential". Achieving the best possible degree of health is the foundation of a fulfilled life.

Being "healthy" is really a global description of many different, but connected factors. Depending on the individual's needs and situation, any one of the aspects of health, or all of them, could be highlighted:

Physical health is about bodily function – breathing, walking, freedom from disease or infection.

Mental health is the ability to think clearly and objectively. It has a close association with emotional and social health.

Emotional health is the ability to recognise emotions and express such emotions appropriately, eg anger, grief, joy. It also implies being able to cope with stress, and tension.

Social health concerns the ability to make and maintain positive relationships with other people.

Spiritual health is connected with the practice of personal beliefs and religion, and achieving inner peace.

Environmental health. Health is not just about the individual, but also about things affecting the collective community in which the person lives, for example housing, air pollution, sanitation.

What affects health?

Lots of things! For example: how healthy a person has been throughout their life; what illnesses or accidents they have had; how much stress they have had in their life; their income; the environment in which they live or work.

Lifestyles, of course, do not stay the same for ever, therefore nor does people's level of "health". Once achieved it is not a permanent fixture. Anyone who has been an active sportsperson, but now gets puffed walking up stairs, will appreciate the truth of this comment.

If you were asked to make a recipe for healthy living for yourself you would probably include something about what you eat and drink, maybe about how much exercise you take and perhaps how happy you feel. However your recipe would depend upon your own individual circumstances; how they combine and produce effects that interrelate and are interdependent.

This can be graphically illustrated by considering how "unwell" a person can be following the sudden death of a close and loved relative. Their depression and anger can be so profound as to affect their relationships with others. It can affect their physical health as they may well neglect their personal hygiene, diet and prescribed medications. They may drink too much or smoke too much.

Or an elderly man whose arthritis worsens and affects his level of physical ability. It prevents him walking as far as he used to. Therefore he stops going to the shops, or his local for a pint. He misses the company of others, doesn't eat as well and feels very isolated. In this case the person's physical health affects their social and emotional wellbeing.

Thus the notion of health can change depending on the person's age, their situation, whether they are female or male, their social class, their culture, and their expectations.

In addition the expectations of others in contact with that person can be very influential. For example, if it is expected that elderly people will become incontinent, one "accident" due to infection is then treated as the inevitable consequence of ageing. The person's incontinent state is then accepted passively by both the affected person and the staff.

As you can see there is more to health than perhaps at first might be thought.

Specific factors that influence the health of people living in residential care

Personal factors
• The resident's existing physical health problems and their effects – eg heart disease, diabetes. The effects of accidents and falls.
• How fit they have been in their earlier years, how fit they are now and their expectations of health in the future.
• The observation and early detection of

Encouraging residents in the activities that interest them is a vital contribution to their health and wellbeing.

possible health problems, eg in-growing toe nails, sudden weight loss, prevention of pressure sores or incontinence.

• Receiving appropriate treatment, therapy and medications.

Social factors – *for example:*

• The expectations of residents themselves. The idea of preventive medicine is still quite a new concept to some people of this generation, who have a more fatalistic attitude to ill health than younger generations: "What can you expect at my age?" "Don't bother the doctor, there is nothing they could do for me".

• The atmosphere of the establishment, and how well residents get on with one another. This will affect the resident's emotional and mental health.

• Living in residential care can be very boring, therefore a changing variety of planned activities can really help to pro-

vide a stimulating and enriching environment. Apathy is like poison. Prevent it at all costs!

• Also remember that activities are not just for groups; it is just as important to encourage each individual in the activities that interest them, and help them if necessary by providing materials and facilities.

• The amount of choice or control the resident can exercise in relation to lifestyle – eg food choice – is vital. So too is the degree of privacy and independence the resident has. Where the resident is involved in their surroundings and in their care they will be motivated to value their health.

• Visitors and regular contacts with the local community are important too – either the resident going into the community, perhaps to visit the library, or people from outside visiting the home.

• As mentioned above, the behaviour and expectations of staff in residential care can have a major effect – for bad or good.

Environmental factors

• The smoke from cigarettes (passive smoking) can be a major irritant to those people who already have breathing difficulties. If residents have been used to living in a smoke-free environment then they should still be able to exercise that right when living in residential care.

• The layout of the establishment should be conducive to social contact. It should be welcoming. It should be clean, well maintained, well lit and ventilated. Cross infection should be prevented.

• All equipment should be safe for the resident and the staff, well maintained and appropriately used.

Actions for health

How can all the factors listed above be achieved? Commonly health promotion is carried out in three main stages:

Health promotion

Here the aim is to prevent ill health arising in the first place. It is also concerned with generally improving the quality of life. It can include health education classes, health screening (eg cervical smears), adopting a healthy lifestyle – a varied balanced diet, regular exercise, supportive and active social contacts.

Harm reduction

This is the steps taken that will adjust potentially unhealthy habits to make them healthier. For example, if someone does not want to stop smoking altogether, they could at least reduce the number of cigarettes they smoke per day.

It can also include the actions to be taken if a person is already unwell to prevent their condition deteriorating and causing chronic or irreversible ill health. For example, supporting the newly diagnosed asthmatic with their treatment and medications.

Preventing infection

This can include measures to prevent infection in people who are already chronically ill or who have a long-term disability. It will include safe handwashing practices by all staff, and activities that will help to prevent pressure sores developing in vulnerable residents.

How to take action

So, using these categories, what could be done? All of the chapters in this book should give you many ideas. The comments below are just a few suggestions.

Health promotion

• Ensure that the menu choice is balanced and relevant to the needs of older people (see chapter 9). People should be able to choose food they are used to, and which fits with their cultural background

and/or beliefs. The food should be attractively served and look appetising.

• Regular health screening as appropriate, eg yearly dental checks (even if the person wears dentures); medical checkups, eg blood pressure monitoring; diabetes screening.

Of course these checks are particularly important if the resident already has a medical condition that could complicate more "minor" conditions. For example chiropody care is very important for diabetics (see chapter 15).

• Prompt reporting of potential health problems.

• Regular opportunities for exercise, so residents stay mobile and independent.

• Outings and varied activities.

Harm reduction

Avoid the effects of passive smoking. Encourage residents to change their diet if they are overweight. Help them to understand any new treatments or medications. Encourage all residents who have bad chests to be immunised against flu.

Preventing infection

Thorough handwashing is important for both staff and residents. Make sure food, clinical and body waste, is disposed of properly. Effective cleaning is important, as are safe working practices (see chapters 11 and 12).

Not so simple

We have to be careful not to be too simplistic. Our health behaviour is derived from many different influences, and just having the knowledge is not always sufficient. Therefore telling a resident to take more exercise or lose weight may not be the most effective way of altering their behaviour.

Also ensure that your message fits the situation: advising an elderly resident that smoking is bad for them and could cause their death, may be something of a hollow threat if they are now 83 and have been smoking all their lives!

Easier choices

Part of your role will be to help **make healthier choices easier choices.** For example, a newly diagnosed diabetic has been advised to lose weight to help control their condition. The reducing diet they are offered should be just as appetising as the normal meals. They should be aware of the consequences of their not dieting, and the likely positive consequences if they do diet. And make sure you offer plenty of praise and encouragement.

If you are concerned that a resident seems depressed and they spend a lot of time on their own in their bedroom, you may well wish to encourage them to join the other residents in the lounge area. Try to find a suitable negotiating point – maybe once a week, when there is a specific event occurring, rather than expecting them to join you every night.

It is much better to make the goals realistic and sensibly achievable. Be sure that both the staff and the resident are working to the same goal. The resident has got to be part of the decision making, otherwise the activity will not be successful. Good communication skills are essential, as is respect for the beliefs and preferences of each individual.

To be really effective your whole establishment should be working together: all staff, residents and visitors alike. Health promotion is for everyone and should involve everyone.

Points to remember

1. Health promotion is for clients, staff and visitors.
2. Health and wellbeing is more than just physical health.
3. Health promotion relates to all aspects of the resident's daily experience.
4. Are you a positive role model?
5. Many other professionals can offer health promotion advice.

Resources

All the other chapters of this book. Remember health is more than just physical needs!

Local health promotion units – address can normally be obtained from the telephone directory, or ask at local hospital.

Your local health centre may often carry out health promotion activities, and they may employ staff who are involved with health needs of older people.

Local branches of national charities and pressure groups (see Useful Addresses p207).

NVQ Levels 2 & 3 Core Units

O Promote equality for all individuals

U4 Contribute to the health, safety and security of individuals and their enviroment.

U5 Obtain, transmit and store information relating to the delivery of a care service.

Level 2 Core Units

W2 Contribute to the ongoing support of clients and others significant to them.

W3 Support clients in transition due to their care requirements.

Level 2 Direct Care

Z6 Enable clients to maintain and improve their mobility.

Z7 Contribute to the movement and treatment of clients to maximise their physical comfort.

Z9 Enable clients to maintain their personal hygiene and appearance.

Z10 Enable clients to eat and drink.

Z11 Enable clients to access and use toilet facilities.

Z19 Enable clients to achieve physical comfort.

CHAPTER 11

Safety and security

Karen Hynes

• The homely way • Maintaining a safe environment
• In an emergency • Choice and safety • Preventing accidents
• Security of the home • Residents' belongings • Drugs
• Locks on doors? • Civil liberties

How often do we clean and tidy our own homes, in preparation for a visit from friends or relatives? How often do they comment on how clean and tidy the house is? Very rarely; but they *would* notice if it were a mess.

The safety and security of an establishment is rather like that, because the harder we all work at it, the less noticeable it is. While everything is safe and secure people just think that it is "ordinary", but they would notice if there were a problem. We all have to work at making sure problems don't crop up, because there is always the potential for a serious accident.

The homely way?

Our own homes are often used as examples of normality in the various discussions about what is the most homely way to do things. However, there are limits. Taken too far you could end up with a bright spark saying something like "I don't have fire extinguishers in my house. They are not very normal and homely are they? Let's get rid of them." Obviously (I hope) this suggestion would not be taken up but there are sometimes discussions about subjects which are far less clear. We

all need to remember our professional obligations and our contracts.

We (as individuals) have a contract with our employers which immediately means that we have Health and Safety responsibilities as an employee. We don't have such obligations at home.

We (as a staff group) have a contract with our residents/patients to provide an agreed level of service. Our relationship with the people at home is very different.

In chapter 26 your personal responsibilities under the Health and Safety at Work Act are described. In this chapter we will be looking at some issues which may not, at first, seem to be part of your job, but you may come in contact with them. and you will need to know what is going on and why.

General safety

A safe environment needs to be adequately lit, heated and ventilated. The definition of "adequate" will be part of your registration requirements. You will also be required to make adequate provision to prevent and deal with any emergencies. We have already mentioned fire extinguishers, but you should also have first aid equipment in the building.

In an emergency

It is part of your role to make sure you know what you are required to do in the event of an emergency. Evacuation drills are usually viewed by everyone as a total pest but they do save lives, so please make sure that you know the procedure for your workplace. There are special considerations when older people are involved:
• With impaired senses (hearing and smell) older people may not respond as quickly as you or I would.
• Many people with mobility problems would have difficulty moving quickly to escape a fire.
• Confused people may be disorientated so they can't find their way out, and they may wander off once they are outside.

With confused people in the building the chances of an incident are greater because the confused person might not realise they are doing something dangerous. Extra vigilance is essential.

Choice and safety

This brings us to the subject of choice and safety. In a nutshell, residents cannot choose to do something which puts everyone in the building in danger. Smoking is the classic subject which excites heated debate. By limiting smoking to a designated area (in other words NOT the bedroom) you are not removing the residents right to smoke, just limiting where they can choose to smoke for everyone's safety.

Preventing accidents

It is a legal requirement that all accidents at work are reported and recorded. Also it is usually a requirement of your registering body that accidents involving residents are reported and recorded.

The largest number of accidents at work involve "slipping, tripping and falls".

The main ways to avoid these hazards are as follows:

Slips
• Make sure any spills of liquids or powders are cleared up as quickly as possible.
• Make sure mopped floors are as dry as possible.
• Warn people (usually with a sign) when the floor is wet.
• Always wear suitable shoes and encourage your residents to do the same. Slippers don't offer good support to ankles and usually don't have a good tread for grip.

Trips
• Make sure floor coverings are not worn out or in a dangerous condition (particularly on stairs)
• Rugs can slip or people can trip over the edges – try to avoid them.
• Wires and flexes need to be safely placed so that people don't trip over them, but they should not be threaded under a carpet.
• When you are using a vacuum cleaner, be aware of the flex and try to keep it out of people's way. Preferably try to clean the carpets at a quiet time of day when people are not trying to get past.
• Try to keep the floor area free from clutter(including walking frames and sticks).

Falls
• If you cannot reach to do a task, such as getting something from a high shelf, use a step ladder to reduce the risk of a fall (don't climb on a box or a chair).

General points
• If you don't feel safe, stop.
• All equipment and machinery should be properly maintained. If you are not sure whether something is safe, report it to the person in charge.
• You may do various DIY tasks at home but you should not do anything at work

that you are not qualified to do safely.

• Cleaning materials and other chemicals should be safely stored and used (see COSHH regulations, chapter 26).

• Use the correct tool for the job (wheelchairs are not designed for moving furniture, for example).

• Empty waste paper bins by picking the whole bin up and tipping it into a larger bin or a bag. Don't put your hand in and pull out the rubbish – there may be broken glass or other dangerous things in there.

Security

Particularly at night, you need to make sure that all fire escape doors are secure and that all ground floor windows are closed. This is sometimes an unpopular move, so as a staff group you may need to assess the risk of leaving the windows open.

Front doors – to lock or not?

The arguments for locked doors

• With rising crime, most households now keep their doors locked as a matter of routine. Therefore it is "normal" in most areas.

• The Police may have difficulty in prosecuting a thief when there is no sign of forced entry.

• You may have difficulty in claiming from an insurance company if you could be seen to have made it easy for the thief to gain entry.

• Having someone answer the door means that everyone in the building is protected from intruders.

• Each person entering the building is individually greeted and welcomed.

The arguments against locked doors

• Particularly in social services and health authority establishments, there is a feeling that these buildings are public property and people should have free access.

• People sometimes don't want the locked front door to look as though it is keeping wandering residents against their will.

• Leaving the front door unlocked means that staff are not tied up answering it all the time.

If the front door is locked, here are some points to consider:

• Anyone who answers the door (either residents or staff) needs to be aware that they are responsible for the safety of everyone in the building.

• It should go without saying that everyone needs to be vigilant and to check the identity of anyone they do let into the building. Wearing a company overall is NOT proof that you work for that company (the most tremendous cons have been pulled by people posing as workers on official business).

• Does the person to be visited actually want to see the visitor? We are so used to residents and patients who anxiously await the next visit from a friend or relative that it is easy to forget that there may be strained relationships and the resident may NOT wish to see the visitor.

• The front door is a means of escape, so people should always be able to get out.

Residents' belongings

In many homes there is a disclaimer sign saying something like "staff cannot be held responsible for valuables which have not been handed into the office for safe keeping". So let us first look at the items which *have* been handed in.

Items held for safekeeping

In many larger organisations there is likely to be a stated procedure for dealing with money and other items to go into the safe. Often staff find this procedure over-complex and a bit of a pain. But I cannot stress enough that procedures are there to protect the residents and to protect YOU. If you don't follow the system laid out you could find yourself wrongly accused of stealing or mishandling valuable items. You have no way of proving your innocence if you haven't filled in the right forms and got the required signatures.

Some points which should be part of the procedures are listed below. If your home's system does not cover these points it may be worth suggesting that they are included.

• Whenever money or valuables are accepted by a member of staff for safe-keeping, the resident should be given a receipt showing

– the date the item was handed in

– the signature of the member of staff

– a description of the item(s)

– the resident's estimate of the value

– the signature of the resident or someone else who can act as a witness.

• When the resident takes the item back into their care, you need a similar receipt to verify that you are no longer responsible for the item. If the resident has died and you are giving their belongings to the "next of kin", you need to be sure that you are giving the valuables to the correct person. The person who regularly visits the resident is not necessarily the legal "next of kin".

• It is a good idea to keep a register of "items held for safe keeping", because these may not always be in the safe. For instance, a resident may ask you to take responsibility for an item which is not of great monetary value or which is too large to fit into the safe (for example a photo album or a piece of furniture).

• It is also a good idea to keep a "safe con-

tents" list, just in case the whole safe gets stolen.

There are two very important points to remember when accepting items for safe keeping. The first is that you should never describe items as, for example, "gold ring" or "diamond brooch". This is because the item may not be genuine gold or diamond, but when someone comes to retrieve it from the safe they could demand a gold ring if that is what you have said you are holding. Instead you should write "yellow metal ring" or "brooch with white stones".

Secondly, your manager will need to know what your safe limit is. Usually insurance companies will cover a loss up to a limit of £500. If a resident is asking you to take responsibility for an expensive item or one which would put the contents total over the limit, you need to tell senior staff, who may advise the person to make alternative arrangements. In the past I have arranged for valuables to go into a safe deposit box at the bank (it is not as expensive as you might think).

Cash for everyday needs

The system that I have outlined above is not at all suitable for the administration of residents' money which is designed for their everyday needs. Many residents will take responsibility for their own personal allowances, but there are sometimes people who are unable to do so or who choose to keep the money in the safe until they wish to take it out.

If the money is regularly going in and out of an "account" in the safe, then a running log needs to be kept to safeguard everyone. Two signatures should be kept for every sum of money that is put into the safe and for each time some is taken out. By keeping this information up to date you will always have an accurate record of the amount of money in the safe.

Drugs

Some people in the home may administer their own medicines (more details below). First I would like to look at your responsibilities and the procedures for dealing with the medicines for those residents who have chosen to put them in your care. I would emphasise the word chosen, as it is not your automatic right to take charge of residents' drugs.

The legal position is that all medicines should be individually dispensed from a chemist with the resident's name and the dosage clearly marked on the label (in other words, they are the resident's property). This means that you should **not** have a large tub of the common tablets that a majority of residents take and dispense them to everyone from the "central pot".

It also means that doctors have a responsibility to be clear about dosage instructions. Doctors should not be writing prescriptions for tablets to be taken "as required" (sometimes the medical shorthand is PRN) because this gives the resident or the staff the responsibility to make a decision about when a drug is required, and that is not your role as a care assistant.

So, each establishment will have a whole range of different packets and bottles of tablets for the various different residents who need to take something. These drugs need to be stored in a cool dry place and they need to be securely locked away.

We sometimes don't realise the attraction that a large store of drugs can be. Not all of the drugs commonly taken by older people have other uses, but there are some drugs which have a "street value" amongst drug abusers; everyone needs to be aware of this.

For reasons of security and for ease of administration it makes sense to try to minimise the number of tablets that residents regularly take. Staff and/or residents can make a doctor feel that there is a subtle pressure to give a prescription when they have been asked to see a patient in a residential or nursing home. It may be worth mentioning that you are quite happy to accept advice instead of a prescription.

It is also worth checking with the doctor for how long they feel the resident needs to take the tablets. I have seen cases of people taking a cocktail of drugs which the chemist warned was undesirable, simply because staff had requested a repeat prescription when the doctor had intended the patient to take only a single course.

Administering drugs

Administering drugs to the residents is most often done at meal and bed times. This is sensible for a few reasons:

• The majority of tablets are most readily taken into the body with food and drink so the instructions say "take with food". (You do need to be aware of the unusual tablets which say "take on an empty stomach" as they need to be taken about half an hour before meals.)

• Mealtimes are traditionally a time when people get together. With all the residents in the dining room it is easy to give out the medicines without having to trail all over the building looking for people.

• People need a drink to swallow the tablets and this is usually available at the table. However, a major consideration is that the drink to help the tablets down must be cold. Just for an experiment, try taking a tablet with a hot drink of tea. I have, and my findings are that you either burn your throat or you choke on a half melted tablet stuck in your windpipe.

The system adopted in most small establishments is that the tablets are stored in a locked cupboard and transferred to a tray to be taken to the residents. In establishments where there are more residents who regularly take tablets this may not be practical, so an alternative which many homes adopt is to have a locked medicines trolley which can be pushed into the dining room. Many people feel that this is very institutional and not at all homely (I would be one of them) but it does mean that the drugs are safely stored and administered.

Drug records

Accurate records of all the drugs in the building is an absolute must. You may find that there is a system which is preferred by your registering body, or the home will have its own system. In either case the records should include:

– a record of all drugs received into the building (both for the residents to take themselves and those for which you are responsible)

– a record of each tablet taken

– the signature of the staff member who actually administered the tablet

– a record of any occasions when a resident refuses to take the tablet

– the signature of the chemist who accepts returned drugs (you should not flush left over tablets down the toilet or into the drains).

Remember the golden rule: If in doubt ask the person in charge.

Belongings

Although staff are not *legally* responsible for **items not handed in for safe keeping,** you do have some responsibilities for these things. When something is lost or stolen it would be wrong for staff to say "You did not hand it in, so we are having nothing to do with this".

If something is lost, all staff must do whatever they can to find the item. If it

cannot be found and it seems that it may have been stolen, you need to report the situation to the person in charge who may call in the Police.

It is important for residents to have a lockable drawer or cupboard in their room for the storage of personal items. This is particularly important for residents who look after their own money and/or drugs. The money obviously needs to be secure and the tablets need to be kept safe as confused residents could "collect" them, and could become ill if they were to take any.

A lockable drawer allows people to store a few small items securely but it does not protect the rest of the resident's belongings from the unwanted attentions of residents who may wander into bedrooms.

Locks on doors?

When the issue of locks on bedroom doors is discussed, the usual response from staff and managers is "We can't do that because we wouldn't be able to rescue a resident if there was a fire", and that is where the discussion usually ends. I really think that we should think more about how to overcome the difficulties rather than just put more obstacles in the way of change.

Why not have a pass key so that the staff can get in if they really need to? Most residents want to lock their doors when they are out of the room, so this is not a problem if they undertake not to lock the door when they are in bed.

This is not a subject that you can change overnight on your own. There will need to be discussions with your registering body and obviously with the management. However, in these discussions, what the staff say is often taken into account, so please don't be the one who makes difficulties. Instead you could be the one who thinks of a solution.

Civil liberties

Many staff, families, members of councils and members of the public think that the staff in a residential or nursing home have a legal right to stop people leaving the building. In the vast majority of cases this is totally untrue. Most of the residents in residential and nursing care have chosen to live there and they are covered by the same Acts of Parliament as you or me. We would not take kindly to an infringement of our civil liberties by being taken to a building and not allowed to leave. If it happened to us it would be called "unlawful imprisonment" or possibly "kidnap".

That's all well and good for people who can competently take themselves to the shops and find their way back, but how do you deal with the residents who desperately want to go home to make the tea for the husband who died ten years ago?

These situations need some sensitivity, staff time and the most enormous helping of patience. You can try to talk the person out of going out and you can try to keep people occupied so that they don't feel bored and want some other form of stimulation, but you can't tell people that they are not allowed to go out, because they are.

Generally you do need to know where people are at all times, not to "clip their wings" and limit their freedom but to protect them from abuse. People who go out on their own need to tell you that they are out of the building and what time they expect to return; that seems to me to be a common courtesy of living in a group. It is very difficult to offer a service to someone whose whereabouts are unknown.

Summary
In this chapter we have looked at various aspects of safety and security in care homes. Very often health and safety requirements seem to be used in opposition to a "normal and homely" environment. I would argue that the two go hand in hand, since residents cannot feel "at home" if they don't feel safe and secure.

Points to remember

1. We cannot draw too many comparisons between our own homes and the homes in which we work. We have different responsibilities at work.
2. In a dispute between residents' choice and safety, choice will not always win.
3. Accidents should be avoided if at all possible; when they do occur they need to be recorded and reported.
4. Everyone needs to be aware of security in the building. Challenge strangers to make sure that they are in the building on legitimate business.
5. Follow the correct procedures when handling money and valuables. They are there to protect the residents and you.
6. Ensure that drugs are correctly stored, administered and recorded.
7. Try to know where residents are at all times and prevent confused residents from becoming distressed and wanting to leave.
8. Keep safety and security in your mind at all times. It makes people feel "at home".
9. With the management and other staff, assess any risks against the benefits. A totally risk-free life would not only be incredibly boring but ultimately bad for both health and wellbeing.

NVQ Levels 2 & 3 Core Units
O Promote equality for all individuals.
U4 Contribute to the health, safety and security of individuals and their environment.
U5 Obtain, transmit and store information relating to the delivery of a care service.

Level 2 Direct Care
Z19 Enable clients to achieve physical comfort.

CHAPTER 12

Health, hygiene and infection control

Judith Roberts

• A hazardous profession? • How a healthy body overcomes infection • Residents at risk • Preventing cross infection • Staff health

Caring is a hazardous profession. At first this may seem a rather strange thing to say, but just consider how many times a colleague has had time off work due to a work-related injury or illness. Perhaps you can remember a bout of gastro-enteritis, or a cut hand due to the careless discarding of broken glass, a bad back from lifting, being threatened or even attacked... I'm sure these examples are familiar.

So it is vital to be aware of the risks and take steps to avoid them. We must also consider how our own ill health or actions could affect the health of our residents. There is a definite link between poor personal hygiene, unhygienic working practices and the development and spread of infection. The process and methods of preventing infection and its spread are relevant to all areas of your work.

Controlling infection

Infection is the successful invasion of the body by disease-causing organisms called pathogens, popularly known as germs. These organisms are very small and cannot be seen by the naked eye. There are various types or groups of pathogens, each of which has its own characteristics. Some of the commonest examples are bacteria, viruses, parasites and fungi. To grow and multiply they all need food, warmth, moisture and a friendly host.

To actually cause disease, germs have to enter the body and overcome its natural defences. They then go on to produce the signs and symptoms of a particular condition.

The ways in which germs can enter the body include the following:
• Contact with infected people, for example sexually transmitted disease, or catching athlete's foot.
• Contact with contaminated objects, eg a care worker's apron or gloves, toilet seats, crockery, hairbrushes.
• By eating or drinking contaminated food or water. Food can get contaminated by unwashed hands, infected cuts on the skin, flies landing on food, and contact with contaminated water.
• Through a puncture of the skin, for example from a used needle, standing

on a rusty nail, or a biting insect such as a mosquito.

• By breathing in contaminated dust or droplets of moisture breathed out by infected people. Sneezing and coughing help to spread the infected droplets of moisture up to four metres away.

Cross infection

Cross infection occurs when an infection is passed from one person to another, via the routes described above. It is also possible to infect yourself, for example by picking at grazes or cuts with unwashed fingers.

When a lot of people live together, whether in an army barracks or in a care home, cross infection is a particular hazard. (This will be discussed in greater detail later in the chapter.)

Protection from infection

The risks of a normal healthy adult getting an infection have to be looked at realistically. Although people may have a yearly cold or tummy upset, most of the time they will remain infection-free. This is not because they have avoided contact with germs; it is because although the germs have entered the body, the body was able to overcome the germs and fight off the infection. This is done in a variety of ways, sometimes through natural defences and sometimes through immunisation. The various defences are as follows:

• The normal acid secretions in the stomach help to cleanse food and water, and eliminate bacteria.

• Tears are naturally antiseptic, and the fluid itself helps to wash away harmful bacteria and dust particles.

• The skin itself forms a physical, waterproof barrier. It is effective as long as it stays intact. The lubrication (sebum) it

produces also contains an antiseptic chemical which helps to kill some bacteria as they touch the skin.

• The respiratory system produces mucus and the cells it contains help to trap particles of dust and germs and prevent them entering the lungs.

• The senses, especially our sense of taste and smell, help to warn us that food is likely to be infected if it tastes and smells "off".

• The blood contains white blood cells which destroy germs. Antibodies also circulate in the blood; they help to kill germs or make them harmless. Antibodies are produced after exposure to an infection, either naturally or through immunisation/vaccination.

The likelihood of a person catching an infection depends on the number of germs, how active the germs are and how well the person can fight off the infection.

Other factors that help protect us

Fresh air, good nutrition, adequate fluids, exercise and freedom from cross infection are all important. Some medical conditions predispose a person to getting an infection more easily, eg diabetes or asthma. An existing wound, for example an ulcer or burn, or equipment that invades the body, eg an intravenous line (a drip) or a catheter, add to the risk of infection. Stress and fatigue are now also considered to be important factors.

Residents at risk

Group living, even for healthy adults, is an acknowledged risk, as it can increase the likelihood of cross infection occurring. In addition elderly people, wherever they live, are more vulnerable to infection for a variety of reasons:

• The ageing process slows down the

response of the immune system.

• Taste and smell decline, making it less likely that they will detect infected food.

• They may have an existing medical condition that can make them more vulnerable to infection, eg a bad chest, diabetes, urinary incontinence.

• They may not be able to carry out personal hygiene routines independently and will need support, for example to wash their hands after visiting the toilet.

• They may have an inadequate fluid intake, or a diet lacking in the essential nutrients.

• They may be confused or apathetic, which could prevent them valuing and carrying out their own personal hygiene.

• They may be taking certain drugs, eg steroids, which could prevent their immune system working efficiently.

• They are vulnerable to the unhygienic working practices of staff, and the unhygienic living practices of other residents and their visitors.

Preventing cross infection

It is important that all possible sources of infection are regarded as potentially dangerous and treated accordingly. You may argue that at present there is no need to be concerned about contact with the blood of an elderly resident, as it is unlikely that they will be infected with HIV or Hepatitis B. At present you could well be correct; but you may not. Increasingly the spread of these infections is likely to involve our elderly population.

Now is the time we should adopt the proper procedures when we are dealing with blood or other body fluids. Care staff must get used to always carrying out the correct procedures, so that they become automatic.

If the same precautions are used for everyone then it should not matter if you deal with a resident who is HIV positive – the care you give will be the same. It also means that their diagnosis is not broadcast to everyone, and confidentiality can be maintained.

The practice of taking the same precautions with everyone is known as the Universal Infection Control Procedure, or **Universal Precautions**. The specific procedures are set out below.

Effective handwashing and thorough drying

This is by far the most important factor. Hands are very efficient at passing germs to others. Like any skill it has to be learned, and appears more simple than it actually is. Look at your hands next time you wash them. Did you clean your left thumb? Did you clean beyond the wrist margin? How well did you clean the ends of your finger tips and nails? How well did you dry them? Did you dry them off by rubbing them down the sides of your uniform? I expect you probably didn't wash you hands as well as you thought you did (neither did I, the first time I really looked at the way I washed my hands).

Automatic thorough washing of our hands before and after dealing with each client really is necessary. So is washing our hands before dealing with food, or the giving of tablets and drinks. Any cuts or abrasions on your hands should be covered; this is to protect both you and the residents.

Protective clothing

If you will be dealing with blood or body waste then you should wear plastic gloves and a protective apron. You should use a different pair of gloves and apron for each resident. Gloves are just as able to transmit germs as hands!

Never share personal effects

Each resident must have the use of their

own personal towels and toiletries; they should not be shared no matter how busy you are. This includes toothbrushes, combs and electric razors. Each resident should also have their own bowl, and their flannels and towel should be allowed to dry after use, not left in a slimy soggy mess at the bottom of a toilet bag.

A clean environment

Regular general cleaning of the environment is important, and at times it may be your responsibility to mop up any spills, even if a cleaner is employed. Make sure you wear any necessary protective clothing when doing so, and carry out the procedure according to your establishment's policy.

Clothing and jewellery

Staff should appear clean and wear appropriate clothing and jewellery. Clothing should allow flexibility of movement and should be easily washed at high temperatures. Shoes should have low heels and be well-fitting. Hair should be clean and kept tied up. Long, loose hair can spread infection very easily as bacteria cling to hair. Loose hair can give confused residents something to hold on to, and freely allows head lice (nits) to spread to you or from you. Chipped nail varnish, long nails, rings with large settings, all can harbour large numbers of bacteria and should be avoided. In addition, nails and jewellery could damage residents' skin.

Food safety

The storage and disposal of food products is also important. All actions have to comply with the Food Safety Act 1990 (see chapter 27).

Food has to be stored at the correct temperature, in a clean environment; it must be kept covered and free from contamination from other foods. It should be cooked thoroughly using clean equipment and served at the correct temperature (below 5°C for cold food and above 63°C for hot food). Food should not be re-heated – this includes milky drinks. Waste food should be disposed of immediately in covered bins.

Staff health

So far we have looked at the health of residents and how the actions of staff can affect them. But the process is not one-way: staff health must be protected too. We have already looked at preventing staff getting infections, but there are additional factors to consider.

It is important always to adopt safe lifting procedures, for both residents and goods! Use appropriate lifting aids, and seek help from your colleagues. If you have not attended a safe lifting course, ask your employer if they could arrange one for you (see chapter 16).

Think about security. A secure establishment protects both you and the residents. If you work nights in a large home, make sure you tell staff where you are going. If they don't know where you have gone how can they tell if you are missing, or lying injured somewhere? If you are involved with a safety or security incident, you must record and report it.

Your emotions

Care work can be emotionally very taxing and stressful. Don't be surprised if it affects you more than you thought it would.

In the past there has been debate about whether care staff should get emotionally involved with residents in their care work. It has been argued that the care worker should remain detached, not showing their distress by crying, for example.

But if we are part of the process that gives good care, I don't know how not to get emotionally attached. The important thing though is still to be able to carry out our caring tasks and functions, not to be disabled by our emotions. For example, if a resident you have known for many years dies, of course you are going to feel a loss. But your sense of loss should be kept in proportion, so that you can still give your support to relatives, friends and other residents.

At times however, often when various factors coincide, events can occur that leave us feeling very anxious and distressed. There is no shame in this.

If you feel stressed or angry, talk to your colleagues. Often, discussing common concerns at the next staff meeting can be very helpful. If this avenue is not available or suitable, perhaps seek counselling or support from senior staff, your GP, union representative, or a minister of religion.

Points to remember

1. The potential to pass on infection to the resident is always present.
2. Thorough handwashing is the most effective way of preventing cross infection. It protects both residents and staff.
3. Remember, elderly people are more vulnerable.
4. Never share personal toiletries or equipment.
5. You must use protective clothing (plastic gloves and aprons) when dealing with spilt blood and other body waste. Make sure all residents are treated the same to maintain confidentiality.
6. Think about what you wear. Is it suitable to protect your health and safety, and that of the residents?
7. Think about security. Make sure your colleagues know where you are.
8. Don't be afraid of becoming emotionally involved, but don't be afraid to ask for support.

NVQ Level 2 & 3 Core Unit
U4 Contribute to the health, safety and security of individuals and their environment.

CHAPTER 13
Accident and emergency

Teresa Mearing-Smith

• The aims of First Aid • What to do in an emergency
or following an accident • Common conditions and how to cope
• When to call for help

Sooner or later, as you work with elderly people, you will find yourself having to cope with an emergency. There may be an accident; someone may suddenly become very ill and distressed; or they may collapse and become unconscious. Whatever the situation, there are important and simple principles of First Aid which you can apply, while waiting for qualified help to arrive.

First Aid

The aims of First Aid are:

• To preserve life

• To prevent the condition worsening

• To help recovery

No one will expect you to make a precise diagnosis, but you are in the ideal situation of knowing the residents, what medical conditions they have, what drugs they are taking, and whether, for instance, they have a tendency to fall, or suffer from fits, chest pain or breathlessness.

The following steps will help you to act in the right order of priorities:

Assess the situation

You must appear calm and confident. This is important not only to help you to cope, but also to prevent fear and anxiety spreading to other residents or staff who may witness the emergency. If appropriate you should take charge, and make use of any other residents who are well enough to fetch another member of staff. You must ensure the safety not only of the casualty, but also of yourself and other residents. There is for instance no point in a second resident slipping on the wet patch on the floor on their way to get help.

Decide what has happened

There are no marks for getting the answer right, but it will be helpful for both yourself and others who may take over to know exactly what has happened. Ask other residents or relatives what they saw or heard, or even smelt. Of course, if the resident can tell you herself, that makes life much easier.

Now have a look at the resident. What can you see that might give you a clue? Has the resident fallen and hit her head,

General rules

• If the person is unconscious, place in the recovery position.
• **DO NOT** give anything to eat or drink unless advised.
• Be observant.
• Record what happened.

or cut herself? Is she conscious? What is her colour like? Then use your hands gently to remove any harmful object, undo clothes to get a better look, or feel her skin or limbs. Is she hot? Cold? Sweaty? Or is one limb swollen, indicating a fracture?

Obviously you must get the right balance between finding out what is wrong, and preventing further deterioration or doing unnecessary harm. If you remain calm and confident it is unlikely that you will do the wrong thing.

Treatment

The first and most important steps are to ensure the person has:

• An open airway
• Adequate breathing
• Sufficient circulation
• If appropriate and you have been trained to do it, start cardiopulmonary resuscitation (CPR) – see opposite page.

The **Recovery Position** is important for unconscious people who are still breathing and do not need CPR. It is similar to the position in which you would put a very frail or dying person; on their side with the upper leg bent and resting forwards to take the weight of the lower half of the body while the upper half rests forwards on the upper arm (see Fig 1). The importance of this position for someone who is unconscious is that the head is on its side and there is less obstruction to breathing. The tongue is less likely to fall backwards, and vomit or mucus is less likely to collect at the back of the throat. You may need to place a resident in this position; certainly if their breathing becomes noisy this is the best position for them to be in.

The next important step is to **dress any wounds** using a simple gauze dressing and

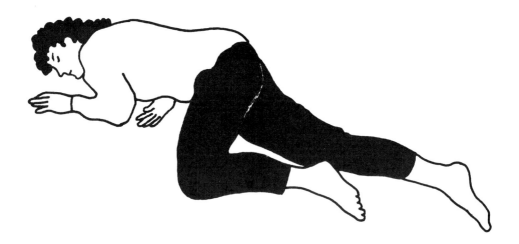

Fig 1. The recovery position – the safest way for an unconscious person to lie.

Cardio-pulmonary resuscitation of adults

Breathing

Lay the person on their back on a firm surface. Tilt the head back and lift the jaw (Fig 2). Pinch the nostrils together, place your mouth securely over the person's mouth to create a seal and breath into the mouth.

If the person has a tracheostomy (a breathing hole in the centre of the neck) it needs to be cleared and air blown into it.

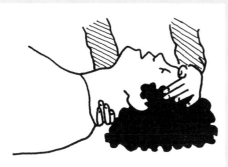

Fig 2. Preparing for mouth to mouth resuscitation: tilt the head back and lift the jaw.

Look to see if the chest is rising and falling. If breathing starts spontaneously after this has been carried out, place the person in the recovery position. Continue to observe them. Their skin should return to a lighter, more normal colour. Wait for help to arrive.

Circulation

If the heart has stopped, you will notice that the lips, tongue, ear lobes and finger nails may become bluish-grey in colour. The pupils of the eyes may be fixed and very large. If you cannot feel a pulse or hear a heartbeat you will need to start cardiac resuscitation.

Place the heel of one hand over the lower centre of the breastbone (one finger breadth below a line joining the nipples). Place the heel of the other hand on top, keeping the palms and fingers forward. With your arms straight, rock backwards and forward (Fig 3). Each time that you rock forward you will be compressing the chest and heart to stimulate the pumping action. If you are on your own repeat this fifteen times, stop, and then breath into the lungs twice. Keep going until help arrives or the person shows signs of responding. When a second helper is present one should give five heart massages, then the other two breaths, then keep repeating the sequence.

With successful resuscitation the person's skin colour will look more normal, a carotid pulse will be felt and the pupils will look less dilated. If the person has stopped breathing, the heart may still be pumping. If the heart has stopped beating, breathing will certainly cease.

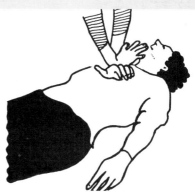

Fig 3. The correct position of hands for cardiac massage.

micropore tape, or gauze held on with a bandage. If bleeding has not stopped you will need to apply pressure on the wound until it does. More serious large wounds or fractures can be covered with a clean (non-fluffy) cloth, but dressing should be left to a trained nurse.

Put the casualty in the correct position. I have mentioned the recovery position, but a conscious patient may well wish to sit up propped slightly forwards. She will probably tell you which position is most comfortable. If the situation appears serious and you have taken the preliminary steps listed already, it is better not to move the person more than is necessary.

Perhaps most helpful of all in this situation is the care assistant who **remains calm and has a calming influence** on the victim and others around. **Be sympathetic**, reduce pain and discomfort as far as you can, handle the person gently to prevent more harm or pain, and protect them from cold and damp.

It is your responsibility as the first person on the scene to **make sure the resident is not left in an unsafe condition.** Therefore you should call the doctor, or officer in charge of other staff as appropriate and inform the relatives if necessary.

Reporting

This is where your account is important, for other people whether trained or not will want to know what has happened, and what treatment, if any, you have given. If you have managed the situation yourself, you should enter the details in the Kardex or Day/Night Book as appropriate.

When to call for help

As part of your general training, it is a good idea to discuss with the officer in charge and other staff, what the home's policy is on calling for help in an emergency. You should know whether you are

expected to call the doctor or an ambulance yourself, or whether other trained staff or the officer in charge will do this. You should know which residents often have little "turns" from which they recover quite quickly with basic help, and which residents have more serious conditions. If you are unsure of what to do, it is far better to call for help than to struggle on by yourself.

Do you know?

Telephone:
Where all the telephone extensions are
GP's number(s)
Nearest Accident Centre number
Officer in charge or other staff at their home (if appropriate)
Where to find residents' relatives' numbers

How to switch off:
Gas
Electricity
Water

Fire:
What the Fire Drill is
Where the Fire Extinguishers/Fire Blankets are

Medical:
Where the First Aid box is
What drugs each resident is taking
How to open the drugs cupboard

It is worth finding out all this before the emergency happens!

Now I will describe some emergency conditions and how to cope with them.

Breathing

Choking: Try to feel in the mouth for the obstruction (eg food or false teeth) and remove it. To do this gently open the mouth and use two fingers to sweep around inside, but be careful not to push

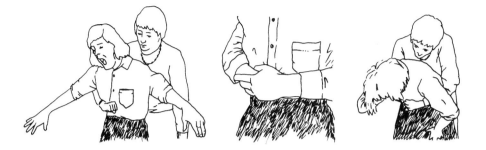

The Heimlich Manoeuvre. 1. Stand behind the choking victim and clench one fist, thumb towards her stomach. 2. Hold this fist tight with the other hand – it should be placed under the ribs, between the navel and breastbone. 3. Pull sharply inwards and upwards, three or four times (pushing the upper abdomen against the lungs to force air violently upwards).

the object further in. If a resident turns blue while eating, puts a hand to their throat and cannot speak, strike them on the back between the shoulder blades and tell them to cough. If this does not dislodge the obstruction, use the Heimlich manoeuvre (see above).

Asthma: You will know which residents suffer from this condition and how badly it affects them. A sudden deterioration may be helped by an inhaler if the resident has one: occasionally they may need oxygen. Try propping them up in a chair or in bed, talk calmly, offer a drink to sip and call for further help if there is no improvement.

Winding: This occurs with a heavy blow or fall onto the upper abdomen. Sit the resident down, loosen tight clothing and gently massage the stomach. This treatment normally works well.

Hiccups: These can be very distressing if prolonged. Holding the breath, taking long drinks or breathing in and out of a paper (not plastic) bag often stops the attack, but seek further advice if the hiccups persist for more than three hours and the resident is distressed.

Circulation

Shock: This can happen if blood or other fluids are lost from the body (from severe cuts, burns or diarrhoea and vomiting). The resident will be weak and faint, pale, cold and sweaty, and may be breathing faster. If you think shock is the problem, you must seek further help, but you can reassure the resident, lie her down on her back with her head on one side and elevate the legs, cover with a blanket and loosen clothing; but do not give anything to eat or drink until advised to.

Fainting: This is a brief loss of consciousness caused by insufficient blood reaching the brain. It may occur as a result of sudden pain, a fright or sometimes hunger. Lie the resident down. Tell her to take deep breaths and loosen any tight clothing. Make sure there is plenty of fresh air; sometimes a sip of cold water will help.

Angina and heart attacks: Angina is pain in the chest (and sometimes left arm) caused by poor blood supply to the heart, which may be brought on by exercise or stress. There may also be sweating and difficulty in breathing.

Get the resident to rest by sitting or lying propped up, and loosen clothing. Here your knowledge of the residents is important. If you know that a person suffers from angina and has little tablets or a spray to put under the tongue (Glycerin Trinitrate) or other treatment for an attack, give it or find someone who can.

A **heart attack** is a blockage in one or more of the blood vessels carrying blood to the heart muscle and may look like severe angina, or it may cause death, either sudden or preceded by severe chest pain.

Summon help and make sure that other residents are not distressed by what is going on. Put the person in the Recovery Position, whether or not there are signs of life. Sometimes, although apparently dead, a person may start breathing again and this position will aid their recovery.

Bleeding: One day you may discover one of the residents in a pool of blood. This may have resulted from an injury, perhaps to the scalp or shin.

Don't panic! A little blood goes a long way and the resident may have spread it around herself, either in confusion or in an attempt to clear it up. Aim to control the bleeding and prevent the wound from becoming infected. So first quickly wash your hands and find the First Aid box or supply of cotton wool and gauze. If small, clean the wound itself either by gently placing under running water or with cotton wool swabs, then cover the wound up with a piece of gauze and clean the surrounding skin. In this way you can tell exactly how big the wound is and what other damage, if any, has been done.

Cover the wound with a suitable dressing. If you are unsure what to do, ask a trained nurse to dress it.

If the cut is more serious then call for help straight away. If the bleeding persists, press firmly on the wound for five to ten minutes, or until the bleeding stops, and elevate that part of the body if you can.

Nose bleeds: These may cause the loss of a lot of blood which can be swallowed or inhaled, and could cause vomiting and/or difficulty in breathing, so the resident may be very frightened at the sight of all the blood she has lost.

Remain calm and sit her down with her head forward over a bowl or basin. Pinch the soft part of her nose just below the bone and get her to breath through her mouth avoiding swallowing, coughing, spitting or sniffing; carry on pressing for ten minutes then release. If the bleeding persists carry on for another ten minutes. If after thirty minutes the bleeding still has not stopped, then summon help. If the bleed has been a severe one it is probably a good idea for the resident to sit propped up in bed for a few hours, and avoid any exertion.

Varicose veins: These may bleed quite dramatically, and frighten the resident, so remain calm, apply pressure on the site of bleeding, and elevate the leg. Lay the resident on her back, remove any clothing over the leg and press directly on the vein with either your fingers or the palm of your hand over a dressing. Make sure there are no tight stockings or suspenders constricting the leg higher up. If the bleeding is not controlled quickly, raise the leg in the air and get help.

Bruising: This is caused by bleeding just under the skin which causes a bluish purple mark, and sometimes swelling. Elderly people bruise very easily, so you should know how to help. If the injury has just happened, raise the injured part, if possible, and place in a comfortable position. Apply a cold compress (ice-pack - or a bag of frozen peas is ideal). Once the acute stage is over, it is important that the resident is encouraged to move, so as not to become stiff.

Nervous system

Concussion: This is caused by a fall or a blow to the head. Injuries of this sort often cause unconsciousness, if only for a few minutes. If the resident comes to very quickly, place her in a chair or lying down and comfort her. She may well feel sick or actually vomit, so be prepared.

If she is unconscious place her in the Recovery Position if possible, and seek help. Head injuries in elderly people do not always follow the usual pattern, so always tell a trained member of staff if you think the resident has suffered such an injury.

Stroke: This is caused by the blood supply to part of the brain becoming suddenly cut off, either because of a clot in a blood vessel or a haemorrhage into the brain. This is another condition that is common in elderly people, and is often associated with high blood pressure.

In its mildest form, a stroke causes weakness on one side of the body or face or difficulty in talking, which may last for half an hour or less, and is followed by complete recovery. More serious is the weakness that is very severe and shows only minimal improvement after days or weeks. The most serious form of stroke is associated with loss of consciousness and total inability to move one or the other side of body; death commonly follows.

Your role here is to help and comfort the resident who is probably very frightened and confused. You may not be able to understand her, but she may well understand you. Get her to a safe comfortable position if possible.

If she is unconscious, place her in the Recovery Position where she is not a danger to herself or others. People who have had a stroke usually cannot move themselves and are a dead weight, therefore NEVER attempt to move them yourself; get help.

Epilepsy: This disease results from abnormal electrical discharges in the brain and causes involuntary movements of the body, usually lasting no more than five minutes, followed by confusion or a dazed feeling. You should know, if any residents in the home suffer from epilepsy, what may cause the attacks, and how they are best treated. While the attack continues you should help the resident into a safe position on the floor (unless they are in bed at the time). Loosen any tight clothing, do not try to restrain and do not put anything in the mouth.

Allow the spasms to stop, and the resident to regain consciousness, and then help them into bed or a chair until fully recovered. There is no need to call for an ambulance or the doctor immediately unless the fit lasts for more then fifteen minutes, several fits occur in short succession, or the resident has not had a fit before. The fact that a fit has occurred should be noted in the records and the doctor informed in due course.

Diabetes: This is caused by the body's inability to use sugar properly, and is common in the elderly. Most diabetics will have treatment either with diet or tablets rather than insulin injections. It is unlikely that a diabetic with dietary control alone will suddenly deteriorate, but conditions such as chest infection or stomach upset could upset the blood sugar levels. Those being treated with tablets or injections, however, may become suddenly ill if they have not eaten (and therefore have *low* levels of sugar in their blood) or if an infection or other illness causes the blood sugar level to become *high*.

Low sugar (hypoglycaemia) causes paleness, sweating, rapid breathing, trembling and confusion. The treatment is to give the person sugary drinks or boiled sweets. Symptoms should improve dramatically; if not, seek help quickly. High blood sugar (hyperglycaemia) should be suspected in any diabetic who has become unwell. Drinking excessively and passing water very frequently are the first signs, followed by deep breathing and drowsiness. This is serious and needs immediate attention.

Bones, muscles and joints

Fractures: As you will know from experience, elderly people are often unsteady on their feet, perhaps from arthritis, a previous stroke, painful feet or poor vision, and are therefore liable to fall and injure themselves. Older ladies in particular often have brittle bones (osteoporosis) and can break a bone very easily.

If you suspect that one of the residents has fallen, it is important that you report this to senior staff, as the resident herself may not remember what has happened. Sometimes an elderly person becomes confused or takes to her bed, with no complaints of pain or a fall, but a broken bone, especially in the hip, must be suspected.

A **fractured hip bone** (head of the femur) is a serious injury. It typically causes the leg to appear shorter and to be turned outwards, sometimes with swelling and pain around the hip, but this may be difficult to see. In fact you may be amazed to find that an elderly person has walked on a broken hip with very little complaint.

Normally a doctor would need to confirm the diagnosis, but the home may have a policy of calling the ambulance immediately if the diagnosis is obvious. An operation is normally needed, and it is remarkable how quickly elderly people can recover from this, and be back on their feet within a few days (as long as appropriate treatment was given immediately following the accident).

Another common **fracture** is of the **wrist** (Colles fracture) caused by falling on to an outstretched arm. This is normally easy to see, as there is pain and swelling at the wrist, and sometimes an obvious "bend" in the bones. Again this requires hospital treatment; usually the results are very good, but there may be permanent stiffness, swelling and pain.

Other bones may break, such as the **collar bone** (which normally heals by itself with the arm in a sling) and the ribs which can be very painful, but again heal by themselves. The shoulder can dislocate in a fall and require hospital treatment. Although elderly people often fall and cut their head, fractured skulls are uncommon.

Sprains and strains: A strain occurs when a muscle is overstretched and torn by a sudden movement, while a sprain occurs at a joint when it is suddenly wrenched. There is swelling, pain and stiffness. Treatment for these injuries is rest, ice (a bag of frozen peas is particularly good), compression with a thick layer of cotton wool and bandage, followed by elevation.

All this may not be possible; for instance you may find it difficult to elevate a leg when there is bad arthritis of the hip. It is also important that an elderly person does not get put into bed for days on end, because they then risk developing pneumonia, pressure sores, constipation or incontinence, and will have difficulty in getting up and about again.

Cramp: This occurs when a muscle suddenly goes into spasm, and can be very painful. It often happens to elderly people during sleep. Gentle stretching of the muscle and massage will help. You need to straighten out the leg or the toes carefully and gently massage the area that hurts.

Burns

It is often difficult to assess the seriousness of a burn: if in doubt, call for help. Any significant burn requires medical attention, and any burn affecting the leg, arm, chest, back or head requires hospital treatment. Elderly people are less able to stand the shock of a burn, and will need hospital treatment more often than fitter, younger people.

You can help further damage occurring from a burn by cooling, either by placing the area gently under running water or soaking the skin in cold water for at least 20 minutes. Hot, wet clothing should be removed as quickly as possible after a scald (which happens with wet heat such as steam, hot water or fat). Cooled dry burnt clothing should be left in place.

Once the burn has been cooled it may only need a simple dressing to protect it. If a blister forms, do not burst it, as infection is then possible, which will delay healing. New skin will grow under the blister, and over the next week or so the skin of the blister will gradually dry and peel off. If a blister is large and does break, then a trained nurse must dress it to ensure the wound is germ-free, as it is very vulnerable to infection.

Sunburn: Exposure to strong sunlight can cause sunburn in varying degrees with anything from redness and itching to burns with blisters and swelling. Burning can be increased by wind, salt, water or light reflected from sea and snow. Fair haired people burn more easily because they have less protection from skin pigment. People on certain types of medication may be more at risk of burning.

Encourage residents to use a high protection sun cream, and to reapply regularly. Mild sunburn can be soothed with calamine lotion or by bathing in cool water. In cases of severe sunburn, do not burst the blisters. Obtain medical advice if the sunburn is distressing, and accompanied by headache, nausea, or fever.

Hypothermia

This develops when the body temperature falls below about 35 degrees Celsius (95 degrees Fahrenheit). One would hope that elderly people living in residential care would not suffer from this condition, but a resident could well fall out of bed and be unable to attract attention for some hours. In this case it will be obvious that she is cold, and the possibility of hypothermia, like that of a stroke or a heart attack, must always be considered.

Re-warming should be done gradually, with any wet clothing removed first and the resident placed in bed in a warm room. You must ask for further help.

Points to remember

1. Remember:
• Assess the situation
• Decide what is wrong
• Take action
• Report.
2. Always call for assistance.
3. If you are not a certificated First Aider, you should not carry out first aid – unless you are first at the scene or the only person available.
4. The information in this chapter cannot prepare you fully for NVQ assessment. You must undertake a recognised course in practical First Aid.

NVQ Levels 2 & 3 Core Skills
O Promote equality for all individuals.
U4 Contribute to the health, safety and security of individuals and their environment.
U5 Obtain, transmit and store information relating to the delivery of a care service.

Level 2 Direct care
Z10 Enable clients to eat and drink.
Z19 Enable clients to achieve physical comfort.

CHAPTER 14

Keeping older people mobile

Helen Ransome

• Be alert to signs of disease • Loss of activity when in care
• Assessing the level of help needed • Walking aids and how to use them
• Motivation, risk and independence • Getting up after illness
• Getting into and out of a chair or bed, on and off the toilet

Does old age cause decreasing mobility? Many old people enjoy very active lives – physically and mentally. By doing this they prove to us that there is no direct link between old age and declining mobility. However certain changes which occur in the body as people get older make them likely to become immobile if they do not keep moving. This should persuade us all to encourage old people to keep active because **"What you don't use, you lose"**.

Why?

If active young people become noticeably less mobile it is correctly assumed that a disease process is the cause. When old people become less mobile it should also be assumed that a disease is responsible. Therefore if a resident gradually or suddenly loses their usual level of mobility the logical response is to refer the resident to the GP for diagnosis and treatment.

Unfortunately, like most of the rest of us, GPs sometimes find it difficult to accept that many of the immobile old people they see have become like that not because they are old, but because they have either spent too much time sitting about or they (or their carers) have not sought diagnosis and treatment for a disease, or both.

However, hospital doctors who specialise in the care of old people (physicians in geriatric medicine or geriatricians) believe that old age does not inherently mean disability, ill-health and less activity. They know that early medical treatment of the disease causing the deterioration can weaken or delay its disabling effects.

It is thus vital to refer residents whose mobility is *just beginning* to show a marked deterioration, to the GP who in turn can refer the resident to the geriatrician for early diagnosis and treatment. Speed is essential, because if nothing is done and immobility sets in, it is usually difficult, if not impossible, to restore mobility again.

You can help

Here is an example of how care assistants helped a resident to remain more mobile for longer by early referral.

An elderly lady had real pain, not just

discomfort, in her knees for a few weeks and found it increasingly difficult to get to the dining room from her bedroom. Like most older people she had a low expectation of her health and mobility and said to the care assistants, "My knees are seizing up, don't worry dear, it's all I can expect at my age – just get a wheelchair for me."

Had the care staff accepted her explanation of the problem and blamed it on age, she would soon have been permanently immobile. However they understood that there was a treatable disease causing the lady's pain and difficulty in moving and told the officer-in-charge about it. The lady was referred to the GP and then to the geriatrician, and the pain was largely relieved by appropriate medicine.

Once the pain was better, walking became easier again. The community physiotherapist also visited to show her and the care staff how to strengthen the important knee muscles and how best to manage activities of daily living, despite her knees. Having been "caught early", this lady had not lost her mobility and could therefore continue to be active at or very near her previous level.

This is one example of the vital role care assistants have in helping residents to remain mobile in residential homes.

The environment

In order to consider the particular problems which make it so difficult for elderly people to keep active in residential homes, we need to look at the environment in which the majority of our residents have spent most of their lives as elderly people – in their own homes.

A group of care assistants accurately answered the question "What keeps an elderly person who lives at home mentally and physically active?" like this:

"Getting out of bed, dressing (with as much time as they need), personal hygiene, going to the toilet, getting a cup of tea, making a bed, answering the door, reading, knitting, going to meals, preparing meals, washing clothes – even if only smalls, dusting and housework, shopping, gardening, tending the fire, looking after pets, going to bed".

Out of this rich (but by no means exhaustive) list of activities, most are lost when an older person is admitted to most homes. Apart from reading and knitting, often only getting out of bed, dressing and personal hygiene (all usually in a hurry), going to meals, to the toilet and bed are still available to old people in residential homes.

Even residents who had very limited mobility before admission and who could only potter about at home, were having regular exercise (like getting in the milk, letting out the cat and making cups of tea) which they immediately lose on admission. The long periods between meals, instead of providing opportunities for vital, varied activity are now filled with sitting – the well-known independence robber!

In addition, opportunities for mental activity are also usually lost, such as choice, decision-making, preserving self esteem and being needed/contributing. The difficulties of coping at home are removed, but because residents do not themselves have to provide the basic necessities of life (food, clean shelter, clothes, warmth), a new problem arises on admission to residential homes: lack of activity, both mental or physical. These two types of activity are inextricably linked: if an old person is physically immobile, her mental activity level will tend to decrease; if mentally unstimulated, her level of physical activity will tend to fall off.

How can care staff in homes change this independence-robbing environment into an independence-encouraging one? A group of care assistants answered this question correctly as follows:

• Assess each resident individually on admission and regularly thereafter.

• Find ways of responding to the various identified needs of each individual resident. In the case of the need for exercise, encourage the resident to remain as active as she was when admitted.

• Involve residents in making decisions about and running the home.

• Encourage them to carry out household tasks – in their own rooms, the dining room, laundry room, kitchen etc.

• Help them to feel valued – encourage independence, not dependence.

• Discover their interests and enable them to continue with hobbies and activities they enjoy.

Assessing independence

So that we can encourage each individual resident to remain as active as she was when admitted, we must know what she is capable of. An accurate assessment of each new resident's level of performance of the various activities of daily living should be made within a few days of admission.

The assessment gives a guide to this "functional level" of the new resident and care assistants can then encourage her all through each day's activities to "keep up" to this. The different levels at which activities of daily living can be performed are:

1. Alone (with the use of an aid if needed, eg walking frame). This is independence and should be our constant aim.

2. With supervision but no physical help from a person. Unhurried supervision is important as a confidence-booster. As confidence and performance improve, the care assistant will only need to "pop back" from time to time and the resident should eventually progress to carrying out the activity alone.

3. With verbal help (ie spoken instructions/advice) – but still no physical help.

Verbal help boosts confidence, and can enable a motivated resident by careful, consistent instructions to relearn how to do an activity and so regain independence.

4. With physical help. Verbal instruction should be tried on several occasions before using physical help. The aim should be to give the *least possible* help to enable the resident to carry out the activity. Once physical help is used a resident is dependent, even if only partially.

For a variety of reasons a resident's functional level may fluctuate, improve or deteriorate. For care staff to continue to respond to these changing levels and needs with the right amount of independence-encouraging support, regular and frequent reassessment is essential. Where this is carried out residents have the best possible chance of retaining and even improving their level of independence.

Independence in walking

Walking is the most important activity of daily living. Only if a resident can walk alone (so long as she can get out of a chair, which she can usually learn if she is capable of walking) can she make choices and be independent.

Independent walking enables her to go *when she chooses* to the toilet, meals, the sitting room, her bedroom and elsewhere in and outside the home. This means she does not have to wait for someone to take her, and the mental and physical stimulation she gains by moving freely helps to keep her active.

Independent residents are also good news for care assistants: less exhausting work and physical risk of back strain, and more time to respond to the needs of other more dependent residents.

Lively residents are best kept independently mobile by providing lots of varied activity in the home. Frailer residents, who may have specific physical problems (eg arthritis, stroke or Parkinson's Disease) may need walking aids to help them walk independently.

It is often very tempting to "give an arm" to a frailer resident who is able to get from room to room without help but who is slightly unsteady and appears vulnerable. When care assistants yield to this temptation they instantly deprive the resident of her independence.

This kind of "help" is given with the best of intentions – because care assistants feel sorry for the resident and are worried she might fall. However, if we stop and think, we realise that there is an alternative which will enable the resident to remain independently mobile. A walking aid (walking stick in this case) should always be tried before considering using the physical help of a person.

A resident who walks alone with a walking aid can move about the home when she wishes, remains confident in her ability to move alone and will not have to sit until someone comes to help her. On the other hand, a resident who is beginning to rely on care staff will sit for longer and walk less. This causes her muscles to get weaker, her joints stiffer, her balance to deteriorate and her walking to become worse.

She also becomes frightened of walking alone, as it feels so unsafe – so she sits rather than moves and as a result she becomes more dependent in all her other activities of daily living. The vicious circle of dependence has begun.

Soon she will be in a wheelchair requiring total help from the already hard-pressed care assistants, who thought they were being caring and helpful by offering her an arm, but who were actually depriving her of her dignity and independence. This lady lost her independence because she did not continue using her mind and body to accomplish activities of daily liv-

ing. Another case of "What you don't use, you lose"!

So all residents who can walk when they enter the home, must be consistently encouraged to remain **on their feet** with as little help as possible. Always try a suitable walking aid before giving physical help.

A physiotherapist is the most appropriate person to assess which walking aid a particular resident needs. However if you cannot find a physiotherapist, the following will help you to do it yourselves.

Walking aids

Walking stick

A resident who is slightly unsteady and who seems to need the physical help of one care assistant will usually be just as safe (and also independent) if given a walking stick. Before giving a resident a walking stick, carry out the following steps:

Equipment needed: Adjustable metal walking stick, saw, new wooden walking stick.

1. **Decide on the length.** Walking sticks should be individually measured. An adjustable metal walking stick is useful for deciding on the correct length for a wooden one. Adjust the metal stick to the approximate height and ask the resident to hold it in the the hand *opposite* to her "bad" leg if she has one. Otherwise she will usually use it on the side best for her. With the resident standing, adjust the length so that:

• the resident's hand on the stick handle is level with the top of the thigh
• the elbow is *slightly* bent
• the shoulders are level.

When you think the stick height is right with the resident standing, ask her to walk. See how it looks and how she feels. If either of you is unhappy, move the stick down or up a notch and try again until you find a height which basically follows the rules above but which also looks and feels "right."

Most people have their sticks too long. The elbow is thus very bent, which makes the stick less useful, and/or the shoulder is too high which leads to a painful shoulder. You may need to persuade residents that a shorter stick is more useful and comfortable; ask them to try it and review a few days later.

2. **Measure a wooden stick** to the same length as the metal one without its ferrule (the removable rubber end). Saw off the wooden stick to the correct length.

3. **Put a strong, wide-based, suction ferrule** on the bottom of the stick.

Make sure that all sticks have ferrules in good condition. When they are worn unevenly, have a hole or no suction ridges, replace them, as they are dangerous and can lead to falls.

4. **Teach the resident to hold the stick in the correct hand.**

5. **Teach the resident to walk correctly** with the stick as follows. There are two ways of walking with a stick:

(a) **When more support is needed** – eg stroke, arthritis
– put stick forward slightly to the side
– take a normal-sized step with the opposite foot *to the level of the stick*
– take a normal-sized step with the other foot past the walking stick
– repeat the sequence.

(b) **When less support is needed** – eg general unsteadiness, or when resident improves from (a)
– put stick and opposite leg forward together
–put the other leg forward past the stick
– repeat the sequence

When a resident using (a) is walking faster and taking less weight on the stick, she is probably ready to change to (b) and may do so automatically.

If a resident needs the help of a person temporarily (eg when recovering from a bout of flu) it is best given from behind – with the care assistant supporting the resident's hips (one hand firmly on each side of the pelvis on the hip bones, just below waist level). Although help is often given under the arm on the opposite side to the stick, it is good to avoid this, as it can damage the shoulder of a resident who has had a stroke, which causes great pain.

Walking frame
A resident who finds walking more difficult, who leans heavily on one care assistant or who needs two care assistants to walk, probably needs a walking frame.

All homes need a good stock of standard sized frames (approximately 33" height) as most residents needing a frame use this size. A few large adjustable frames (33"-36") are needed for taller residents and an occasional tiny resident will need the junior adjustable size (approximately $27\frac{1}{2}$"-$31\frac{1}{2}$").

The following steps are necessary before giving a resident a walking frame:

1. **Decide on the height.** Try what "looks like" a frame of the right size first. With the frame on the ground, the resident holding the frame and leaning forward slightly on it (the back legs of the frame should be level with her feet) her arms should only be slightly bent. If she hunches forward and looks "bent" over the frame, it is too low; if her elbows are very bent and her shoulders pushed up, then the frame is too high.

If the standard size frame is unsuitable, try the appropriate adjustable frame, adjusting it until the resident looks and feels comfortable.

2. When you think you have a frame of the

correct height, you will need to **teach the resident to walk with it.** Most people given a frame and no instruction will walk wrongly or even dangerously with it. In order to gain support and benefit from a walking frame, the following walking pattern is essential:

• put the frame well forward so that it can be leant on with arms nearly at full stretch
• take a normal-sized step with the "bad" leg (if there is one – if not, either)
• step *past* the "bad" leg with the "good" leg
• repeat the sequence

NB: The walking frame should be on the ground when either foot is off the ground.

3. Before giving the frame to the resident **check that it has a strong, safe suction ferrule** on each leg.

4. Walking with a frame is a complex activity, so you will probably need **several training sessions** with the resident to make sure she has learnt to use it correctly.

5. If the resident needs the physical help of a person as well as a walking frame (hopefully only temporarily while gaining confidence in it or recovering from illness) it is best to give help from behind. As a walking frame is held and moved forward by the resident using *both* hands it unbalances the walking pattern and resident to help under *one* arm. Help should therefore be given from behind as described in the section on walking sticks. This is also safer for the care assistant. Should the resident suddenly collapse for any reason, the care assistant can lower her to the ground with full control, by bending her own knees and keeping a straight back.

This is impossible when holding a resident on one side – both resident and care assistant may fall. Another advantage of holding "from behind" is that help can gradually be reduced without the resident being aware of it.

How NOT to use a walking frame:

1. **Carrying the frame.** This is a hazardous activity and should be discouraged. The resident might try walking without an aid or using a walking stick.

2. **Pushing the frame.** This too is unsafe. The resident may need a frame-on-wheels.

3. **Lifting one side of the frame after the other** with a rotary motion. The resident who does this probably does not need a frame; a stick should suffice.

4. **Walking "into"** the frame. This happens when steps are taken which are too large. After two steps, the resident has her tummy right against the front bar of the frame, which is unbalanced and unsafe.

5. **Moving the frame and feet "at random"** with no pattern. This wastes the balance-aiding, weight-bearing value of the frame. Residents using the frame in these last two ways should be taught the correct walking pattern.

The Frame-on-wheels

The frame-on-wheels is a walking frame fitted with wheel units on the front legs which is pushed gently along. The ferrules at the back prevent any "running away" because as soon as weight is put on the frame it stops. Side-slip does not occur, as the wheels are restricted to forward movement. The frame-on-wheels is available in two adjustable sizes: for large/average adults and small adults/children.

The frame-on-wheels is very useful for elderly people who need a lot of help from one person or help from two people, but who cannot cope mentally with learning the walking pattern necessary to use a walking frame correctly. It is also surprisingly (it does not run away) useful for older people with Parkinson's Disease as it can make their walking more fluent.

Decide on the correct height of a frame-on-wheels for a resident in the same way as for a walking frame. Any help required should be given from behind.

Special bags can be obtained which enable personal possessions to be carried on both kinds of frame. Handbag hooks can also be obtained.

Quadruped

Residents who have one "bad" leg (from severe arthritis in one hip or knee or a stroke), who need more support than a walking stick but less than a walking frame, may need a quadruped.

The following steps are necessary before giving a resident a quadruped:

1. **Measure,** using the same principles as for a walking stick - the quadruped is itself adjustable.

2 **Check that the four suction ferrules are safe** and replace them if necessary.

3. The quadruped should be **held in the opposite hand** to the resident's "bad" leg.

4. Teach the resident to walk using the following **walking pattern:**

• put the quadruped forward
• take a normal-sized step with the opposite foot
• take a normal-sized step with the other foot so that it lands level with or just past the quadruped
• repeat the sequence.

5. **If a resident improves** and starts to walk faster putting the quadruped and opposite leg forward together, she is probably ready to change to a walking stick.

6. If physical help is needed give it "on the hips" from behind as for a walking stick.

When a quadruped is not in use, ie. is free standing on the floor, it can easily be knocked over. This is a potential hazard which care staff need to remember.

Trolleys: Residents who usually use walking aids can be independent when transporting items (eg a cup of tea) by using a high trolley on wheels.

Assessment and teaching

It is essential for walking aids to be used correctly. Therefore all care staff must be able to teach how to use them, and continually remind residents of the appropriate correct, safe walking pattern. As it is difficult to teach a skill you have not mastered yourself, you should "try out" the walking aids covered above using the correct walking patterns.

As a resident's needs may change, it is important regularly to re-assess her walking, to ensure that she is still using the appropriate walking aid.

If a resident's walking deteriorates (which is usually very obvious) she may need a walking aid which offers more support.

If a resident's walking improves (which often goes unnoticed) she may need a walking aid which offers less support, or no walking aid at all.

Encouraging walking

Even when a resident has the correct walking aid and knows how to use it you may find she is reluctant to walk. Pain and stiffness caused by prolonged sitting may be the cause, in which case bending and stretching the legs a few times before walking may help.

However the usual reason for not walking is lack of motivation. Older people in a residential home need an enticing destination in order to feel that it is worth making the effort to walk.

The longer a person sits in a chair the more mental and physical effort it takes to get out of it. Therefore long periods of sitting must be "broken up" by providing many and varied destinations in addition to the basic reasons for moving, ie visits to the toilet, the dining room or returning to the bedroom.

A group of care assistants gave the following good list of activities to entice residents out of their chairs:

• providing tea and coffee in the dining room, rather than the sitting room

• group activities in another part of the home, eg keep-fit, disco, music and movement, bingo, craft sessions, card games, etc

• gardening (indoor or outdoor)

• outings outside the home: to the pub, library, church, community centre or further afield.

If walking to another room is very difficult for a particular resident, start her off first and position chairs along the route for necessary rests.

If a resident *can* walk, always use *every* possible alternative to the dreaded independence-robber – the wheelchair. Do not give in to persuasion. Only use a wheelchair if the resident is really ill.

Risk and independence

Let us imagine an old gentleman who uses a walking stick as he is a little unsteady on his feet. It is Friday night and he wants to go to the pub nearby for a drink. He is perfectly capable of locating the pub and returning from it, but he is discouraged from going by the staff at his residential home because "he might fall".

Is the slight risk of his falling such that he should be discouraged or even "not allowed" to pursue his usual (when he lived in his own home) Friday night activity? Or is this an acceptable risk which must be taken to enable this gentleman to remain independent and purposeful?

Just because he cannot continue to live alone at home does not mean that he cannot retain responsibility for some areas of his life when in a residential home. Indeed he must retain this responsibility if he is to stay truly alive.

Defining what constitutes "acceptable" risk for an individual resident is very diffi-

cult and can only be done after careful discussion of all the factors involved between the staff and the resident. There are very few, if any, situations in which a resident wishes to attempt an activity which in fact turns out to be an "unacceptable" risk. Encouraging elderly people to be independent, despite an acceptable level of risk, is to encourage them to remain active in body and mind.

Care assistants may also need to take the initiative in stimulating residents to take risks. An elderly lady who likes to walk holding a care assistant's arm, but who really does not require this help, may be taught to use a walking aid and then be encouraged to use it independently.

After the "supervision" stage has been successfully negotiated, this lady can walk around the home, albeit with a slight degree of risk. She could lose her balance and fall – but this is judged "unlikely", so the risk is "acceptable". If falling were thought to be "likely", then the risk would be unacceptable.

Getting up after illness

Elderly people must get up as soon as possible after illness because if they stay in bed the following threaten their health and mobility:

• they become stiff and weak very quickly because they are not using their legs for walking

• their lung capacity becomes smaller

• they do not breathe deeply and fluid collects in the lungs

• they find this fluid difficult to cough up and they quickly succumb to pneumonia

• circulation deteriorates

• they are more likely to suffer a thrombosis, because of poor circulation. (This can cause a number of serious problems, any of which can lead to death.)

It is therefore essential for residents to be encouraged gradually to regain their previous mobility as soon as their illness has passed its acute stage (usually when the temperature has returned to normal).

When helping older people to get up for the first few times after illness into a chair by the bed, do everything *slowly* with them. For example, you might say:

1. "Sit over the edge of the bed *slowly*".
2. "Sit on the edge of the bed *for a few minutes*" (to get used to having legs down and head up).
3. "Stand up *slowly*" – use a walking frame for them to hold onto when in the standing position if necessary.
4. "Turn around and lower yourself into the chair *slowly* ".

Shoes or slippers?

Most residents wear unsuitable footwear. Slippers and soft shapeless shoes allow an elderly foot to spread and fall over so that shoes may eventually not be able to be worn and walking becomes unstable. They also "slop" at the heel which is dangerous and encourages elderly people to shuffle in order to keep the soft shoe/slipper on. Shuffling is dangerous as feet can catch on carpet edges or scatter rugs, causing falls.

High-heeled shoes, worn by a few residents, are clearly unsafe as they provide such an unstable base.

After explanation of the value of shoes for safe walking, all residents should be encouraged to wear shoes, if only for part of the day. Men should wear ordinary outdoor shoes. Women should be encouraged to wear a "sensible" pair of shoes. These can be difficult to find, but some mail-order firms provide excellent shoes for elderly women, often at very reasonable prices.

Surgical shoes are needed by a few residents with special (often arthritic) foot problems or when a surgical appliance (caliper or heel raise) has to be fitted onto the shoe. Incontinent residents may need machine washable shoes which some large department stores stock. They are not suitable for most other residents.

If a resident cannot get her shoes on she may need chiropody, new shoes or special shoes. Swollen feet may also be the cause; or if diabetic, the circulation in her feet may be deteriorating. These conditions should be reported to the GP. See also Chapter 15 on care of the feet.

Varicose ulcers

It is vital to notice a mark on the skin, or broken skin, early and treat it immediately as leg ulcers cause pain and immobility. As well as nursing treatment, walking must be encouraged as it boosts the circulation and maintains mobility.

A resident with an ulcer, however small, should never have her feet down on the floor when sitting. They should be up on a stool which supports the whole leg and raises the feet above hip-level. Only then can gravity help the circulation so that the extra fluid drains out of the legs, giving the ulcer the best possible chance of healing quickly.

Chairs

Chairs are probably the most important items of equipment in a residential home. Not only because so much time is spent in them, but also because much energy is used to get them and risk taken getting into them. Unsuitable chairs give care assistants unnecessary work and discourage independence.

Gradual replacement of obsolete dining room chairs without arms with stable chairs with arms is essential if the comfort and safety needs of frail elderly people are to be met. Even more important is the replacement of unsuitable low sitting room chairs (which only suit the needs of a few very frail residents) with supportive, high-backed chairs with a variety of seat heights and depths (Most will need to be 18-20" high).

Once these are available, they are only useful if the correct chair is matched to the needs of each individual resident. A person who cannot get up from a low chair without help may be independent from a high chair. Providing a chair with a high seat for this resident will encourage her to maintain her independence and her dignity.

Getting out of chairs

If chairs are suitable, and a chair has been carefully chosen to meet a resident's individual need, yet she still says she cannot get out of it, what can care staff do?

Help her? No! *Teach her* how to do it by the method which works for most elderly people. The instructions to give her are:
1. "Wriggle to the edge of the chair" (by wriggling hips forward)
2. "Bring your feet back as far as possible" (knees should be bent to at least a right angle)
3. "Now put your hands on the chair arms"
4. "Lean forward" (when learning how to get out of a chair, a resident may need a firm but gentle hand on the top of her back to encourage her to bend forward)
5. "Now push with your hands on the chair arms, keep on leaning forward, and stand up!"

If after considerable teaching, the resident does need physical help, it should be minimal, and the helper should avoid dragging on the shoulder.

All care staff need to acquire the vital skill of teaching this method, to enable elderly people to get out of chairs independently. Getting out of a chair independently provides excellent muscle-strengthening and joint mobilising activity which

helps to keep an older person fit and active.

Getting out of chairs with a walking aid

With a walking stick: Hold the walking stick in the curled fingers of one hand, while using the "heel of the hand" to push up from the chair.

With a quadruped: Do not hold onto the quadruped while getting out of the chair (unsafe), but take hold of it when standing firmly.

With a frame: Do not hold onto the frame while getting out of the chair (unsafe), but take hold of it when standing.

Picking up items off the floor

Some residents find leaning forward to get out of a chair difficult and uncomfortable. This may be because they habitually avoid the bending forward position as it is awkward, makes them feel slightly dizzy and therefore anxious.

Thus when something needs picking up off the floor (a handkerchief or a newspaper) a "helpful" care assistant always does it – depriving the resident of the opportunity to practice and therefore retain the ability to bend forward at the hips.

Since "what you don't use, you lose" it is preferable for the elderly person to pick up the items off the floor with supervision or as little help as necessary.

For some residents a "helping-hand" aid or "pick up stick" can enable this activity to be carried out independently.

Getting into chairs

This is a hazardous activity because many elderly people have a compulsion to sit in the chair as soon as possible, once they are within reach of it. They therefore sit down in a great hurry before getting close enough to the chair, and may land on the floor. This can have disastrous consequences, including the possibility of a fractured neck-of-femur.

Uncontrolled movements like this are always unsafe; to avoid danger and to encourage controlled, safe movement the following sequence should be taught:

1. "Move towards the chair but do not try and sit on it yet".

2. "When you are close enough, turn all the way round until you have your back to the chair."

3. "Walk backwards until you feel the chair behind the back of your knees".

4. "Lean forward while feeling for the chair arms with first one hand and then the other".

5. "*Gradually* lower yourself to sit gently on the chair" (doing it slowly is important because it gives additional exercise to important muscles and prevents jarring of the spine).

It is essential to emphasise the first instruction and stop the elderly person *before* she lurches dangerously into the chair, by reminding her not to sit in the chair *until* she has turned all the way round and can feel the chair.

Toilet and bathroom

The sequences for getting on and off the toilet are the same as those for getting on and off chairs, just described.

Many residents find it difficult to get on and off the toilet. Rather than care assistants helping them physically, which creates dependence, it is preferable to fix suitable rails for their use. A great variety of rails are available for different situations; it is therefore essential for an occupational therapist to advise on toilet fixtures. (Many homes have rails which are useless because they are the wrong type or fixed in the wrong place).

A removable high toilet seat can make a resident (eg with severe hip arthritis) who finds the toilet too low, independent. A hook in each toilet is useful for residents to hang their walking sticks on, as these are a nuisance or dangerous if just propped up.

Many residents will be able to manage the bath alone if they use a bath seat, bath board, non–slip mat and well–positioned grab rails. A range of smaller bath aids will enable many residents to wash in privacy. **NB** an occupational therapist should advise on the use of toilet and bath aids with particular residents.

Beds

Most homes have beds approximately 16" high (including mattress) which is rather on the low side. Low beds are difficult to get up from and more risky to sit down onto. The optimum height for an elderly resident to manage safely and easily is usually 18"-20" high.

As a firm surface is easier to move on, sit safely down onto and rise from, beds should be firm. Softer beds can be made firmer with a board/boards under the mattress. Low beds can be raised on special, solid blocks.

Scatter rugs are dangerous for older people as they can easily be slipped or tripped on.

Moving while lying in bed

The basic instructions for moving sideways or up and down in the bed are:

1. "Lie on your back"

2. "Bend up your knees with your feet flat on the bed"

3. "Put your elbows firmly on the bed near your waist"

4. "Lift your bottom off the bed"

5. "Push on your elbows and feet and move your bottom up/down/to right/to left".

Rolling in bed

Usually achieved by:

1. "Turn your head to face in the direction you are rolling to"

2. "Bend up the leg of the side you are rolling away from with your foot flat on the bed"

3. "Reach with your arm for the side you

are rolling to"
4. "Push on the foot of the bent-up leg and roll over".

Getting out of bed

Usually achieved by:
1. "Roll towards the edge of the bed"
2. "Swing your legs over the edge of the bed"
3. "Push up on your hands and sit up".

Having got to this point elderly people, particularly those with low blood-pressure, may need a little time to get used to the upright position before getting off the bed.

Getting off the bed

This is the same basic procedure as getting off a chair or the toilet:
1. "Wriggle to the edge of the bed"
2. "Bring your feet back as far as you can, so that your knees are bent to at least a right-angle"
3. "Now put your hands on the edge of the bed"
4. "Lean forward"
5. "Now push with your hands on the edge of the bed, keep leaning forward and stand up".

NB Residents who use walking frames should be taught not to pull on them when getting off the toilet, bed or chair, as it is dangerous. It is also dangerous for a care assistant to stabilize the bottom bar of the walking frame with a foot and the top by leaning on it, so that the resident can pull on the frame to get up. Why? If the care assistant is not there and the resident tries to get up by pulling on the frame, they may fall.

Getting on to the bed

This activity can be hazardous and worrying for elderly people. Using the following sequence makes the activity safer and more comfortable:
1. "Approach the side of the bed, but do not try and sit on it yet"
2. "Turn all the way round until you have

your back to the bed"
3. "Walk backwards till you feel the bed behind the back of your knees"
4. "Make sure you are about half-way along the bed. If not move sideways till you are"
5. "Lean forward and feel for the bed edge with first one hand, then the other"
6. "Gradually lower yourself to sit on the bed gently".

Getting into bed

This is an awkward activity, which can result in a lot of unnecessary humping and lifting, if the elderly resident is not aware of how to position herself before lying on the bed.
These instructions should make it easier:
1. "Make sure you are seated about half-way along the bed"
2. "While sitting on the edge of the bed, move your bottom so that you are facing the foot of the bed"
3. "Swing your legs up on to the bed, meanwhile flinging your body back on to the bed". This must be done *quickly* or the resident may remain on the edge of the bed feebly trying to gather up sufficient courage to have another go; or she may get her body back on the bed and fail to get her legs up, which is uncomfortable; or worse she may just ask for and receive help – all of which may be avoided by following the steps above.

Wheelchairs

Wheelchairs for individual residents

A permanently disabled resident who has been carefully assessed as needing a wheelchair permanently, is entitled to one of her own from the DoH. The GP and a physiotherapist or an occupational therapist should be involved in obtaining the correct chair individually chosen for the resident. Once supplied, this chair should only be used by the particular resident for whom it was obtained.

The few residents who because of permanent disability (eg double amputation) need a wheelchair of their own, but who can transfer independently from bed to chair, chair to toilet etc, should be encouraged to do this, in order to maintain their independence. They should also wheel *themselves* from place to place whenever possible.

Wheelchairs for residents with declining mobility

The majority of residents who are in wheelchairs need them because of deteriorating mobility. This chapter has looked at many ways of avoiding loss of mobility when this is possible.

However despite medical treatment and all attempts to keep them moving independently, some elderly people with diseases like arthritis and Parkinson's Disease do become less mobile and may eventually need a wheelchair.

It should then be used for as little of the day as possible and a maximum amount of walking should be encouraged. Even one short walk a day provides invaluable exercise, and will help the resident to remain active in body and mind as long as possible.

Wheelchairs for general use

A home for elderly people probably needs at least one communal wheelchair plus thick foam cushion, for residents who are recovering from illness. This wheelchair should never be used to save time wheeling residents who are capable of walking, as it eventually leads to permanent dependence.

Wheelchairs must be maintained as they are dangerous if tyres are flat, brakes do not work or foot plates get loose.

Wheelchair transferring – with help

Residents who are dependent and in wheelchairs for part or all of the day may still be able to do a lot of the work involved in transferring from bed to chair, chair to toilet, etc themselves.

Even if they require help in transferring, residents should be encouraged to use their arms to push with and to take as much weight through their legs as they can. This will help maintain their remaining strength, balance and concentration. Total lifts should rarely be necessary.

Points to remember

1. Encourage older people to keep active because what you don't use, you lose.
2. Remember to think of ways to encourage each resident to stay mobile and independent.
3. Sticks and walking frames are better than depending on a helper to walk.
4. Think carefully before you use a wheelchair, and don't do it just to "save time".

NVQ Levels 2 & 3 Core Units
O Promote equality for all individuals.
U4 Contribute to the health, safety and security of individuals and their environment.
U5 Obtain, transmit and store information relating to the delivery of a care service.

Level 2 Direct Care
Z6 Enable clients to maintain and improve their mobility.
Z7 Contribute to the movement and treatment of clients to maximise their physical comfort.
Z11 Enable clients to access and use toilet facilities.
Z19 Enable clients to achieve physical comfort.

CHAPTER 15

Care of the feet

Judith Kemp

• Normal feet and how they grow • Walking • Skin and nail care • Special care for vulnerable feet • When to call the chiropodist • Footwear

Foot care is of major importance to older people. Three out of four of them will have some foot problems. There are many simple tasks within the capability of any caring person, which I will describe. These can make the feet more comfortable, without needing the help of a professional chiropodist.

Normal feet

Each foot contains 26 bones joined by ligaments and moved by the actions of muscles in the leg and foot. Most children are born with normal feet, and at birth, the foot bones are mostly soft cartilage (like the end of your nose) which is gradually replaced by hard bone over the first eighteen years of life.

If the joints develop in an abnormal position, the way that the foot moves will be affected, and it will not function as efficiently as it should.

This may not cause much discomfort in younger people, but often does in old age. many foot problems are due to poor foot function, but the foot can also be affected by problems with the knees, hips and spine. Many so called "flat feet" are in fact caused by the relationship of the leg with the pelvis at the hip.

Walking

In a normal foot during walking, the outer edge of the back of the heel strikes the ground first. The shock is transmitted up the leg where the bent knee acts as a shock absorber. The outside edge of the foot then begins to take weight, followed by the ball of the foot, starting at the outside edge and then across to the base of the big toe. Whilst this is happening the heel is lifting off the ground and the foot finally leaves the ground as the big toe pushes off. The other foot does the same things but at a different time.

The muscles in the thigh lift the whole limb off the ground in walking whilst those below the knee control the movement of the foot. There are many more small muscles within the foot itself, which also affect toe function and stabilise the foot during walking.

When there is something wrong with the foot, knee or hip the normal cycle becomes disrupted and some parts of the foot may take too much weight, or take weight for too long. Other parts of the foot may not be doing their fair share of the work. This results in foot deformity, corns, callouses, foot strain and in some patients, ulcers caused by pressure.

Skin and nail care

The skin needs to be kept clean, supple and intact, because most germs causing infection like warm, dark, damp conditions. Because the feet are usually covered by hosiery and shoes, they are particularly vulnerable to bacterial, viral and fungal infections. In addition, older skin tends to be drier than young skin and may be undernourished if the circulation is not good. The following routine will help to prevent skin problems:

Wash the feet with warm water and good quality soap. Elderly people's feet may not need washing every day as do more active feet. The temperature should be tested with a thermometer and must not exceed 40C (104F). This is to avoid scalding fragile or insensitive skin. Unless instructed by a doctor or chiropodist nothing should be added to the washing water, nor should feet be soaked.

If the toes are very tight together, do not pull them apart or pass the flannel between them, as this can split the skin. Use a cotton bud to gently wash between them.

Dry carefully, using a soft towel. Dry between the toes gently, using paper kitchen towels to absorb the water.

After drying, cut the toe nails if this needs to be done. If not massage the skin with a cream such as Simple Ointment BP, or a good quality hand cream. Pay particular attention to the heels which tend to be the driest part of the foot. Do not cream between the toes as this area tends to be moist in any case.

If the skin looks white, soggy or peeling, swab gently with Surgical Spirit BPC. This may sting slightly but will quickly restore the skin to health. Repeat as often as needed to keep the skin texture normal.

Nail cutting

Cutting the toe nails does cause some anxiety, especially if you are not used to doing this job, and because toe nails tend to become harder and thicker with age. Ideally, residents should be screened by a State Registered Chiropodist to ensure that anyone whose feet are potentially at risk, receives professional help (see below). If this is not possible, check the

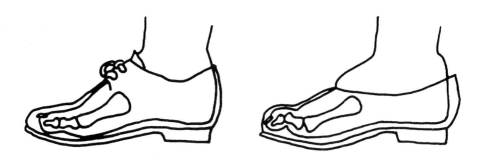

A properly fitted shoe (left) allows for the foot to lengthen and spread out in walking. In a shoe without proper fastenings (right) the foot pushes forward in walking.

person's medical history. If they are diabetic, taking anticoagulants or steroids, check with their GP before proceeding.

The procedure should always be supervised by a chiropodist and/or qualified nurse. You will need:

1. A pair of **chiropodist's nail nippers** which can be bought from a good chemist shop. You will find them much easier to use than nail scissors, especially if you practise on your own finger and toe nails first.

2. A **diamond faced file** which can be boiled between use on residents, or disposable emery boards which can be kept for each individual. This is essential to prevent passing on fungal or other infections. Fungal infections of the nails usually make them discoloured and crumbly. They can be treated with a paint or cream, but this takes about nine months to be effective.

• Make the resident comfortable with their shoes and hosiery off. Their feet should be on a soft stool, covered with a clean, non fluffy cloth or disposable sheet, at a height convenient to you. Make sure the light is good, and place a low seat for you, facing the resident. Then wash your hands.

• Start with the little toe nearest to your "nipper" hand. Hold the toe firmly (so that you do not tickle) with the thumb and finger of the other hand. Start by taking a small cut into the nail, making sure you are not going to clip the flesh before you shut the nippers. Shut the blades by pressing firmly on the handles. A "snatched" movement is less effective and may cause you to pull on the nail which can cause pain.

• Continue to take small cuts until you reach the other side of the nail. Nails should not be cut too short. The nail should be as long as the fleshy part of the toe and you should not cut down the sides of the nail with the nippers.

• Once you have cut all ten nails, the corners can be rounded with the file or emery board. The free edge should be filed smooth. If the nails are thickened, the file can be used to reduce the thickness as well as the length. For residents whose nails do not grow very much, regular filing may be all that is needed.

• Finish with a massage with cream as outlined above.

Special care

The feet can be affected by any disease which affects the body; in particular diseases of the nerves, muscles, circulation, skin, joints or the ability to fight infection. There are some groups whose feet are particularly at risk:

Diabetics. These people tend to have poor circulation especially in the toes, which leads to under-nourished skin, muscles and nerves. They may not feel their feet as well as normal, and can have bleeding blisters or grazes without feeling pain. they tend to develop pressure ulcers because they do not feel pain if they stand or sit in one position too long.

They are also less sensitive to heat and cold and may be scalded or get chilled without realising it. Any damage to the skin, however minor, needs good first aid treatment, careful daily observation and referral to a chiropodist or doctor at the first sign that healing is not occurring. Diabetics are less able to fight infections of all kinds.

People with **diseases of the nervous system** such as strokes, multiple sclerosis, spina bifida or who have had polio. The effects of these diseases vary but there is usually some loss of muscle power and nerve activity. The way in which the person walks (if at all) is altered, putting abnormal strains on the feet, and sensation may be lost.

People on **steroid drugs or drugs for cancer.** These drugs affect the body's ability to fight infection and relatively minor infections can become very serious in these people.

People with **poor circulation.** Many people find their circulation becomes poorer when they get older, but for some the problem is severe enough to need treatment from GP or hospital. They are at risk because the blood supply plays a vital part in fighting infection and healing. If it is diminished, these processes are severely restricted and infections may take hold much more quickly and with much greater damage than in the normal person.

Any resident who is taking **medication of any sort** or who has a foot problem should be seen by a doctor or chiropodist before care staff attempt foot care.

When to call the chiropodist

Ideally, each home should have a State Registered Chiropodist to advise and give treatment as necessary. The local District Health Authority should be approached for advice. They will not always treat on the premises if conditions are not adequate for good practice, but a screening service may be available. Residents should attend the local clinic wherever possible.

Once residents have been screened the chiropodist will advise on individual residents and should be called if anyone develops a new painful area, any increased redness or swelling in the feet, any colour change, any infection area which looks as if it might turn septic. This is especially important for residents with feet at risk as outlined above.

Footwear

Footwear plays an important part in foot health. The basic requirements for a good shoe are:

Length: the shoe should be about 12 mm longer than the toes when standing with the fastenings done up.

Width: the foot should sit on the sole of the shoe and to hang over the edge, causing the uppers to bulge.

Depth: the front of the shoe should be deep enough so as not to rub on the toes or toe nails. This can be difficult to achieve if the toes are curly.

Fastenings: good shoes have an adjustable fastening across the instep to stop the foot sliding forward into the toe area and crushing the toes together. Laces, bars with buckles or "touch and close" (eg Velcro) all make good fastenings.

Heels: these should not be too high, and should be chunky rather than thin, to increase ankle stability.

Residents should be encouraged to wear shoes indoors for the greater part of the day, as slippers rarely fit the requirements of a good shoe as described. Slippers should be kept for early mornings or late at night, and it is essential that they are in good repair.

Further reading
The foot care book: An A-Z of fitter feet, designed for elderly people and their carers, by Judith Kemp. Published by Age Concern England, Astral House 1268 London Road, London SW16 4ER

NVQ Levels 2 & 3 Core Units
O Promote equality for all individuals.
U4 Contribute to the health, safety and security of individuals and their environment.
Level 2 Direct Care
Z6 Enable clients to maintain and improve their mobility.
Z9 Enable clients to maintain their personal hygiene and appearance.

CHAPTER 16

Safe manual handling
(and special mobility needs of the person with dementia)

Tracy Packer

• Are you really encouraging independence and promoting mobility?
• What can affect or restrict movement • The little things that matter a lot
• Good communication • The effects of the environment • Safe manual handling
• When just a little help is needed

Sometimes I can walk into an area of care and very quickly assess how much independence is encouraged and whether as much mobility as possible is promoted. Time and time again, I see a person with dementia sitting forward in his chair just attempting to stand up, only to be pushed back into the chair by a well meaning care worker saying: "Sit down Bob! You can't get up now, there'll be a nice cup of tea along in a minute."

A similar variation on this theme often takes place. Bob has, after a huge effort, successfully managed to stand up and shakily walked a few yards up the corridor. He is again taken by the hands and led back to his chair, often being scolded: "You can't go there Bob, now just sit down for a little while will you?"

Zimmer frames and walking sticks are carefully "tidied away" out of arms' reach, and small tables are firmly positioned in front of people sitting passively in their armchairs. Does this happen purely out of a need to keep an area clutter-free, or to ensure that food and drink can be reached? Or is there, in fact, an insidious kind or restraint taking place?

There is much that care workers can do to limit or encourage the amount of movement a person can be enabled to achieve. Promoting optimum mobility involves a certain amount of risk-taking, but the likely improvement to a person's quality of life always makes it worthwhile.

Promoting mobility

Many people with dementia will never have difficulties getting around, but some people do experience severe problems in this area. Mobility can be affected when people get further medical problems as a result of, or as well as, the effects of their dementia. They may also be affected as a direct result of damage to the parts of the brain which co-ordinate movement and balance.

Conditions which might affect mobility
• Conditions causing pain in the joints and muscles, particularly finger, hip and knee joints, may restrict a person's ability to get around. These may be arthritis, rheumatism, gout or bone fractures.

• Diseases which affect the circulation

can also affect movement. Long-standing diabetes may lead to a dulling of sensations in the fingers and toes. Heart problems and high or low blood pressure can lead to dizziness and fainting, particularly after lying down and getting up too quickly.

• Migraine can severely affect vision and perception, and tinnitus (ringing in the ears) can affect the mechanism in the inner ear which co-ordinates the ability to balance.

• Some drugs can make people drowsy, unco-ordinated and unsteady. Alcohol alone can also do this, but even small amounts of alcohol mixed with some medication can have the same effect.

• Sometimes the ability of the brain to make sense of distance and space, as well as tell the difference between patterns, shadows and objects, can be severely affected by damaged eyesight or even the dementing process. This may make a person feel too frightened to move, or may contribute to unsteadiness or accidents which do not appear to have an obvious cause.

• Chest conditions such as asthma, bronchitis, infections and lung cancer can render a person too breathless to make even the smallest movements or shortest walks bearable. Anaemia may also make someone breathless.

• Any condition which weakens muscles and bones, may lead to a restriction of the ability to bend, stretch or support one's own body weight. Nutritional deficiencies, damaged tendons/ligaments, and obesity are just a few of these.

Encouraging independence

Often, when we know that someone can walk with only minimal assistance, it is easy to fall into the trap of thinking that they are being lazy or stubborn when they refuse to change position or walk anywhere. The other trap is, of course, to blame the process of dementia. This is easily done, and when a person with dementia refuses to "come for a little walk", you may hear comments like:

"Oh don't worry about what he says, he's very confused and doesn't know what's going on. Just do it anyway."

This kind of scenario can lead to great frustration for everyone. It is often the result of care workers automatically "blaming" the dementing process for a person's behaviour, instead of accepting that there might be perfectly good reasons why they should **not** do what you have asked them to do. The difficulty is in finding out what these reasons are, and doing something about them. In an ideal world these reasons should be discovered before a "job" needs to be started. But this is often easier said than done!

Consider the simple things in life

Some ladies are unhappy about going anywhere without their handbags. If they are unable to manage their bag as well as a zimmer frame, there are special net bags which can safely be attached to the frame to hold handbags etc. This may seem a trivial detail to you, but the walk will be much more enjoyable if you take such concerns seriously.

Some people may be afraid of losing a comfortable seat in their absence. Others may be afraid of their trousers or underwear falling down. Be sure that belts and braces are well fastened, buttons are done up, catheter bags have been drained, and that they and other continence aids are discreetly hidden.

Has the person you are about to walk with been to the toilet recently?

Many people live in fear of having an "accident" in front of everybody when they are walking. It is often worth discreetly offering to take them to the toilet before you start. This can of course be part of getting them moving. Other people may have a urinary infection, or stress incontinence which makes them feel as if they need to be very close to a toilet at all times. Even if they have appropriate continence aids, and lots of reassurance, you may have to compromise with a circular walk in the general area.

So that you can chat while walking with them, ensure they are wearing hearing appliances if they use them, as well as dentures and spectacles. Zimmer frames and walking sticks often get mixed up, so ensure they are labelled or easily identifiable. Always make sure they are used.

What is the routine in your area?

Some people may think they will miss out on a cup of tea, their mealtime, or even a visitor, if they go for a walk at a specific time. Emphasise that they will be back on time and make sure that they are.

If they have missed out on a drink, make sure you get one for them on their return. If you do not, they may refuse to come with you in future.

Try to have a chair ready at the end of the walk. Some people will refuse such a journey ever again, because they had to stand in front of a room full of people staring at them while a chair was being found.

Imagine how you might feel walking into a room full of strangers, without having a chair to sit on when you get there: then having to stand there feeling like a trouble maker, or the odd one out, while another chair is being found?

Don't forget the less obvious things

Bunions, corns, calluses, verrucae and ingrowing toenails may seem common to you, but they are serious enough to hinder any active mobility. Make sure a referral to a chiropodist is made in order to sort these out. This should be done as soon as they are noticed, and long before intensive rehabilitation begins.

Not long ago, an unfortunate chiropodist I knew was kicked in the face by a very frightened lady who was having her feet done after a hip operation. The nursing staff had neglected to give her any pain killers! Chiropodists can't do their job properly if this is neglected, and such an oversight will only delay a person's recovery. If you think someone is in pain, let a trained member of staff know about it immediately.

Ill fitting shoes and loose, insecure footwear can all hinder movement. So can pain from arthritis, gout, leg ulcers and many other medical conditions. A headache can be all it takes.

Get to know the person, and the signs they show when they have pain. They may not always be able to tell you about it, or even point to the place where there is pain. However, they may become withdrawn, fidgety or even "guard" the area that is in pain. The more you know, the better equipped you will be to do something about it.

Have you allowed enough time?

In the world of health care, many of us would dearly love to have more time. However, all too often we inflict the everyday busyness of our daily routines upon the people with dementia in our care. I'll give you an example:

It was a very busy shift with all of the staff rushing to and fro trying to catch up with all the work that had yet to be completed. Mrs Smith was waiting for an ambulance to take her to an important appointment. It was late. She had sat there patiently waiting for almost an hour, when suddenly two burly men and two members of staff burst in through the door. One of the men said:

"I hope this won't take too long, as we're already behind and we've got another three pick-ups to do yet."

The two nurses rushed to Mrs Smith's side. She was startled and her eyes widened as they took each of her arms and, without speaking to her, attempted to stand her up.

Mrs Smith was having none of it. She dug her heels down, and pushed her bottom deep into the back of her chair. By this time she was very frightened and refused to go anywhere. It took all four of them half an hour to persuade her to get into the ambulance. You can imagine what state of mind she was in by the time she reached her destination. How would you like to have been the care worker at the other end, looking after Mrs Smith when she arrived?

If only someone had had the foresight to spend just five minutes with Mrs Smith as the ambulance arrived, explaining what was about to happen. It would have saved everyone a lot of time and unnecessary distress.

Are you making yourself clearly understood?

It obviously helps if a person understands what it is you are doing, and what it is you want them to do. We take so much of the spoken word for granted, but it is very important to be clear and concise. Simple words, short sentences, and plenty of repetition can often make life for everyone a whole lot easier (see also chapter 3). It is also important to watch carefully and listen, so we don't misunderstand.

If you had a very poor memory, what would you make of this: "Right, Mr Jones, I'm just going to make sure your slippers are on properly, then if you could stand up for me, we can take a little walk to the dining room. Can you just put your hands on the arms of the chair and push

up, then I'll be able to help you, OK?"

The chances are that Mr Jones is either still thinking about getting his slippers on at this point, or he's wondering what it is you're going to help him with. Either way, you can be pretty sure that no movement in any direction will have taken place. This is a better approach:

"Hello Mr Jones. It's lunchtime." (Pause.)

"Would you like to come to the dining room with me?" (Wait for his response.)

"I'll just check your slippers." (Do this.)

"Are you ready to go to the dining room?" (Await response.)

"I'll help you." (Offer him your arm.)

"Now get a good grip on the arm of the chair." (Guide his hands if necessary.)

"Good. Now push yourself up." (Wait for this to happen, and repeat the instruction if necessary.)

"Are you all right?" (Check that he is.)

"The dining room's this way Mr Jones." (Point out the correct direction before starting to walk.)

"Well done." (Always offer praise and reassurance.)

What are your non-verbal cues saying?

The ability to understand words and language is very often damaged in people with dementia. This may mean that no matter how hard you try to keep things simple and to the point, there are sometimes great difficulties in making yourself understood. This can be frustrating for all concerned.

Always be aware that your body and face tell a "thousand stories" about what sort of mood you are in, how busy or interested you are, or what you think of somebody. People with dementia can become very good at understanding what we mean by observing our complex

Edward refused to get out of bed for the first weeks after he was admitted to a specialist dementia unit. He would either get up around lunchtime, or the staff would attempt to wrestle with him to get him up sooner. It wasn't because he was tired and liked a lie in, which would have been fine, but he would point at the floor showing great fear and shaking his head.

The staff were baffled, but after one of them started some life story work with him, he found out that the gentleman was scared of water and had been involved in a nasty swimming accident when he was younger.

They then realised that the shadow cast on the shiny floor by the fine patterned curtains looked very "watery" as it moved about. When they closed the main curtains and put a light on when it was time to get up, there were no further problems.

body language. We can turn this to our advantage by using gestures, mime, and often specific sounds, in order to make ourselves clear.

When assisting someone to get up out of a chair, or walk, or sit back down again, it is important to give lots of reassurance in the form of smiles, nodding of your head, frequent eye contact, or thumbs up signs. A reassuring squeeze of the hand (or firm touch on the shoulder, if that's too personal) may just make the difference between someone giving up or successfully completing the task in hand.

Use your hands and eyes to indicate clear directions. Always try to appear calm, even if you are in a rush! Apply the same principles to non-verbal communications as spoken ones. That is: one instruction at a time, don't confuse your messages, and *listen*.

What effect does the environment have?

There is no doubt that the layout of a care setting can have a significant effect on the manner in which people with dementia can or cannot get around.

Floors that slope without warning can lead to a feeling of disturbed balance and uncertainty: people with dementia often slow down and grasp handrails more tightly if this happens. The change in texture from linoleum to carpet may affect the way wheels on a zimmer frame function, or the way the ground feels underfoot.

Pools of bright light or darkness across a corridor can be very deceptive, particularly if a person already has visual difficulties, as can heavy shadows and floor patterns. Strips of dark shadow or carpet edging can appear to be a step, and lead to a person refusing to go any further without any apparent reason.

Keep clutter and unnecessary objects out of the main thoroughfares in your area. If the place is turned into an obstacle course, you increase the chance of nasty accidents, "traffic jams" and general mayhem. Remember, if getting from A to B becomes a major chore, it is unlikely that someone will attempt it more than a very few times. Ensure that any spillage of fluids, talcum powder, food, etc, is cleared up immediately.

In many care environments, the most cluttered time of day is the morning, when hygiene needs are being met, beds made, and much of the general cleaning is taking place. At this time a plethora of linen skips, mops and sponges, buckets of water, cloths, detergent bottles, hoover/buffer leads, and the obligatory small pile of odds and ends from the floor which have been swept into a neat pile awaiting the bin, have to be negotiated.

It is important not to take these things for granted. If you can anticipate a problem, make sure you offer explanations

When assisting someone, reassurance and smiles help a lot. Try to appear calm, however busy you are.

and reassurance to the person well before they come across it. Ensure there are handrails along the way and that these are secured safely to the wall, free from splinters and clear of debris.

Does the person actually want to do it?

Sometimes there are things we want to do that involve the person we are caring for. It is important that we don't get so carried away with a task that we don't offer the person a choice over what is happening. Sometimes a person will simply say "No". Other times they may not speak, but simply refuse to comply with what it is you want, and do their utmost to make it difficult to complete.

If you go ahead and make someone do something against their will, you will damage any trusting relationship you have been building up, and in the case of moving someone, you may even hurt yourself.

This is unnecessary. If you've consid-ered some of the simple things that were mentioned earlier, and they still do not wish to comply, it is wise to respect a person's wishes. What is the worst thing that can happen? You can always come back and try again later. People with dementia should be able to take some control over what is happening to them. If they are able to be assertive, consider it a comple-ment. After all if they were too scared of you, they might have just complied and been very unhappy.

Are you confident in what you are trying to do?

Keep yourself up-to-date with the current manual handling regulations. You owe it to your colleagues and those in your care to do this, but most of all, you owe it to yourself.

Always use the equipment that is pro-vided, and if you are not sure how it should be used, it is your responsibility to find out before attempting to use it. Most places allocate a member of staff who is responsible for updating everyone in manual handling skills and regulations. Find out who it is and use them – consult them and ask them to show you the best way to do things. If you do not have one, or do not know who it is, go to the person in charge and ask them about it.

People with dementia can often tell whether you know what you are doing or not. If there is any hint of uncertainty in what you are doing or how you are doing it, they will very often pick it up. How keen would you be to let someone lift you out of a bed or bath with a complicated-looking piece of machinery, if you suspected they did not really know what they were doing? If a person is frightened about this, they may not let you near them in the first instance. It is not surprising that if someone has had a traumatic experience with a poorly handled hoist before, they are unlikely to want to repeat the experience.

Safe manual handling

An estimated 40,000 care staff are off sick with back problems every year, and over 3,600 give up their work every year because of back injury. Do not become another one of these statistics. Take the law seriously; it exists to protect you.

There are three key issues to consider:

• Whenever possible, you should avoid manual handling which involves a risk of injury.

• If you cannot avoid it, a written assessment of the manual handling activity should be made by a trained member of staff. This should give detailed guidance on the way you should approach the load (person), the task in hand, the immediate environment and the abilities of the person undertaking the task.

• Every step should be taken to reduce the risk to the lowest possible level which is reasonably practicable. This means using mechanical aids as much as possible.

An increase in knowledge of safer handling over the last few years has led to new guidelines on handling. This approach focuses on four main areas:

The task
How will the handling affect your body movement or posture? Will it involve:
  – twisting the torso?
  – stooping?
  – stretching upwards?
  – too much lifting or lowering?
  – too much carrying?
  – too much pushing or pulling?
  – sudden movement of the person with dementia?
  – frequent & prolonged physical effort?
  – not enough rest and recovery?

The load
In the context of this chapter, the "load" refers to the person you are thinking of handling and/or moving. Is this person:
  – heavy?
  – bulky or awkward to hold?
  – difficult to grasp?
  – agitated or likely to move?

The environment
The conditions that you work in can have an important effect on your ability to work safely. Is there:
  – plenty of room to use a good posture?
  – uneven, slippery or unstable flooring?
  – any variation in the floor level or work surfaces?
  – too low or too high temperature or humidity?
  – low or dazzling lighting?

The abilities of the individual
The more you know about your own capabilities, the easier and safer it will be for everyone concerned. Does the job:
  – require lots of strength, or a particular height of person?

– create risks for those who might be pregnant or have a health problem?

– require special information or training?

– become more difficult because of protective equipment or personal clothing?

What this all means is that by carefully thinking about what you have to do, well before you have to do it, you can reduce the risks to yourself. The person can often help out considerably if you know what you are doing, and they understand what it is you want them to do. However, a proper assessment may indicate that the risks are simply too great, and mechanical assistance should be used.

Are you looking after your back?

There are many things you can do to protect yourself from painful and un-necessary back injuries. Remember it is important to be responsible to yourself and your colleagues. If you are not, you may suffer the consequences for the rest of your life.

The daily routine

Many of the things that care workers are involved with during their normal, daily routine can contribute towards a future back injury.

Consider how many of the things mentioned below are part of your daily routine. Then think about how many stretches, twists and bends you make to get that task completed. Finally, think about how you might change the way you do these jobs by working with other colleagues, sitting down, or using the equipment or adaptions that are provided.

• Making a bed by yourself

• Making a bed in a restricted space with little room to move

• Bending over a low bed while making it

• Leaning over a bed to reach something on the locker at the other side of it

• Stooping over a person while taking their blood pressure

• Reaching for an item on a shelf much higher than you

• Moving a heavy piece of furniture.

The following are not only bad practice but dangerous for your back too:

• Standing up or leaning across a table to feed someone

• Standing when talking at length to someone who is sitting

• Moving a static chair with a person in it.

Posture

If you have to lift at all, it is important that you are aware of the correct way to position yourself. The main aim is to avoid any movement which may lead to twisting, stretching or loss of balance. Seemingly trivial details such as tight, restrictive clothing and dainty footwear will contribute to bad positioning. Consider these points:

• Is this lift really necessary?

• Is there any equipment you should use instead?

• Is the area around you free of hazards?

• Do the patient and any colleagues you are lifting with, fully understand what will be done?

• Is there enough room for you to bend at the knees?

• Are your feet apart by a hip width to help maintain your balance?

• Is one foot facing the direction you are going in?

• Are you as close as possible to the person, to reduce potential back strain?

• Have you got a good, dependable handhold?

• Is your back straight?

• Are you really concentrating on the task to be done?

Mechanical aids

It is the responsibility of employers to provide suitable equipment for manual handling purposes. It is the careworker's responsibility to make sure they understand exactly how pieces of equipment work, and inform themselves in order to stay up to date. Read the manufacturer's information, attend manual handling update courses, and remain competent not ignorant! Above all, use the equipment you are provided with, do not consider "just managing" or "getting by" without it.

You must also report any damage or operational failure to the person in charge immediately. If equipment is not working, it should be taken out of use and clearly marked as damaged. Failure to do so could lead to other care workers and/or patients injuring themselves needlessly.

Accident forms

If you think you have pulled a muscle or hurt your back in any way during your working day, you must let the person in charge know about it, and you will need to fill in an accident form.

You have a responsibility to yourself, your colleagues and your residents, to refrain from any manual handling at all while you have discomfort. It may even be more appropriate for you to stay away from work.

Accident forms may seem like tedious paperwork, but they are there to protect you. They may also provide evidence on your behalf, particularly if you feel that your injury was a result of negligence by your employer. Always fill in an accident form.

When just a little help is needed

There are many people in our care who are never totally dependant on mechanical aids to get about. However, they may need some help to get out of their bed or chair. There is a fine balance between assisting someone and actually lifting them, and it is important to understand the difference.

Chapter 14 sets out detailed sequences of instructions so that you can give verbal help and encouragement to the person, without lifting or giving any physical assistance. This helps the person stay as independent as possible for as long as possible.

And finally...

Being able to get around when we want and where we want is something we all take for granted. However, most of us at some time or another have experienced sweatiness and discomfort after a lengthy time sitting down on a hard or vinyl covered hospital chair. If not, you should try it sometime!

If you have ever badly sprained your ankle or broken your leg, you will have also experienced the complete reliance on supportive friends and relatives during your convalescence. You will remember the eternal "clock-watching" and the sheer relief and subsequent embarrassment at the arrival of someone to help you to get on to the toilet.

If this has not happened to you, try and imagine how you would cope for six weeks with your leg in a plaster. Then imagine that you are in a strange place surrounded by people you don't know, with only complete strangers to help you. Finally, think about how it might feel if you also had a poor memory.

Checklist for good practice

1. Daily routines and old habits can contribute to both the conscious and unconscious restraint of people with dementia. Take a look at the everyday practice in your area, to see if this is happening.

2. There are many physical conditions that can affect how much a person is able to get around. It is important to find out about these as soon after they are admitted as possible.

3. You need to get to know someone well in order to explain some of the individual differences which might affect their wish to move around. Always make sure the rest of the team know about these, in order to prevent frustrating misunderstandings.

4. Your verbal and non-verbal communication skills are important. Above all listen and observe. There may be a very good reason why someone is having difficulties.

5. Never force a person to do something which they clearly do not want to do. You may both end up getting hurt.

Take the pressure off the situation and come back later, or give someone else a chance to try.

6. Make sure you know where you stand with the law and the manual handling regulations. It is your responsibility to keep up to date.

7. The consequences of an injured back may last for a lifetime. Look after yourself and your colleagues. You may not get a second chance.

8. There are ways of helping people to move around without physically having to lift them. Learn about how the body moves normally and use this knowledge to promote their independence.

9. Imagine how you would cope if you were unable to get around without assistance, and then consider all the things that might make it feel less stressful. How does your practice compare?

Reference

Health and Safety Executive (1992) *The Manual Handling Operations Regulations 1992. Guidance on Regulations.* HSE Books, London.

CHAPTER 17

Pressure area care

by Claire Hale

• Who is at risk of developing pressure sores?
• What happens to body tissues under pressure • How to prevent damage
• How sores should be treated • Your role

A "pressure sore" is a term used to describe an area of damage to the skin and tissue underneath it, which has been caused primarily by unrelieved pressure. Pressure sores most frequently occur in people who cannot move without help.

The most vulnerable group is elderly people, who often sit or lie in the same position for long periods because they are unable to move themselves. This lack of mobility is often caused by some underlying condition such as arthritis, a stroke or a fractured hip following a fall.

A pressure sore leads to unnecessary suffering, pain and loss of dignity, while nurses and their assistants are likely to develop feelings of guilt, frustration and confusion.

The causes of sores

A pressure sore is caused by an interruption to the blood supply to that area. This interruption to the blood supply is usually caused by pressure, of which four types are generally recognised: compression, shearing, direct disruptive damage and friction.

Compression: This occurs when body tissues are squashed between a bone inside the body and a firm surface such as a bed (see Fig 1). The capillaries (tiny blood vessels) lying between the bone and the surface become narrowed or blocked and the blood supply to the tissues reduced. The tissues can eventually die from lack of oxygen (which is carried to them in the blood). A resident left sitting too long in one position will suffer from this type of pressure, and a pressure sore may result.

Shearing: Shearing forces are caused by dragging the skin over hard surfaces; the skin's surface becomes grazed and this damages the network of small blood vessels. Residents left in a semi-recumbent position (ie half-sitting, half lying) are liable to this type of damage particularly at their sacrum (the base of the spine) and heels from sliding down the bed (Fig 2).

Direct disruptive damage: This occurs when a severe blow to the tissues damages the capillaries; this once again causes disruption of the blood supply to the tissues, and tissues can die due to lack of

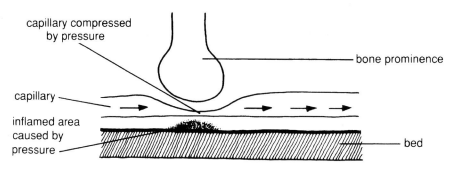

Fig 1: The effects of compression.

oxygen. A resident falling on to a hard surface could develop this sort of damage.

Friction: This causes burns and abrasions on the skin, and is likely to occur when two areas rub against each other. Sores developing under breasts are one example of this form of pressure. Another kind of "friction sore" is caused by a Plaster of Paris cast rubbing against the skin (also called a **plaster sore**). This occurs when the plaster cast is fitting badly. The resident may complain of a burning sensation inside the plaster. If this occurs the plaster will be removed and re-applied, or else a hole will be cut in the plaster to allow the sore to be dressed.

Knowledge of the different forces that can contribute to pressure sores is important so that they can be avoided. However, not everyone exposed to pressure will go on to develop sores.

A number of additional factors have been identified, which are known to make people more likely to develop sores. These include both increased and decreased body weight, diseases affecting the blood and blood vessels, any kind of reduced mobility, pain and malnutrition. Other factors, which are mainly in the control of staff, include poor hygiene, poor lifting techniques, hard beds and trolleys and incorrect positioning.

Some people are generally more likely to get sores than others. These include elderly people, those with spinal injuries causing paralysis and loss of sensation, residents who are sedated or who are taking drugs that are likely to make them sleepy, the terminally ill and any patients with wasting, low resistance to infection, poor nutrition and impaired mobility.

Finally, chairbound people who may seem to be "better off" than those who are cared for in bed are actually at greater risk of developing sores, because their body weight is not evenly distributed over such a wide area, and because preventive measures may not be applied so rigorously.

To help nurses to identify the residents who are at risk of developing sores, a number of "pressure sore risk calculators" have been developed. These list the factors that make sores more likely, and score people on the absence or presence of these factors.

A well known and well used pressure sore risk rating scale is the Norton Score, developed for use with elderly patients in 1962. It is a numerical scoring system on five criteria: physical condition, mental state, activity, mobility and incontinence (Fig 3). A score of 14 or less indicates that a person is at risk of developing sores; people scoring below 12 are considered especially at risk. Other risk calculators frequently used by nurses are: The Waterlow Scale, the Douglas Scale and the Pressure Sore Prediction Score.

Prevention

When residents at risk have been identified, preventive action must be taken. The main aim is relief of pressure, however it is caused. The traditional method of pressure relief is regular changing of the resident's position (at least every two hours). This applies to people sitting in chairs as well as those in bed. Activities such as turning residents from side to side in bed, lifting them off the bed, helping them to take short walks, even simply standing up, can all help to relieve pressure.

Other factors that help prevent pressure sores are **improved nutrition**, especially increased protein in the diet, increased **mobility**, and pain relief.

Pain relief is particularly important because when people are in pain they are often tense and reluctant to move. This can increase their risk of developing a pressure sore. All residents need to be assessed for pain and appropriate pain relieving measures introduced when necessary. These pain relieving measures can include complementary therapies such as massage and aromatherapy as well as medicines (see chapter 21).

Barrier creams are thought to have a limited role in preventing superficial sores developing. They should only be used to give protection from friction, dehydration, grazing and damage to the skin from urine or faeces. However, *massaging the skin with these creams to promote circulation is a misguided practice*. Rubbing or vigorously massaging the skin will cause tissues to break down and *increase* the likelihood of a pressure sore developing.

Washing with soap and water as a method of pressure sore prevention is also *an ineffective and potentially harmful practice*. Excessive washing lowers the acidity of the skin and removes the skin's protective substances, making pressure sore formation a greater possibility. Special soaps and cleansers are now available which do not reduce the acidity of the skin and these can be used on incontinent residents who may require frequent washing.

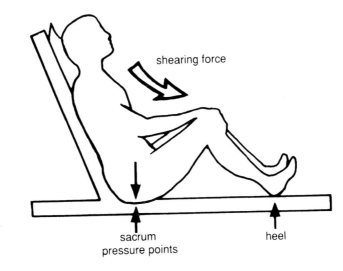

Fig 2: Pressure points.

Aids and equipment

When measures such as these are not possible or are impractical, there are a number of aids available that aim to minimise the forces that cause damage. However, it is important to note that any aid which reduces pressure due to compression may not reduce pressure due to shearing forces, and vice versa. For example, sheepskins placed under the sacrum and heels may minimise the damage caused by shearing in sliding down the bed, but will do nothing at all for the pressure caused by compression.

One of the main causes of pressure sores is the hospital-type mattress. In some positions, eg lying on the side, the total weight of the body is supported by the bony prominences of the shoulders and the hips. When lying on the flat firm surface of the hospital-type mattress the tissue underneath these areas becomes compressed and then damaged. Ideally, as much of the body as possible should be in contact with the mattress to enable pressure to be more evenly spread and so reduce tissue damage.

Because of the need to spread body weight over a large surface area it is often better to look after someone lying on their back or front, with only limited time, not more than two hours, being spent lying on their sides at any one time. By taking this factor into account people can often be allowed four hours absolutely flat on their backs overnight, thus giving them a better chance to have uninterrupted sleep.

There are a variety of substances that can help body weight to be distributed more evenly. The most well known of these are air and water. Air and water are used to suspend the body on a support surface, and the principle of suspension allows the body weight to be spread over a large surface area.

There are a number of pressure relieving aids that have been designed with this factor in mind: these include special beds and mattresses, cushions and heel pads. Although many of these aids have not been fully evaluated, the principles upon which they are manufactured appear sound and thus they should act to reduce pressure if they are used correctly.

Pressure relieving devices are costly and it is important that they are used properly and effectively. Manufacturers usually provide detailed advice about the use and care of equipment and this should be followed for the best results.

One often-used aid which does not, in fact, have any pressure relieving effect is the ring cushion. These placed under the sacrum are far more likely to cause pressure sores than to relieve them. This is because where the ring is in contact with the body, pressures are increased not decreased. Someone left sitting on a ring cushion for long periods of time will develop a ring of pressure damage where the body is in contact with the ring.

Treatment of sores

If, despite preventive efforts, someone develops a sore, then a positive approach to treatment is required. Pressure sores are now usually classified into five stages. In stages 1 and 2, the skin is red but not broken. The redness of the skin indicates that tissue damage is occurring and will get worse if not treated. In stage 3 the skin is broken and there is usually a small ulcer. In stage 4, the ulcer has become larger and deeper, and in stage 5 the sore is usually infected with areas of dead skin, yellow discharge and an offensive smell.

Treatment of a pressure sore depends upon its stage of development. Pressure sores at stage 1 and stage 2 seldom require more than the prevention measures mentioned earlier. However, pressure sores of grade 3 and above are classed as

Physical condition		Mental state		Activity		Mobility		Incontinence	
Good	4	Alert	4	Ambulant	4	Full	4	Not	4
Fair	3	Apathetic	3	Walks with help	3	Slightly limited	3	Occasional	3
Poor	2	Confused	2	Chair-bound	2	Very limited	2	Usually urine	2
Very bad	1	Stuporous	1	Bedfast	1	Immobile	1	Double	1

Fig 3: The Norton Score for pressure sore risk assessment.

wounds and a qualified nurse should always supervise treatment. Nevertheless knowledge of the principles involved is useful to all staff.

Knowledge about wound healing is increasing and earlier thoughts about the best way to treat wounds have altered. In the past a dry wound was thought to be best for healing. However, it has now been established that drying a wound delays skin re-growth.

In fact, wound healing occurs two or three times faster when wounds are covered with a dressing which closely covers the wound but allows the oxygen through, compared with wounds covered with conventional dry dressings. These dressings are rather like clingfilm and are designed to retain fluid produced by the wound and create a moist environment.

Opsite is perhaps the best known of these: this dressing permits the exchange of oxygen and carbon dioxide, and the passage of water vapour, but will not allow bacteria, viruses or water to pass through. These dressings should not be used on infected wounds.

The use of stoma products (primarily designed for people with colostomies) to promote pressure sore healing can be effective. They also retain wound fluid on the wound surface, and so create a moist wound environment.

Another factor important to wound healing is that the wound needs to be at body temperature for healing to take place. Carrying out a dressing and using cold lotions can reduce wound temperature so much that it can take several hours to return to body temperature. For this reason all lotions should be kept at room temperature if possible, and the wound dressing should be disturbed as little as possible.

The choice of dressings available is increasing all the time. When staff are not sure what to use, they should seek help from a wound care specialist nurse.

Your role

Care assistants are bound to become involved with pressure sores, either by trying to prevent them occurring or helping to treat them if they have occurred. The most important point to remember is that **all residents need to change their position regularly.** This applies to patients who are sitting in chairs as well as those confined to bed.

Residents who have any degree of restricted mobility should be assessed for "pressure sore risk" using a recognised assessment tool such as the Norton Score shown on page 133. The responsibility for doing this assessment lies with a qualified nurse. The score, together with a plan of care for dealing with that problem (or potential problem) should be written in the resident's care plan. Care assistants should be aware of their residents' scores, understand what they mean and then familiarise themselves with the required plans of care for each resident.

When helping residents to wash and dress, care assistants should always note the condition of vulnerable pressure points such as the sacrum (base of the spine), buttocks and heels. Any signs of redness should be noted and reported.

The treatment of a pressure sore depends on its grading. Because Grades 1 and 2 pressure sores require little more than the standard preventive measures, care assistants will be involved with treating these sores. Pressure sores in which the skin is broken and which may also be infected will be treated by a qualified nurse. In between, there are sores which may need some kind of protective covering, for example when the skin is red or slightly grazed. In some situations, care assistants will be shown how to apply these protective dressings.

Points to remember

DO

1. Make sure all residents change their position regularly.
2. Observe residents' skin and report any signs of pressure damage.
3. Leave a clean wound alone, covered with a dressing.
4. Encourage a good diet with plenty of protein.
5. Follow each resident's care plan exactly.

DON'T

1. Rub or massage skin vigorously, with or without creams.
2. Wash skin excessively.

NVQ Levels 2 & 3 Core Units
U4 Contribute to the health, safety and security of individuals and their environment.
U5 Obtain, transmit and store information relating to the delivery of a care service.

Level 2 Direct Care
Z6 Enable clients to maintain and improve their mobility.
Z7 Contribute to the movement and treatment of clients.
Z9 Enable clients to maintain their personal hygiene and appearance.
Z19 Enable clients to achieve physical comfort.

CHAPTER 18

Promoting continence and stoma care

Helen White and Stuart Darby

• *How we all feel about bladder and bowel control* • *Passing urine* • *How the bowel works*
• *What is continence and how is it achieved?* • *Problems that can lead to incontinence*
• *Assessing the type of incontinence* • *Incontinence of faeces* • *Toileting programmes*
• *Personal protection* • *Catheter care and hygiene* • *Sex* • *Stoma care*

oing to the lavatory is a basic human activity which we all perform several times a day without much thought and rarely discuss unless something goes wrong. Our culture seems to find it hard to cope with anything to do with bladders and bowels: the public are embarrassed by the subject, many professionals tend to ignore the problems, and too often care assistants are just left to cope as best they can.

This chapter will discuss how residents and care staff feel about this sensitive and intimate part of care; explain how continence is achieved and maintained; describe what may go wrong, how incontinence can be managed, and what resources are available.

Confusing terms

Continence is not an easy subject to talk about. It is hard to find words that are descriptive and easy to use, so we often use euphemisms such as "relieving yourself", but these terms can also cause confusion and embarrassment. Nurses and doctors resort to clinical terms which are little understood by most people.

Feelings

Incontinence can have devastating effects, especially when symptoms are obvious such as wet chairs and smelly clothes. Some people will go to extraordinary lengths to hide their incontinence, either denying there is a problem and refusing to seek help, or isolating themselves from families and friends. Feelings of shame, helplessness, rejection and misery are commonly expressed, especially by older people.

It is generally assumed that care staff are at ease with all aspects of toileting and incontinence, but we can be just as embarrassed as anyone else at having to assist residents perform these intimate tasks. We too can feel disgusted that someone is not able to control their bladder or bowel, and be resentful that we have to deal with the mess and the smell.

It is important to recognise and be aware of these feelings in ourselves, and to be able to share them with other staff, because in our care work we must always put ourselves in the individual's place and imagine how *they* feel. You need to be very sensitive and discreet, especially when someone is denying that a problem exists. People living in residential settings are frequently ostracised and humiliated because of their incontinence: this is always totally unacceptable.

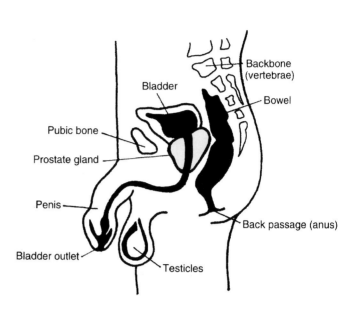

Side view of male showing enlarged prostate gland.

Incontinence can happen at all ages. People over 75 and those in residential settings are particularly at risk, not because they are old but because of physical changes due to the ageing process.

Everyone has an important part to play in the promotion of continence: as a care assistant you are closest to the resident, the person they confide in, the one who performs the most intimate tasks. Talking to residents with knowledge and confidence will give them the reassurance that they are not alone and the guidance to where help is available.

Passing urine

Urine is produced in the kidneys. There are two kidneys situated in the lower part of the back on either side of the spine. They act as a filter and remove waste products from the blood. These, in the form of urine, pass down two tubes, ureters, into the bladder. The bladder is an "elastic" bag made of muscle which expands to store the urine and contracts to squeeze the urine out through a narrow tube, the urethra, which is 4cm long in women, 20cm in men. The bladder and urethra are supported in position by the pelvic floor muscles.

When the bladder fills to about 250-350mls, it sends messages to the nerves in the lower part of the spine. These messages travel up the spine to the brain. The brain responds by sending the appropriate message back to the bladder. If the time and place are convenient, the nerves send the messages back down the spine to the bladder muscles. The bladder muscles contract, the urethra relaxes and the urine is squeezed out.

If the time and place are not convenient it is possible to ignore the desire to pass urine, and it will fade from consciousness. Then it returns at intervals until the need is so urgent that emptying can no longer be delayed.

How the bowel works

In normal bowel action, the formed stool is pushed into the lower part of the bowel, called the rectum, by contraction of the muscular walls of the bowel. This triggers sensory receptors in the wall of the rectum which are felt as a desire to empty the bowel. The ring of muscle controlling the anus (the back passage outlet) is relaxed if the time and place is convenient, and the stool is passed, sometimes with the assistance of the muscles of the abdomen.

In a normal bowel action the stool should be soft, well formed and easy to pass. Little hard pellets can indicate constipation.

What is continence?

Continence is being able to pass urine or faeces voluntarily in a socially acceptable place. That is: recognising the need to go; holding on until it is convenient and comfortable; identifying the correct place; then emptying the bladder or bowel completely.

This requires a urinary and bowel system which is working effectively; a nervous system which can convey messages; the ability to move independently or at will, and toilet facilities which are easy to reach and acceptable.

Successful toilet training requires normal physical development, especially of the nervous system, and certain social skills such as being able to remove and replace clothing as necessary at the lavatory; being able to get up and walk to the lavatory, or ask to be taken, or ask for the lavatory; and being able to plan ahead for the lavatory whether the bladder is full or not.

Going to the lavatory demands a complex sequence of events:

• recognising the need to empty the bladder or bowel – so there must be no interruption in the nerve pathway between the bladder and the control centre in the brain

• holding on until an appropriate place is reached, even if the bladder is full (this can be particularly difficult for dependent residents who may have to wait some time for a helper)

• adjusting clothing – undoing zips, pulling down pants

• sitting or standing at the lavatory, initiating the urine stream (or bowel movement) and sustaining it until the bladder or bowel is empty

• wiping the bottom or shaking the penis

• flushing the lavatory and making sure it is clean (no urine dribbles on the seat or soiling on the bowl)

• replacing clothes correctly and washing hands before leaving the bathroom.

It is also a very exhausting activity for

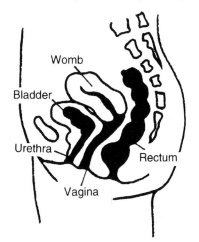

Female side view shows pelvic floor and body passages.

people who have walking and handling difficulties or tire easily, and residents with heart problems, arthritis or multiple sclerosis.

What are the problems?

The following questions will highlight the physical, emotional and environmental factors essential to maintaining continence:

Can they recognise the need to go?
Adults who are confused may not get the message, and there are occasions when both they and others need reminding. This will be discussed further under toileting programmes.

Can they ask to go?
Older people who have lost their speech following a stroke may have a special way of communicating; residents who have severe learning difficulties may communicate in a sign language. It is always advisable to check with family or friends to save embarrassment and distress.

Do they know where the lavatory facilities are?
Clear directions which are reinforced with signs will assist residents in their independence. Signs can also be used in a person's home if they are confused or forgetful. Some residents may prefer or find it easier to use a commode or urine bottle. Whenever possible encourage them to sit on the lavatory or commode as this is less stressful and more efficient than a bedpan. With guidance, each individual should make their own choice. Remember to give instructions on how to use urine bottles. Although they are familiar to you, many people will not know what to do and may be too embarrassed to ask.

Can they get there in time?
The toilet should be within easy reach. If your resident has walking problems and is slow it may be important that their bed or chair is as close to the door as possible. Shoes and a walking aid may help. If despite all this they don't get there in time, it is better to wheel them to the lavatory if necessary, and allow them to walk back slowly rather than suffer the humiliation of wetting on the way.

Care should be taken to ensure that the entrances to the toilet are free from obstruction and not used as an extra storage place, causing added delay.

Can they manage their clothing?
Easy-to-adjust clothing, such as an extended fly with dabs of velcro on trousers and pyjamas, will overcome the difficulty for men of getting the penis out quickly enough, and women may find a fuller skirt where the back can be tucked into the belt, and split-crotch or French knickers quicker if there are problems with handling. Shoes give more support than slippers for easier walking.

Is the lavatory seat at an appropriate height?
The correct position is to sit with the bottom and back well supported and feet firmly on the ground. Some older people can be scared about falling into the bowl, and many people crouch so as not to touch the seat for fear of infection.

In some cultures it is customary to squat with the feet on the seat. Do make sure that the seat and any surrounding rails are secure and able to take this unusual distribution of weight.

Residents who have difficulties balancing, or getting on and off the lavatory, will find aids such as grab rails helpful. The occupational therapist will advise on the positioning of the rails. Residents who need to push themselves up off the loo will require horizontal rails, while those who pull themselves up will need a vertical rail. A foot rest, and if necessary straps to support the trunk, give extra security and confidence. A raised seat is helpful for residents with stiff joints, and men with prostate problems may find sitting a more effective way of emptying their bladder.

Is the lavatory acceptable and private?
Finding the lavatory quickly and easily can be one of the problems encountered by people with incontinence problems, especially if they are unable to wait. Residents will feel at greater ease if they know where the nearest clean, well lit, warm and ventilated lavatory, with a door that locks, is available.

Trying to pass water and even worse having a bowel movement, when you are aware someone can hear and smell you, is most inhibiting. These problems can be overcome by running water, lining the pan with paper and spraying with a deodoriser.

Is cleaning adequate?
Residents who are soiled through faecal incontinence should be cleaned as soon as possible, using large soft tissues or special wipes, then washed with warm water and dried thoroughly. If the soiling has dried on to the skin, cleansing agents which can be sprayed on to the skin and then wiped off with a moist tissue are very helpful, particularly where the skin is already fragile.

Urine is acidic and can cause skin soreness, which in turn can lead to rashes and infection. Avoid scented soap and talcum powder as these can add to the irritation. A flannel for washing face and hands should be kept separately from the one used for washing between the legs. If the skin is particularly sensitive, patting between the legs with a soft towel or drying with a cool hairdryer can be helpful. A qualified member of staff will advise you on skin and barrier creams.

People from certain cultures, such as Moslems and Sikhs, hold strong views about personal hygiene, and may for example require a special jug so they can wash with running water. If in doubt it is best to ask family or friends.

How much are they drinking?
The vast majority of older people believe they should drink less so that less urine will be passed. What happens, though, is that the urine becomes concentrated, the bladder capacity may become smaller and other problems can result, including constipation. A good guide is eight to ten cups of fluid over 24 hours. Do encourage more water and less tea, coffee and cola, as these drinks stimulate the kidneys to produce more urine than necessary.

Many people have the habit of going to the loo at every opportunity in case of "accidents". This trains the bladder to empty before it is full, so these people will never venture far from a public toilet. Anyone who requires to pass urine more than every two hours or who gets up more than twice a night, unless they are on medication, requires investigation.

Bowel frequency is very individual – once a day, twice a week – what is important is the *consistency*, not frequency. Stools should be soft, formed and easy to pass; straining to pass a stool can indicate constipation.

Certain medicines, such as water tablets (diuretics) increase the amount of urine, sometimes very rapidly, so there is little warning. Sleeping tablets (sedatives) can delay the message being relayed and responded to by the brain; pain killers (analgesics) can cause constipation.

What is their attitude to continence?
Anxiety can cause anyone to wet themselves, and an unfamiliar situation or moving into new surroundings (eg coming into care) can be very stressful. For an older person, having an "accident"

like this is a humiliating experience, and a memory which will never fade.

Depression can affect older people, and may lead to a loss of motivation. This should not be confused with laziness and attention-seeking. Loss of independence can lead some residents to use bladder and bowel control to their advantage; for many it is the only means they have left to express themselves. Forcing residents to the lavatory can have the opposite effect to the one you want.

Incontinence

Incontinence means the uncontrolled (involuntary) loss of urine or faeces. It is not a disease but a symptom of an underlying problem which can happen to anyone at any time of life. It affects more women than men but it is not an inevitable consequence of old age or disability. Indeed the majority of people remain continent all their lives.

Incontinence at any age causes physical, emotional, social and financial hardship and severely disrupts people's lives. Many see incontinence in older people as a natural stage of regression to infancy and treat them accordingly, increasing dependence and loss of adult status.

There are many causes of incontinence and an individual can suffer from several symptoms. Treatment or management must be based on individual assessment and investigation to discover the type of incontinence and possible causes.

Assessment

Assessment is based on answers to questions such as the following:

Do you leak when you cough or sneeze?
Leaking of urine on exertion, **stress incontinence**, can occur when there is extra strain on the tummy, such as cough-ing or sneezing. It is a common complaint in women of all ages, who have weakened muscles around the bladder and urethra during pregnancy and childbirth, after the menopause and if there is a history of constipation.

It can be cured by exercises, correctly done, to strengthen these muscles, and in extreme cases by surgery to tighten the muscles. It can be successfully managed by not letting the bladder become overfull, avoiding constipation, doing pelvic floor exercises, and wearing protective garments.

Do you have to go frequently and quickly?
A strong need to pass urine quickly and often, sometimes not reaching the lavatory in time because the bladder muscles become overactive and contract with little warning, is known as **urge incontinence.** The person rushes to the lavatory immediately they are aware of their bladder in an effort to prevent urine loss. The bladder seldom holds more than a few millilitres of urine because it is emptied so frequently. This quickly becomes a habit, and the time between emptyings becomes less and less – in extreme cases every 15 minutes.

It is common to men and women, particularly those who have problems affecting the nervous system, such as multiple sclerosis or stroke, those with dementia, and children and adults who are bedwetters. Sometimes people become so depressed and anxious about having an accident that they refuse to be far from a lavatory.

This type of incontinence is particularly common in older people. Again it is curable in many cases, by introducing a programme of bladder exercises to extend the intervals between trips to the lavatory, and wearing light protective garments for confidence. Medicines to quieten the bladder muscles may also be prescribed.

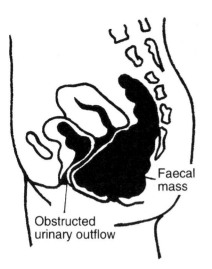

Faecal mass

Obstructed urinary outflow

Side view of female showing how constipation can affect the bladder outflow and cause incontinence of urine.

Do you have to get up at night?

Dribbling or continuous leakage of urine, sometimes leading to wetting the bed at night, is known as **overflow incontinence**. It is often associated with an obstruction at the bladder neck such as an enlarged prostate gland (in men), or constipation. Atrophic vaginitis, due to lower hormone levels, is a common cause in older women.

Overflow incontinence may also be due to the bladder muscles not contracting properly, for example where there is damage to the nerves of the spinal chord, so the bladder does not empty completely, retaining a substantial volume of urine which causes a feeling of fullness even after urine has been passed.

If left untreated this can lead to repeated urinary infections and other serious complications, so a medical assessment is important. How the condition is managed will depend on the cause, but always check for constipation and provide personal and bed protection to preserve the resident's comfort and dignity. In some cases an intermittent or indwelling catheter (see page 144) will be recommended.

Do you find you get no warning?

The bladder may empty without any warning – **reflex incontinence** – because the nervous system is not conveying the messages to the brain. This may happen following acute illness or infection and can cause extreme confusion and fear.

In some cases a chart recording the times of the reflex can indicate a pattern which will allow toileting at set intervals to anticipate the loss, or it may be necessary for the urine to be contained with highly absorbent pads or another recommended method.

Can you get there in time?

Simply not getting to the lavatory in time because of walking and handling difficulties – **functional incontinence** – can usually be managed with easy-to-wear clothing, commodes and urine bottles as appropriate. **Not being able to get out of the chair** is a very common cause of incontinence.

Incontinence of faeces

Loss of either solid or runny unformed stools, or soiling of clothing, is referred to as faecal incontinence. Although this is not nearly as common as urinary incontinence it can be far more distressing because of the resulting mess and smell. The most common cause is **severe constipation**. This is common in less mobile older people, because lack of physical activity has an effect on the bowel, making it work more slowly.

In severe constipation a hard mass of stool forms in the the lower part of the bowel. Liquid stool trickles past the blockage as a continual faecal loss, causing soiling of clothes and bedding. This is called **constipation with overflow**. It has a very distinctive smell and should not be confused with soiling because the older person has not been able to clean themselves, or diarrhoea due to tummy upset or allergy.

There are many causes: embarrassment at using a strange lavatory, poor diet including insufficient fluids, lack of exercise, certain medicines, difficulty in passing hard lumps or a solid mass, or an interruption of the nerve messages to the brain, such as can occur in dementia.

The simple management is to avoid the situation by ensuring that the toilets are acceptable, the diet is adequate, and a routine is established. The best time for a bowel movement is very individual, but for older people about half an hour after a meal or hot drink, when the gut has been stimulated, is often good.

Bulking and softening agents, suppositories, and in extreme cases an enema to clear out the bowel, may be necessary. It will be a medical or nursing decision, but you have an important part in contributing to this.

In the ageing bowel the sphincter mus-cles may become lax and less efficient, or there may be a lifetime of straining to open the bowels or a persistent use of laxatives which contribute to the loss of control. In most cases the symptoms can be treated. New techniques in surgery can sometimes improve the function of the muscles controlling the back passage, which may have been damaged at birth or as the result of an injury.

Bowels are a very private affair and should be dealt with discreetly. If protective garments are necessary they should be snug fitting to avoid seepage. Special attention must be given to skin care and personal hygiene; in severe cases it may be necessary to provide a deodorising agent to maintain the resident's dignity.

Toileting programme

Toileting is the term applied to the intervals when residents should visit or be taken to the lavatory to maintain bladder and bowel control. The programme will depend on several factors including the bladder function, mental ability and mobility of the resident. Residents must be assessed as individuals so that the most appropriate programme can be introduced. Even for people with dementia success is possible.

Toileting cannot be imposed on an unwilling or uncooperative resident, even if they are intellectually competent. It is therefore important that resident and staff alike are convinced that success is achievable. Age is no barrier, however.

The assessment will include keeping accurate charts of the times urine is passed in each 24 hours, and the amount if possible. This record should be kept for five to seven days so that a pattern may emerge on which to base the programme. This requires the motivation and cooperation of all staff as well as the resident. Whenever possible encourage

---

Effects of ageing on the bladder:
• Increased frequency of passing urine, especially at night
• Decreased capacity for urine
• Urgency – sometimes the first warning is when they can't hold on any longer
• Over-active bladder.

Effects of ageing on the bowel:
• The bowel works more slowly if the person is less physically active
• Faecal incontinence may occur when ageing muscles work less well
• There may be reflex emptying of the bowel.

the resident to fill in the record themselves. Many companies provide simple easy-to-record charts like the one illustrated (right).

It is important that both the residents and staff understand what is expected of them, and then stick to the programme.

Set interval toileting is reminding or taking the resident to the toilet. It does not teach independence but is useful for people who forget, have no bladder sensation or have no regular pattern of passing urine.

Individualised toileting is working out when the resident is most likely to pass urine, by

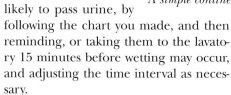

TIME	MON	TUES	WED	THURS	FRI	SAT	SUN
6am							
7am							
8am							
9am							
10am							
11am							
12am							
1pm							
2pm							
3pm							
4pm							
5pm							
6pm							
7pm							
8pm							
9pm							
10pm							
11pm							
12pm							
1am							
2am							
3am							
4am							
5am							
TOTAL							

Please tick in this column every time you use the toilet.

Please tick in this column every time you are wet.

A simple continence chart.

following the chart you made, and then reminding, or taking them to the lavatory 15 minutes before wetting may occur, and adjusting the time interval as necessary.

Bladder retraining is a programme to extend the intervals between going to pass urine. The aim is to hold on for two- to three-hourly intervals. It is useful for people who have lost their confidence and go just in case, but it does need much understanding and support for resident and helper.

Personal protection

Sometimes it may be necessary to provide protective garments or appliances for residents who are not able to be completely dry or who are awaiting treatment.

There are thousands of aids available which can make selection difficult. The final choice of product must be made by the resident whenever possible, but the type of product will depend on the nature of the incontinence – urinary, faecal or both; the quantity of loss – leak, gush or soiling; the personal details of the resident including sex, dexterity, mobility and mental ability.

If reusables are to be tried the laundry facilities need to be flexible to allow for the manufacturer's washing instructions.

You should aim to become as familiar as possible with the products used, their application and management, so that you can advise and support your resident and relatives as well as provide a high quality of care. Too often aids are inappropriate, or are used incorrectly because of ignorance or lack of instruction. This can be costly to the resident's dignity as well as your time and the resources of the unit.

The continence adviser can advise on selection, although this is often restricted by cost and local purchasing policies. Some products are expensive for regular use if bought independently.

Pads and pants: Absorbent garments and pads are the most commonly used, and reusable products are becoming popular for people who have a long term urinary loss. They are not recommended for a faecal loss because of staining and washing difficulties. An absorbent aid is designed to keep a resident comfortable and free from leakage for 3-4 hours.

For men and women who have a light loss, machine washable pants with an absorbent gusset can give a feeling of confidence. Where the loss is more severe, there is a range of disposable or reusable liners which can be worn inside the person's own pants.

Body worn liners should be cupped to form a gully, with the absorbent surface facing upwards and kept in position with close fitting pants.

Pants and all-in-one garments should be selected by hip fitting. Check the manufacturer's instructions if you are unsure. Make sure the user and carer at home know how to use the product, dispose of soiled pads and how to get supplies. Many authorities have a computerised system which automatically allocates a regular supply and reassessment.

Sheaths: Men may prefer to wear an appliance such as a disposable sheath, which should remain in position for 24 hours. There are other appliances which can be worn for longer periods. The initial sizing and fitting should be under the supervision of a nurse or appliance practitioner. These products are available on

prescription from the GP. Older men who have a retracted penis may have difficulty in keeping disposable sheaths on and should be offered an alternative.

Sheets: There are also highly absorbent washable bed sheets which can help to improve sleep patterns because they keep the person warm and dry. It is important to follow the manufacturer's instructions to obtain the maximum benefit, and check the resident's laundry facilities as an automatic washing machine with a range of wash temperatures is essential.

Catheter care

Sometimes a hollow tube called a catheter is placed in the bladder in order to drain the urine away. A catheter may be used once and then removed (intermittent catheterisation) or left in position to drain continuously and changed at intervals (indwelling catheter).

Intermittent catheterisation is passing a fine, usually plastic, catheter through the urethra into the bladder to completely drain it of urine at regular intervals. Poeple can be taught at any age, and even women in their 90s have had success – but sight, dexterity and willingness are important.

This method of bladder control has revolutionised the lives of people of all ages who had previously suffered repeated urinary infections which have severely restricted their lifestyle. It is suitable for residents whose bladder is unable to empty completely for some reason, such as older people with multiple sclerosis, diabetes or dementia. Whenever possible the resident is encouraged to catheterise themself, enabling them to be more independent. Catheterisation once a week, under medical supervision, may be all that is needed.

The **indwelling catheter** is passed in to the bladder, usually through the urethra, but sometimes directly into the bladder via the abdomen. It is made of a latex or silicone material, depending on the length of time it is to remain in the bladder, and is attached to a drainage bag, which collects the urine. It is important always to ensure that the connecting tubing is not kinked or compressed so that the urine can flow freely, and that the bag is below the level of the bladder, as urine cannot flow uphill.

The bag can be supported by leg straps or a garment such as a pouch sewn on to the leg of underpants or trousers. The method of support is important as it not only assists in the drainage but also in the dignity of the resident. No one likes to see bags of urine and many residents do not want their family and friends to know this intimate aspect of their care.

Residents and relatives can find the prospect of a catheter daunting and you may find yourself having to allay their fears, by explaining clearly so they understand the reasons and the care of the system. Most of the catheter manufacturers provide excellent guides.

Any indication of infection, such as the resident feeling ill or having a raised temperature, should be reported to nursing staff immediately.

Hygiene guidelines

• Always wash hands before as well as after emptying the drainage bag.

• Attach the night bag to the leg bag rather than changing one to the other.

• Never allow the tap of the drainage bag to touch the floor.

• Pay special attention to personal hygiene and washing between the legs.

• Ensure that the catheter and drainage tube are draining freely, and there is no blockage.

• The bag should slope towards the tap to allow complete emptying.

• Support and maintain the shape of the bag using a garment or straps. Remember legs can become swollen by evening so check straps have not become too tight, or hang the bag on a stand on the wheelchair or bed.

Sex

Incontinence can have a devastating effect on relationships. As many people are sexually active in their 70s and 80s it is important to let them know that they can continue to have intercourse.

Reassure them that a catheter can remain in place, but the drainage bag should be emptied first and secured to the leg or tummy. A sheath or similar appliance should be removed first. Assure them that urine is not infectious, and advise them that an absorbent sheet placed under the couple will act as a precaution and give greater confidence.

Stoma care

A "stoma" is the term used when a part of the bowel or tubes leading from the bladder are surgically brought out onto the abdominal wall because of disease. Colostomies and ileostomies carry faeces to a collecting bag attached to the skin on the abdomen. Urostomies carry urine. The site of the stoma and collecting appliance needs to be well looked after in the first few weeks after surgery.

People will usually be taught in hospital to care for their stoma and to apply and change collecting appliances. They may also require further help to overcome the psychological stress of having a stoma or need assistance with physically applying and changing the appliances.

Fears and anxieties

People with stomas naturally have a number of fears and anxieties and it is important to discuss these. Often people need as much help to overcome fears and anxieties as physical help with fitting a stoma appliance. Many hospitals, community health services and manufacturers of stoma appliances will also have specialist nurses who can be called upon for expert advice and guidance in stoma care, such as how to get stoma bags on prescription. You can help by listening to people's worries and reinforce any advice and information given by these experts.

Many people fear that they will not be able carry on working or playing sports. In addition people have an altered image of themselves: they fear that their stoma will be noticeable to everyone or that they will no longer be sexually attractive to other people. People can be supported through this period by assuring them that they can continue with their normal lifestyle, including sexual activity, and helping them to manage in the same way that we all manage our own toilet needs.

A common fear for people is that they will smell. Stoma appliances are usually odour free if fitted correctly, and charcoal filters and deodorisers are available with certain appliances.

Food and drink

All individuals with a stoma will normally be encouraged to eat a wide variety of foods. Some foods may however cause diarrhoea and excess flatulence. One way of overcoming this may be to take smaller amounts of a particular food, rather than give it up altogether. In addition certain foods are digested more slowly and it will help to ensure that they are chewed well in order to reduce the work of the stomach and intestines.

There are no dietary restrictions for people with a urostomy, but some residents may not drink their normal amounts of fluids in order to reduce the number of times that their appliance bag is changed. An adequate and normal amount of fluids should always be encouraged.

Choosing an appliance

A qualified member of staff should always be responsible for assessing people and fitting stoma appliances in the first few days of care. Appliances are labelled according to the size of the opening that fits around the stoma and a measuring guide for correct choice is usually made available with the appliance. To keep the skin undamaged the stoma must be protected from the adhesive and bag. The appliance should therefore fit snugly around to within 0.5 cm of the stoma edge.

Appliances now widely used are designed to be leak- and odour-proof, unobtrusive, noiseless and disposable. As a general rule they fall into two categories:
• One piece appliances comprise a bag with an adhesive attached to it. The bag and the adhesive are removed when the appliance is changed.
• Two piece appliances consist of a *flange* that adheres to the skin and a bag that clips onto the flange. This method means that the adhesive can be changed less frequently and helps to protect the skin.

Stoma accessories

Mild soap and water is all that is required for cleaning the skin. Creams and skin barriers should only be used if these are designed specifically for people with stomas. Lotions, sprays and gels, protective wafers and rings are also available to protect the skin around the stoma. Again these should only be used where the advice of a qualified member of staff or a stoma therapist has been sought.

Points to remember

1. You are central in reassuring residents that their problems are recognised and will be given sympathetic help.
2. Your knowledge will give you the confidence to encourage residents to talk about their problems. Ask senior staff if you feel unsure about a query or problem.
3. Bladder and bowel control (continence) is a skill we learn in early life and normally retain till the end. Losing this control – incontinence – is a very common problem.
4. The symptoms are embarrassing for residents and care workers alike. It is not an easy subject to talk about: recognising your own feelings is important.
5. Incontinence is a symptom which has many causes.
6. It can often be cured, and always improved and better managed.
7. Success depends on the accurate recording and reporting of your observations to the team.
8. Treatment is a team effort involving the resident, their family and all care staff.
9. Attention to the fears and worries of people with incontinence or a stoma is at least as important as their physical care.

Resources

Caring for Continence by Mandy Fader and Christine Norton. Practical guide for care assistants. *Better Care Guides* series, Hawker Publications (1994) London. *Incontinence and Inappropriate Urinating* by Graham Stokes. Winslow Press (1994) Bicester.

Incontinence Helpline Disability North at the Dene Centre, Castle Farm Road, Newcastle-upon-Tyne NE3 1PH. Helpline: 091 213 0050, weekdays 9am - 6pm.

Association for Continence Advice, 2 Doughty Street London WC1 2PH. Tel: 071 404 6821. Multi-disciplinary organisation for professionals.

InconTact, at the same address, is a consumer-led organisation offering information and support for people with bladder and bowel problems.

British Colostomy Association, 38-39 Eccleston Square, London SW1V 1PB. Tel: 071 828 5175.

British Digestive Foundation, 3 St Andrew's Place, Regents Park, London NW1 4LB. Tel: 071 487 5332.

Ileostomy Association of Great Britain and Ireland, PO Box 23, Mansfield, Nottinghamshire NG18 4TT. Tel: 0623 28099.

Urostomy Association, Buckland, Beaumont Park, Danbury, Essex CM3 4DE. Tel: 0245 224294.

NVQ Levels 2 & 3 Core Units

O Promote equality for all individuals.
U4 Contribute to the health, safety and security of individuals and their environment.
U5 Obtain, transmit and store information relating to the delivery of a care service.

Level 2 Direct Care

Z6 Enable residents to maintain and improve their mobility.
Z9 Enable residents to maintain their personal hygiene and appearance.
Z10 Enable clients to eat and drink.
Z11 Enable residents to access and use toilet facilities.

CHAPTER 19

Personal hygiene

Sue Millward

• A trusting relationship • Bathing, showering and the strip wash
• Giving a bed bath • Care of the hair • Nails and feet
• Care of mouth, teeth and dentures

To help elderly people in care homes maintain good personal hygiene requires a great deal of tact and skill on the part of care staff, but it can be extremely rewarding.

Accepting the need for help can be difficult for anyone, even for a short time. In a residential situation, where the invasion of privacy will seem likely to go on, the need to establish a relationship of trust between resident and carer is absolutely vital.

Elderly people can develop quite negative feelings about themselves when they have to rely on other people. This may lead to their "giving up" and becoming even more dependent.

So it is important that residents are given as much choice as possible in all matters of personal care. Deciding whether to bath or shower and at what time of the day, choosing favourite toiletries and which clothes to wear, will all help to minimise these feelings.

If the resident retains a degree of independence and the care assistant experiences job satisfaction, any "generation gap" between them will not matter. In fact, it may have advantages for them both. A trusting relationship with good communication can be the foundation of happy and dignified residential care.

The bath

No topic, except perhaps the day's menu, is guaranteed to arouse such strong feelings among people in residential care as the timing and frequency of their baths. But it is unlikely that everyone, given the choice, would want to have a bath at the same time of day, and a little negotiation will usually maintain harmony.

Having a bath should be a pleasant experience in a relaxed atmosphere. It provides a good opportunity for a chat and time for reminiscing.

Get organised: Everything needed should be assembled at the outset. No one wants to wait unclad while the talcum powder is retrieved from the other end of the building. All toiletries, flannels, towels and clean clothes should be taken to the bathroom with the resident and the door closed to maintain privacy. You should wear a plastic apron (see chapter 12), explaining that this is as much for the resident's protection as for you.

The bath should be run to the preferred temperature and depth. This is largely a matter of common sense and individual choice but it should be deep enough to cover the legs when sitting down. It is vital to check that the water is not scalding hot, and a non-slip mat placed at the bottom of the bath is a sensible safety precaution.

Help as required: Most people appreciate having their back washed, but can manage everything else themselves. If this is not possible for any reason then help should be given to make sure the resident is thoroughly washed all over. The use of bath foam, liquid soap or a soap substitute is a matter of individual choice and staff should be guided by the resident's wishes. Extra attention may be needed to the ears, navel and areas between the toes.

Be observant: This is a good time to look out for any possible problems such as loss of weight, skin conditions, swellings, lumps or sore areas, which should be noted and reported to the person in charge. Any necessary treatment can then be given promptly. Not only physical ailments but emotional problems will often be revealed under the relaxing conditions in a bathroom.

Once out of the bath, quick thorough drying of the skin with a warm towel will be appreciated. Extra care should be given to areas where skin surfaces touch, such as under the arms and between the thighs. A light dusting of talcum powder is soothing but it should be used in addition to efficient drying, not as a substitute.

Allow enough time: Help with dressing should only be offered where necessary. The carer must avoid trying to speed up the process by doing too much. It is better to clean the bath and tidy the bathroom while the resident dresses at her own pace.

Be familiar with guidelines: Whether or not a resident should be left unattended during bath time will depend on the policy of the home. In any event the resident should have access to a system of calling for help should they require it. All care

staff should be familiar with their own relevant guidelines.

If someone is taken ill in the bath, pull out the plug, support the head above the water level, then call for assistance and keep the resident warm.

Care of nails: General care of nails is easier after a bath as they are often softened by soaking in warm water. Finger nails can be trimmed if necessary, and a little hand cream applied to counteract dry skin. Toe nails should be kept short, cut straight across at the top (see chapter 15). However, if the nails are really tough, the services of a chiropodist may be essential, as there is a risk of injury to a toe from inexperienced hands.

Vigilant attention to feet is an essential element in the care of elderly people. Many problems of mobility can be eased by competent treatment of corns, bunions, or an ingrowing toe nail before it becomes infected. Extra care must be taken if a resident has diabetes. The circulation of the blood is usually less efficient: any cuts or wounds will take longer to heal and be more liable to infection.

Use of bath hoist: If a resident is unable to step in and out of the bath for any reason and a mechanical hoist is provided, it should always be used. Instruction and advice will be given by a senior member of staff. It is foolhardy to lift anyone alone as the risk of injuring your back is very high.

Tidy up afterwards: This is a vital part of any procedure, and leaving the bathroom clean and tidy is important for many reasons. Elderly people can be absent minded and items like watches can easily be left behind on a bathroom shelf. Everything must be taken back to the resident's living area and put away. Any dirty washing should be dealt with in accordance with the policy of the home.

The bath must be cleaned with suitable cleansing cream and rinsed well. The floor should be mopped and allowed to dry. This will reduce the possibility of infection being spread from one person to another and is part of maintaining a general high standard of care.

Points to remember:
• Get everything ready before you start - save your legs.
• Encourage residents to do as much as possible for themselves.
• Pay attention to details - nails, ears, navel and between toes.

The shower

A shower can be a considerably safer prospect than having a bath for any elderly person who is rather frail. It also requires less physical effort.

If a strong comfortable shower seat is provided and the water temperature properly controlled, preferably with a thermostat, then many people will enjoy a shower and find it invigorating. It is important to make sure the shower room is warm enough to avoid the resident feeling chilled either before or after the procedure.

A shower may however be more difficult for people who are not able to wash themselves, and it is difficult for staff to help someone else to shower without getting very wet themselves! Some homes provide wellingtons for them to wear, and it has been known for carers to don swimsuits.

Some elderly people are very resistant to the idea of showering. It may just be that they did not have one at home and have never used one before. Others prefer a soothing bath. The final choice must be made by the resident. But as long as there is sufficient time and the individual does as much as possible for herself, a shower can prove a very satisfactory alternative.

Care of the skin: Once again, it is a good time for the carer to be observant. Remember to be gentle when drying elderly people; the skin becomes less elastic with age. Apply talcum powder sparingly as it can make the skin even drier.

Clearing up afterwards is most important. The shower should be cleaned after use and the floor mopped to avoid the risk of anyone slipping over. Accidents can happen so easily to staff or residents that this cannot be stressed too highly.

Points to remember:
• The resident should be happy about having a shower.
• Check water temperature.
• Dry skin gently but thoroughly and be sparing with talcum powder.
• Clear up carefully; alert others if floor is wet.

The strip wash

Most homes now provide facilities in each room for residents to wash themselves. If this is not the case, a screen should be placed around the sink so that privacy is maintained.

Some elderly people may have difficulty turning taps on and off. Providing special taps with large handles can mean the difference between managing themselves and relying on others – a great advantage at modest cost.

A strip wash can be done sitting down on a seat or wheelchair beside a sink or with a wash bowl on a convenient table. Help should be given where required.

Care of flannels: It is a good idea to remind people occasionally that face flannels need regular laundering. There is nothing worse than finding a soapy, soggy mess at the bottom of a toilet bag when helping someone freshen-up.

The bidet: This can be a very useful item for making a wash of the genital area much quicker and more thorough. It is not easy to wash this area while standing up, if the resident is unsteady and needs support.

The bidet could be more widely used in care homes, particularly for the frequent washing sometimes needed when there are incontinence problems.

Shaving: There should always be a mirror available for men to shave in a good light. The routine of shaving does not get easier with age. Sometimes folds of skin under the chin are impossible to flatten out with one hand and a little tactful assistance may be welcomed.

It must be a firm rule that razors are never shared. Each resident must have his own shaving equipment, and never lend it or borrow from anyone else.

Facial hair: The Volunteer Beauty Care Service of the Red Cross is skilled in providing help to remove unwanted facial hair. This caring service operates throughout the British Isles. The teams are controlled by each county branch headquarters and will help elderly people who are not able to care for themselves. They will also give a relaxing massage of the face and neck, hand care and cosmetic camouflage. Provided volunteers are available, the service is free.

Points to remember
• Maintain privacy.
• Residents can wash sitting down if it is easier.
• Mention to senior staff if more toiletries are required.
• Help with details – make-up for ladies, after-shave for men – can boost morale.

A bed bath

From time to time it may happen that a resident is confined to bed although not ill enough to need admission to hospital or a nursing home. Extra care will then be required, of the kind of caring that a relative would give at home.

A bed bath is simply a way of bathing someone in bed. It is not an awesome task, and if two people can work together it should only take about 20 minutes.

Begin by placing everything that is needed at the bedside: bowl of water; soap; two flannels and towels; brush and comb; toiletries; toothbrush and paste with beaker and small bowl; nail scissors; barrier cream; clean night-wear and bed linen.

Principles:
1. It is a good idea to ask the resident if she would like to use the toilet first. A commode at the bedside is probably easiest for someone feeling unwell.
2. Ensure privacy. Screen the bed if necessary.
3. Remove top bed clothes carefully, leave resident covered by a cotton blanket, and take off night dress or pyjamas.
4. Wash and dry face, then neck and ears followed by arms.
5. Expose only the part being washed. Pay special care to under arms and apply deodorant if used. The area beneath the breasts in a woman may need a light dusting of talcum powder.
6. Use a separate flannel for the genital area. The resident may be able to do this herself if the blanket is held up. Again a light dusting of talcum powder can aid comfort.
7. Change the water and with the first flannel, wash legs and feet. If possible, rinse feet in the bowl. Cut toe nails straight across if necessary.
8. Roll resident over gently, wash and dry the back, gently apply a little cream to base of spine, heels, elbows and hips. This may be a convenient time to insert a clean sheet.
9. Help the resident to put on clean night-wear, then re-make the bed.
10. Trim finger nails and tidy hair.

11. Clean teeth and give a mouth wash.

12. Leave resident warm and comfortable. Clear away and tidy up. Make sure bed-table and locker are within reach.

Points to remember:
• The temperature of the water should be as hot as is comfortable for the carers' hands.
• A separate flannel is always used for the groin.
• The resident is exposed as little as possible at all times.

Care of the hair

Hairdressing is a skilled occupation. Cutting and setting hair with all the extra treatments available today, is best done by a professional. Many salons have special reduced prices for senior citizens on certain days. Most ladies will enjoy a regular outing for a "hair-do".

Alternatively a hairdresser may be found who is happy to visit a residential home for regular sessions. Men can equally enjoy a trip to the barbers. Everyone feels better when they are looking good with the hairstyle of their choice.

Hair may need washing in between visits to the hairdresser but it can quickly become dry and brittle if shampooed too often. It is not necessary to wash hair at every bath time. If a resident has paid for a shampoo and set, she will not be pleased to have it washed out a day or two later by an over-enthusiastic member of staff!

Older people often say their heads are more tender than they used to be, so if you wash their hair do massage shampoo into the scalp very gently. (If someone with a tender scalp also complains of a headache, inform the staff member in charge, as it could be a sign of serious illness.) Rinse thoroughly and pay dry with a towel. Set the hair in the preferred style and dry with a hair dryer if available.

Points to remember:
• Hair care is best left to professionals.
• Be gentle, older heads are often tender.
• Observe the condition of the scalp.

Head lice may occur in any community. They can be a source of embarrassment, which is really unjustified. Lice seem to like clean, healthy hair and pass easily from one person to another when heads touch. Treatment, with special shampoo, is simple and effective.

Inspecting the head for lice or nits requires patience and great care. If staff are asked to assist with such an inspection, which is done with a special comb, the following points should be remembered:
• Maintain strict privacy for the resident.
• Be as kind and tactful as possible.
• Staff are as likely to be the source of infestation as residents.

Care of the mouth

Mouth care tends to be rather low on the list of priorities involved in giving personal care. By the time a resident has bathed, put on clean clothes, had a shave or applied some make-up, it is all too easy to forget about the mouth and teeth.

But taking care of teeth and gums is important all through life. It should be part of the routine involved in getting up in the morning and preparing to go to bed at night.

The sort of advice given to children at school applies equally to elderly people:
• Regular visits to the dentist to check for tooth decay and gum disease should continue.
• A healthy diet should be encouraged with no sticky, sugary snacks between meals.
• Thorough brushing of the teeth at least twice daily will remove particles of food which can decompose and cause infection.
• Change toothbrushes as soon as they

begin to wear and ensure that residents are able to obtain supplies of toothpaste or powder.

Complications of neglected teeth include:
• Tooth decay.
• Unpleasant taste leading to refusal of food.
• Spread of infection to other parts of the body.

Denture cleaning: Most residents will have their own established routine for dentures. However, if help is needed, the best method is to place them in a container, rinse under cold water, then brush with special denture cream or powder.

To remove stains the dentures should be soaked or scrubbed in a proprietary solution. Bleach should never be used on dentures as it can damage the surface, as can very hot water.

Avoiding misplaced dentures: Great care must always be taken to keep dentures in a container at the resident's bedside when they are not being worn. Never leave them in a bathroom or beside a wash-basin which may be used by others.

However it is not just staff who lose dentures; residents themselves may leave them around. Ideally the dentures themselves, not just their pot, should be named.

Caring for an ill person's mouth: During illness the mouth can become very dry. If the tongue gets furred and the breath offensive, they will feel even worse.

It is important that the sick person has enough to drink. Sharp-flavoured drinks such as lime juice can be refreshing and leave a pleasant taste, and they may like ice to suck.

Extra mouthwashes, in addition to the usual, and cleaning with sodium bicarbonate solution, can be helpful.

A little vaseline or lip-salve can be applied to the lips to counteract any dryness.

Points to remember:
• "Prevention is better than cure" when caring for the mouth.
• Regular dental checks should continue.
• If the resident has dentures, they should be checked regularly for correct fit and any damage.
• Extra attention is necessary if a resident is ill.

Problems

If a resident obviously needs a bath but refuses to have one, it is better to "take time out" and avoid a head-on confrontation. Where a good relationship exists between resident and care assistant, this type of problem is rare. With good communication and some skill at negotiation, a compromise can usually be reached. This avoids loss of dignity for anyone.

The carer who is skilful at managing those who are less than enthusiastic about personal hygiene, will always be appreciated by everyone else in the home. A sense of humour is also a great asset when coping with this type of problem.

It is also essential, of course, that staff should pay scrupulous attention to their own standards of hygiene and personal freshness. It is difficult to demand higher standards from others than you are prepared to maintain in yourself.

Sometimes a written care plan related to hygiene needs can be helpful so that progress can be assessed and recorded. Advice can always be sought from a more senior member of staff.

It is important to keep a sense of proportion. Many older people will recount how they were brought up to have one bath each week. For them it may have been a major operation involving a lot of hard work. Although modern appliances make the procedure a lot easier, this memory remains. The most protracted negotiations may not produce any desire to

Everyone feels better when they are looking good with the hairstyle, clothes and jewellery of their choice, and their favourite possessions around them.

change the routine of a lifetime. A thorough daily wash may have to be accepted as a reasonable alternative.

Maintaining good personal hygiene contributes to a healthy life. Residents have the right to expect proper care and attention, to help them achieve the proverbial "health and happiness" so often expressed as good wishes on special occasions.

Resources
British Red Cross Society, 9 Grosvenor Crescent, London SW1X 7EJ. Tel: 071 235 5454.

Afro skin, hair care and recipes – booklet from the Commission for Racial Equality, and *Hair Care* by Carol Baxter, National Extension college for Training in Health and Race. Also available from CRE.

NVQ Levels 2 & 3 Core Units
O Promote equality for all individuals
U4 contibute to the health, safety and security of individuals and their environment.
U5 Obtain, transmit and store information relating to the delivery of a care service.

Level 2 Direct Care
Z9 Enable clients to maintain their personal hygiene and appearance.

CHAPTER 20

Personal grooming and dressing

Sue Knell

• Our personality stays the same as we get older – we feel the same inside as we did when young • Everyone should be able to choose how they look; some residents will need you to help them in individual ways • Dressing, special clothes and aids • Care of property

Our personality is the one feature which remains constant throughout our life. Ask any of your residents, "How old do you feel inside?" and you will be surprised at their answers.

As we get older our ability to control our own affairs may fade, we may become frail or even confused, but our personality remains constant and those things which have given us happiness all our life continue to make us happy, even though we may become dependent on others to provide our basic needs.

A very important but sometimes neglected part of caring for elderly people is personal grooming and dressing. The way we dress is after all a direct expression of our personality and/or our cultural background and beliefs. We all like to feel and look good; age does not alter this.

It is very important that people are allowed to choose how they look. If a woman has always worn lipstick and powder, or a man a shirt and tie, they would probably not feel right dressed any other way. A favourite pair of earrings or a necklace – it only takes a few minutes but it makes a world of difference.

In this situation the relationship between care assistant and resident is of crucial importance. You have by far the closest, most frequent contact with residents; you are best placed to observe and meet individual needs and preferences.

How much help?

It is important to establish the amount of help each individual needs. Too little help and they will feel unable to cope, and perhaps not even try. Giving too much help is as bad, it will not encourage independence. So observe each individual to judge what help is required, and back it up with lots of encouragement.

As you help a resident to help dress and undress, always talk to them explaining what you are doing, telling them for example which arm you are about to put into a sleeve – they may well be able to co-operate and make it easier.

If a resident likes make-up, she may need help to apply it. A resident who has had a stroke may only be able to see half of their face; eyesight may be poor or perhaps they have limited use of their hands. They may guide you in the amounts used even if they can't apply it themselves.

Privacy

When dressing and undressing clients, it is important to preserve their modesty and dignity. Never leave them inadequately dressed sitting on a chair or commode, even if the door is shut. An elderly resident will be horrified to think somebody could walk in and find them.

Special clothes

There are specially adapted clothes available that may help individual residents: zips instead of buttons, velcro fasteners, elasticated waists, front fastening garments. For someone who is incontinent it is better to use clothing that is easy to undo, in material that can withstand frequent laundering. Women who may be incontinent will find it easier to wear skirts with half slips or trousers, so that their blouses and tops should not need changing as frequently.

People with indwelling catheters may find roomy trousers are more comfortable and useful for concealing catheter bags.

Communicating choice

If you spend time chatting to residents about their appearance, you will get to know what they want, so that they are satisfied and comfortable with their appearance and feel that it is their choice.

If a resident can converse with you, it will be easy to discuss what they wish to wear, which earrings and beads to put with the clothing chosen, or how they like their hair combed. But what happens when someone is unable to answer you?.

It is very important to keep trying and offering choices: the resident may be able to communicate their choice with a smile, a nod or a gesture. Remember that relatives are likely to know about the resident's preferences, and will be pleased to be asked – but this shouldn't replace your attempts to communicate with the resident herself.

You may need to choose clothes for someone who is confused. Make sure they do not always wear the same clothes, and check that clothing is laundered, not put away dirty by the resident.

Standards

Each resident has the right to dress according to their own standards, beliefs and preferences.

Their decisions should be respected and not changed by anyone else who may feel the choice is inappropriate.

Prostheses and other aids

A prosthesis is an artificial part of the body, such as a false limb, eye or breast. People with prostheses may need extra psychological as well as practical support. It is possible that no one other than partner/carer has seen the resident without the prosthesis. You must be aware of and able to control your own reactions and facial expressions, as these can cause distress to the resident. Staff must strive to be as calm, discreet and supportive as possible.

If a prosthesis appears to be ill-fitting or is causing pain or discomfort to the patient, this must be reported immediately.

Other aids and equipment prescribed can range from the common (hearing aids, chapter 23; spectacles, chapter 22; dentures, chapter 19) to corsets, wigs, surgical shoes, and camouflage creams for scars and birth marks.

Care assistants need to find out at the outset how to fit and use such equipment so that help and support can be given and any problems or queries quickly solved.

You should also observe the condition of the aids. Corsets, for example, may be so old and worn, and straps so frayed, that they may no longer give adequate support. You are the most likely person to make this observation, so tell senior staff. Newer or more modern aids may be available, and help and guidance to replace old and worn equipment should be offered.

Remember also that as residents' medical condition changes it is advisable to have their vision and hearing checked, in order to be sure they are getting the best from their hearing aids and spectacles.

You may need help and advice to fit the aid. Ask the resident first – but you may also need to consult an occupational therapist or the supplier of the aid.

Residents who need any type of aid should always be given discreet and friendly help and encouragement and help to wear it. Confidentiality and discretion are very important.

Care of clients' property

Helping residents to take an interest in and look after their property is a very important part of care. Staff must always treat residents' belongings with respect:
• Toiletries should not be left in the bathroom or used on other residents.
• Cosmetics and brushes should be labelled and kept clean.
• Clothing should be labelled and laundered, before putting away safely in the resident's own room.
• Jewellery, whether of monetary or sentimental value, should be kept safe. Maybe a small cash box could be used and the resident keep the key. If the resident is confused it is the responsibility of all staff to keep their property safe. (See chapter 11).

A special time

Helping a resident to get up and dressed may seem a small and straightforward part of your day's work as a care assistant. But when you stop to think about what our appearance and clothes mean to all of us, and how important it is for us to feel good about ourselves, you begin to see what an important time it is.

So never rush, however busy you are; be as attentive as you can and use the opportunity of giving physical care to boost your residents' self-esteem. Try to put yourself in the resident's place as you help them in personal grooming.

Points to remember

1. Personality remains unchanged with age. Older people feel the same inside as they did when young.
2. Personal grooming and dressing is a direct expression of our personality.
3. Establish a minimum level of assistance required in order to maximise the resident's level of independence.
4. Talk to residents about their clothes, and other personal items. Listen to what they say and let them choose wherever possible.
5. Ensure all available aids are offered.
6. People who are confused are entitled to the same rights and considerations given to others, including privacy and confidentiality.
7. A resident's standards, beliefs and preferences may be reflected in the way they like to dress, and should be respected.
8. Try to put yourself in the resident's place as you help them.

NVQ Levels 2 & 3 Core Units
O Promote equality for all individuals.
U4 Contribute to the health, safety and security of individuals and their environment.
U5 Obtain, transmit and store information relating to the delivery of a care service.

Level 2 Direct care
Z9 Enable clients to maintain their personal hygiene and appearance.

CHAPTER 21

Physical comfort, rest and sleep

Anne Eaton

• Needs for rest and sleep are very individual • Why people can't sleep • Daytime rest • How to help • Drugs • Alternative therapies

We all need rest and sleep, and we all need the environment to be suitable before we can achieve either. As a care assistant it will be a part of your role to help residents gain the rest and sleep they need to enjoy their daily activities and stay as healthy as possible.

Individual needs

There is no set amount of sleep that anyone needs. As with all other aspects of daily living, the amount varies from person to person, and indeed from day to day. We are all individuals, and you will find by talking to your elderly residents and learning about their lives that the need for rest and sleep differs for everyone.

After a lifetime of rising at 5.00am in order to go to work, and retiring at 9.30pm, for example, an elderly resident may find it very difficult to alter their routine to fit in with the environment in which they now live.

It is vitally important that an individual's normal routine relating to rest and sleep patterns is identified and recorded by the caring team, so that you can encourage and enable the resident to continue with a lifelong routine.

Why can't you sleep?

Many factors affect the way we rest and sleep during the day and night, and the care assistant needs to be aware of these factors, and control them if it is within your power to do so.

Adapting to change

An elderly resident who is newly admitted to your care home may initially find it very difficult to sleep at night. This may be for a number of reasons including fear, unhappiness, loneliness, a strange bed, absence of a partner.

You need to identify these problems, and may be able to help alleviate some of them by listening and talking to the resident. If they know that there is always someone there, even through the night, this may help to allay their fears. They will need to know how to summon your help, and so you must tell them about the call system and how to use it.

The room may be too hot or too cold for them. Some adjustment in temperature may be possible, bearing in mind the needs of other residents close by.

If they are now sharing a room, this may be a new experience which will take time to adapt to. How would you feel sharing a room with a total stranger? Your patience and understanding will help the resident get used to this new situation.

Psychological factors

Elderly people worry just as anyone else does. Whether they are new or established residents, some problems may arise which will cause them to have difficulty in sleeping. There may be worries over money, their family or property, and all worries seem worse at night. The observant care assistant will notice the resident who is not sleeping and use all her caring skills in order to identify any problems and if possible help to alleviate them.

Physical factors

You may observe that a resident is not sleeping because they are uncomfortable for some reason. This discomfort may be due to the position they are in or because they are in pain, which could be caused by arthritis or another physical complaint. We all "feel" pain differently; the level at which we complain is called a "pain threshold".

As with many other things, pain is very individual: the resident's opinion of its severity must be believed and acted upon appropriately. Reactions to pain may differ between different ethnic groups and their feelings may be expressed in a different manner (see chapter 5). A pain assessment chart (see p161) may be used. You will need to interpret and pass on to other staff all verbal and non-verbal signs of pain the resident may show. Non-verbal signs may include:

- restlessness
- withdrawal
- tearfulness
- becoming unco-operative
- lack of appetite
- lack of sleep

They may also be restless because they need to pass urine, or to have their bowels open; they may find it difficult to get to the toilet. Hunger and thirst may also cause problems. Tea, coffee and cola all contain caffeine and can cause wakefulness. Alcohol may be relaxing, or it may make someone restless. All these drinks make people pass more urine than usual.

Daytime rest

Most elderly people not only need an adequate amount of sleep during the night, but also some undisturbed rest during the day. We all need rest in order for our bodies to undertake normal healing and repair of all body tissues, and this function takes longer in an elderly body.

After lunch is often a favourite time for an hour's sleep. This rest may be taken wherever the individual chooses. Some people like to stay in their favourite chair in the sitting room; others like to retire to their bedrooms and lie on their beds. You will need to identify each person's individual choice and satisfy that choice.

How to help

The environment

During any rest period, day or night, your role is to make sure that the environment will help rest and sleep.

All staff must be aware of noise levels when people are trying to sleep. Be aware of how loud your voice sounds, especially in the middle of the night, and keep as quiet as possible.

Kitchen noises should be kept to a minimum during rest periods, and visitors during the day need to be aware of the needs both of their relatives and of other residents.

The temperature of bedrooms should be adjusted to suit individual needs, and opening bedroom windows may be appropriate, bearing in mind the safety aspects relating to ground floor bedrooms. Bedding can be altered to suit individual needs. Some elderly people do not like duvets and may prefer blankets; you can take this into account when helping to plan individual care.

Familiar objects, and possibly furniture, may make a new environment seem more familiar, and the new resident should be encouraged to bring their own personal belongings with them into the care setting.

Psychological factors

Worry prevents anyone sleeping well; elderly people are no exception. Through talking to your residents and getting to know their normal sleep and rest patterns you will quickly identify any problems. Sometimes all they need is to be able to talk about their worries with someone who has the time to listen. However, you may feel they need professional or specialist advice; if so you should pass on your findings to a senior member of staff in order for the necessary action to be taken.

Physical factors

We all need to be comfortable in order to rest and sleep. A favourite armchair may be all the resident needs during the day in order to rest. At night each resident should be able to choose what time they go to bed and you can help them to establish a routine which will aid sleep. This routine may include a set bedtime, a favourite milky drink, a light snack, perhaps a warm bath, comfortable night attire and a warm, comfortable bed. Individual choice is vital and some people do not like to change the routine, even for one night.

You may need to assist an individual to achieve a comfortable position in bed. To do this you may need to utilise various aids, for example special mattresses, sheepskins, strategically placed pillows. People who cannot move themselves in bed may need you to change their position during the night, both for comfort and in order to prevent pressure sore formation; however it is vital that sleep is disturbed as little as possible.

This disturbance also relates to toileting during the night: although incontinence should be prevented if at all possible, establishing a normal bladder routine during the day, and being aware of the resident's normal fluid intake may enable an individual care plan to be established which allows for long periods of undisturbed sleep.

All these things help to promote rest and sleep. Sometimes, however, other measures may be needed.

Drugs

There are many drugs, which need to be prescribed by a general practitioner and administered by senior care staff, that may help your residents to sleep. Some residents have taken sleeping tablets for many years, some long before they come into their current care environment.

If a resident is prescribed these tablets, part of your role is to ensure that they are taken at the appropriate time and that all other measures to promote sleep are used as well.

If the resident finds difficulty in sleep-

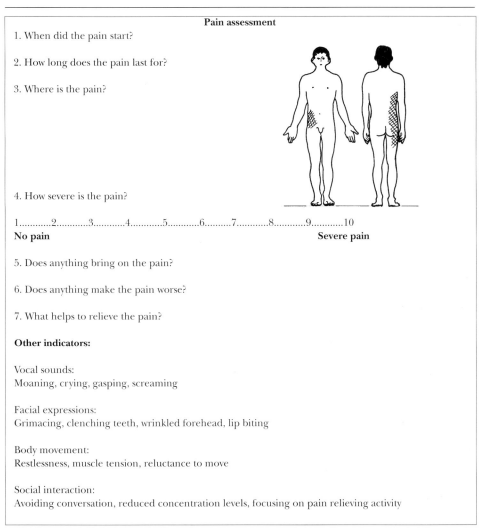

Pain assessment

1. When did the pain start?

2. How long does the pain last for?

3. Where is the pain?

4. How severe is the pain?

1............2............3............4............5............6.........7............8............9............10
No pain   **Severe pain**

5. Does anything bring on the pain?

6. Does anything make the pain worse?

7. What helps to relieve the pain?

Other indicators:

Vocal sounds:
Moaning, crying, gasping, screaming

Facial expressions:
Grimacing, clenching teeth, wrinkled forehead, lip biting

Body movement:
Restlessness, muscle tension, reluctance to move

Social interaction:
Avoiding conversation, reduced concentration levels, focusing on pain relieving activity

A pain assessment chart

ing due to pain caused by a specific condition, arthritis for example, then prescribed drugs in the form of painkillers (analgesics) may be vital in ensuring that the resident is pain-free and therefore able to sleep. Paracetamol, aspirin, or more powerful drugs such as pethidine or morphine, are examples of analgesics.

Your role is to assist with the administration of these drugs and to monitor their effect. For example, do they keep the resident comfortable and pain free?

Are there other side effects such as rashes, stomach upsets or excessive drowsiness in the daytime? You must report the effects of drugs to the senior staff as you record them.

Alternative therapies

Other methods of promoting rest and sleep, without using prescribed drugs, are becoming more popular.

Massage: Some residents find that a

massage, perhaps of the head, neck, shoulders, feet or hands, helps them to relax, rest, and ultimately sleep. Massage can be performed using a base oil, eg baby oil, or by using special aromatic oils, with different aromas that have different effects on the body.

Care assistants should seek advice and consent before undertaking massage, especially with specialist oils as this may utilise the art of aromatherapy. The effect of touch and the feeling of individual care plays a large part in the effectiveness of massage.

Aromatherapy: This alternative therapy was first developed by the ancient Egyptians. It uses the essential oils of flowers, plants, trees and resins. The basic idea is that aromatic oils can have a beneficial effect on mental and emotional states, and these oils can be given orally, or inhaled or massaged into the skin.

The care assistant may wish to find out more about aromatherapy with the idea of utilising it with some residents. You will need to seek advice from professional care staff, the resident's GP and a qualified aromatherapist before proceeding with this therapy. Obviously the consent of the resident and/or relatives is also vital.

Aromatherapy is becoming more popular in its use within care environments as definite positive effects are being achieved.

Herbal remedies: Herbs have always been used to restore good health, and are derived from a variety of plants. Many modern drugs are produced from plants. Herbal preparations are made into ointments and tea, and many are used by individuals by simply buying them from the appropriate shop.

Herbal remedies such as valerian and motherwort can be used to help residents rest and sleep. If a remedy does not interfere with the resident's overall care and it enables them to sleep, then the care assistant can help the resident to use the remedy after gaining the appropriate permission.

Remember, with all "non-prescribed" treatments it is vital that you consult the appropriate qualified staff and seek permission from the relevant people before you become involved with or administer these therapies.

Points to remember

1. We all need to rest and sleep.
2. Your elderly residents are individuals and their needs should be assessed and care planned on an individual basis.
3. Communication skills are vital in your role of assisting residents to rest and sleep, particularly on night duty.
4. Good basic care is necessary to make sure your resident is comfortable, and therefore to promote sleep.
5. Always seek permission from senior staff, as well as the resident, when considering the use of alternative therapies.

Resources
Complementary Therapies for Older People. A Better Care Guide from Hawker Publications, 13 Park House, 140 Battersea Park Road London SW11 4NB. Tel: 071 720 2108. ISBN 1 874790 21 3.

NVQ Levels 2 & 3 Core Units
O Promote equality for all individuals.
U4 Contribute to the health, safety and security of individuals and their environment.
Level 2 Core Units
W3 Support residents in transition due to their care requirements
U4 Contribute to the health, safety and security of individuals and their environment
Level 2 Direct Care
Z7 Contribute to the movement and treatment of residents to maximise their physical comfort
Z11 Enable residents to access and use toilet facilities
Z19 Enable residents to achieve physical comfort.

CHAPTER 22

Sight problems and blindness

Joan Mitchell and Rose Ashbee

• How the eyes work • Common disorders • Normal changes with age • Changes that need expert attention • How to help and communicate with sight-impaired and deaf-blind people • Guiding, and safety in the environment

Any disturbance of vision can be distressing and worrying. Most of us have a dread of permanent damage to our eyes, which might lead to blindness and loss of independence.

This fear usually causes people to seek help early if they notice a deterioration in vision. However elderly people may delay because they think that a reduction in their vision is simply due to old age.

Sometimes age changes are the cause of visual loss, and indeed with increasing age everyone suffers a change in his or her vision. For those who care for elderly people, an understanding of what is a normal age process and what requires further investigation, can be helpful.

The eyes

Each eyeball is a sphere, about one inch in diameter, and is protected by the bony orbit which is part of the skull. The eyeball has a tough white outer covering called the sclera. The curved area at the front of the eye is known as the cornea. This is transparent like a window. It is unprotected and so it can be damaged very easily.

Behind the cornea is the iris, the coloured part of the eye, composed of muscle with an inner contractible circle known as a sphincter. This "hole" is known as the pupil and appears dark to the onlooker. The size of the pupil varies according to the light (see below).

Behind the iris is the lens. This can change its shape by the action of muscles attached to it. In this way it can focus an image on the back of the eye. This region is known as the retina and can be likened to the film in a camera. Through a hole in the back of the orbit the optic nerve reaches the eye from the brain.

Changes with age

The eyes are suspended within the orbit in fat which acts as a cushion. Elderly folk lose some of this fat, so their eyes may appear to be sunken.

Change in the size of the pupil. The pupils are round and equal in size, but with increasing age the pupil often becomes smaller because the iris becomes more rigid. When wide open the pupil lets in light (like an open shutter in a camera). Thus the smaller pupil of the elderly per-

Good lighting is very important for older people. It is a false economy to turn off lights in passages or to have dim lighting in dining rooms and reading rooms.

son lets in less light and causes difficulty in vision if the light is poor. Elderly eyes adapt less quickly to changes in lighting.

Arcus senilis. In a considerable number of elderly people, a narrow greyish white line develops near the margin of the pupil, leaving a clear rim outside it. This is due to fat deposits and has no effect on vision.

Pinguecula. Sometimes a triangular cream-coloured patch of fatty deposit appears under the conjunctiva on either side of the pupil. No treatment is necessary because it does not affect the eyesight. These patches can be removed for cosmetic reasons, but the resulting scar may be no improvement on the patch itself.

Xanthelasma. This is a long name given to the flat yellowish areas often seen in the skin of elderly eyelids, due to special deposits. They are usually symmetrical and have no effect on eyesight and do not require treatment. They can be cut away if they are disfiguring.

Disorders of the eyelids. The eyelids protect the eyes. They are covered with skin on the outside and a thin layer known as the conjunctiva beneath. As people grow older the eyelids become lax and the skin may be in folds. The eyelids frequently turn inwards or outwards due to weakness with increasing age.

Senile entropion is the term used for the lower eyelids turning inwards. This causes the lashes to turn inwards too and so irritate and damage the cornea and conjunctiva. Usually this can be corrected by a sim-

ple operation. Entropion does not affect the eyesight, but scarring of the cornea due to irritation and infection from the inturned lashes can impair vision if the condition is not treated.

Ectropion is the name given to the eyelid turning out due to the slackening of the skin and muscle of the lower lid. Tears cannot get away normally and soreness develops near the eye. The eyes also water a great deal. Again the condition can be corrected by a simple operation performed under a local anaesthetic.

Drooping eyelids may follow a stroke. Usually it is the upper eyelid which is affected. If the drooping hinders vision, special spectacle frames can be provided to raise the margin of the lid and clear the field of vision.

Changes in focusing

Ordinary visual difficulties such as long or short sight do not change much over the years until about age 45.

In youth the lens is transparent. It is covered by a membrane known as the lens capsule and the lens can change its shape by the pull of muscles attached to it, so bringing into focus objects at variable distances. In elderly people the lens becomes firmer and cannot change its shape so readily. It therefore becomes difficult to focus on a page of a book or other near objects including food.

This change becomes troublesome around age 45 although it has been going on long before this age. At first the printed page only needs to be held further away, but soon reading glasses become essential. The condition, known as presbyopia or long-sightedness, gradually becomes worse until by about age 65 virtually everyone needs reading glasses. Distance vision usually improves.

Wearing glasses before or after the onset

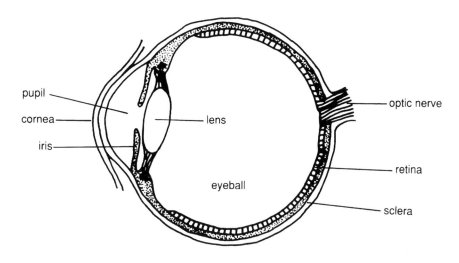

Anatomy of the eye.

of long-sightedness has no effect on the course of the change, and there is no known method of preventing it. The changes vary from one individual to another and no exercises, diet or medicines have any bearing on the development of the condition.

Spectacles can be very helpful and there are many improved kinds on the market from which to make an individual choice. Variable focus lenses are particularly useful for musicians, painters, typists, etc.

Slow loss of vision

Slow loss of vision may not bother an elderly person, who may attribute the change to age. But it is very important that their eyes are checked regularly, because progressive loss of sight can sometimes be halted.

There are three main causes of blindness: cataract, glaucoma and senile degeneration of the macula. These three conditions nearly always develop very slowly and are not usually noticed until there is considerable loss of vision.

The first cause, cataract, can be remedied. The second, glaucoma, cannot be cured but it can be arrested. The third, senile degeneration of the macula, often progresses to blindness.

Cataract. This accounts for about a quarter of the applications for admission to the blind register.

As well as the covering of the lens becoming firmer with increasing age, the lens also becomes less transparent. Everyone over 65 will show some loss of lens transparency. Usually the lenses of both eyes are affected, although not necessarily to the same extent. Treatment is only required if the loss of transparency of the lens interferes with the vision enough to hamper a person's normal occupation or recreation.

Cataracts usually increase in thickness slowly, causing a gradual deterioration in vision, but there is no way of knowing how quickly the process will proceed. Some thicken very rapidly over a few months, others barely at all in a lifetime and may never give any trouble.

Cataract formation is a process of ageing and, as in the development of long-sight-

---

edness, no diet, exercises or other medical treatment can prevent it, any more than it is possible to stop a person's hair from going grey. Indeed, there is as much variation from individual to individual over cataract formation as grey hair.

The development of a cataract frequently increases short-sightedness. A change in glasses is all that is needed in the early stages. Sometimes drops can be used to dilate the pupil.

Cataracts do not necessarily need to "mature" before being removed. The decision to remove a cataract is made when poor sight interferes with an individual's lifestyle. Thick spectacle lenses are required after operation to replace the lens that has been taken away.

Simple glaucoma. This is due to a rise in pressure of the fluid inside the eyeball. When glaucoma occurs gradually, the eye remains white and painless, but sight can be irretrievably lost.

It is probably due to ageing but the true cause is obscure. Heredity plays a part and therefore people with a near relative suffering from glaucoma should be screened for the condition. It is usually detected by the optician, but sometimes elderly people notice a restriction in their field of vision which may cause them to blunder into objects. They may also complain of aching eyes.

Treatment by an ophthalmologist is necessary and involves regular follow-up examinations.

Degeneration of the retina. Degenerative changes affecting the lining of the eyeball (the retina) are a common cause of visual loss in elderly people. The degeneration frequently affects an important area of the retina known as the macula. The only treatment for the resultant poor vision is strong reading glasses and the use of a magnifying glass or low vision aids.

Diabetics are more prone than other people to these changes of the retina (they are often more prone to cataract formation too). Sometimes laser treatment can help.

Vitreous floaters. Age changes in the thick fluid behind the lens (the vitreous) often cause black spots to float about. These are called "floaters" and tend to move when the eye moves and settle when the eye is at rest. No treatment is needed for these and vision is not threatened, but it is important to be sure that the person has indeed a floater and not some other condition, such as retinal detachment.

Sudden loss of sight

The gradual loss of sight in one eye may not be noticed unless the good eye is covered up for some reason. If loss of sight occurs suddenly it is usually noticed soon afterwards. There are many causes for sudden loss of sight, including vascular causes, detached retina, or causes associated with other medical conditions. All require expert ophthalmological attention.

Toxic amblyopia. One uncommon cause of loss of sight, but one that is treatable, is toxic amblyopia. It is almost confined to heavy pipe smokers who complain of loss of vision in both eyes. Treatment with vitamin B12 and reduction in smoking bring about a marked improvement in vision. The improvement occurs in six to eight weeks after reducing smoking. Cigarette smokers do not seem to suffer from this condition.

Loss of vision associated with a painful eye. This usually happens suddenly, and the affected person is also ill. It is obvious that medical attention is urgently required.

There are four main causes of a **painful red eye**:

• Inflammation of the outer covering of the eye, eg conjunctivitis. In this case there is discomfort rather than pain and sight is not threatened. Treatment is usually by appropriate antibiotic drops.

• Inflammation of the iris, known as iritis, is more painful and requires expert treatment. It is curable, but if neglected the sight can be affected.

• Similarly ulcers of the cornea are very painful and can lead to scarring and blurring of vision if untreated.

• Acute glaucoma is the most serious cause. The sufferer is usually prostrate and may even vomit. Prompt attention and admission to hospital is usually needed.

Herpes Zoster (shingles) affects one eye, but the other may be red and swollen "in sympathy". This condition usually follows the reactivation of the chicken pox virus which has lain dormant since an attack of chicken pox in childhood. Symptoms are more severe in elderly people and they are often left with severe pain at the site of the shingles for a long time afterwards. Expert medical treatment is needed as soon as possible.

Registration

Registration of a person as blind or partially sighted is made by a consultant ophthalmologist. It opens the way to a large range of help from the services devoted to the care of the blind.

Braille or the more simple "Moon" can be learnt. Talking books and cassettes are available through a special Freepost service and there are many helpful devices which are being improved all the time. Large print books available at public libraries are valuable if visual loss is less serious.

PART TWO
• How to help and communicate with sight-impaired and deaf-blind people
• Guiding and safety in the surrounding environment

There are some 190,000 registered blind or partially sighted people in the UK today, two-thirds of whom are aged over 75. But a recent RNIB survey has shown that the total number of people with some kind of visual handicap may be as large as 960,000 – most of whom, for one reason or another, are not registered. It is likely that some of these unregistered sight-impaired people may at some time find themselves in residential care.

There are also hundreds of people who are hard of hearing or deaf as well as being sight-impaired. The partial loss of sight and hearing together can cut people off from their surroundings and isolate them from companionship.

Being deaf *and* blind is not just twice as bad as losing either sight or hearing, the problems are multiplied. A sight-impaired person can still join in conversation and someone who cannot hear may compensate by lip reading or sign language. A person with both handicaps is unable to do so. It is rare for anyone to suffer a total loss of both senses. If an individual has some sight or hearing, opthalmic and audio examinations may indicate means of improvement.

Entering care

For many people coming to terms with losing their homes and (by implication) their independence, is a very traumatic experience, akin to that of bereavement. Pause for a moment and reflect how additionally disadvantaged an individual may feel coping with the extra burden of failing eyesight and hearing .

Try doing some everyday activity like eating your lunch or trying to find something in the cupboard without using your eyes. Sit by the television with the sound turned down or try and listen to the radio that is slightly off tune so that it continually whistles and buzzes. Although no one can really understand what it must be like to be deaf and blind all the time, these exercises may help you to realise the enormous impact of these handicaps.

Adapting to change is difficult for most of us, and the older we get the harder it is to make any transition. For example, we have all moved house at some point in our lives and lived with the ensuing anxiety and fears that accompany such a move. These feelings intensify as we get older, and many elderly people coming into care may feel them insurmountable .

However there are many ways that we can help them to adjust to and enjoy their new environment. Encouraging independence, retaining dignity and maintaining self respect, are goals for which to aim for every individual.

Communication

When you approach a sight-impaired person, always introduce yourself, say who you are and what your job is. Do stop and chat if you have the time, and always say what you are doing. Try and remember to address each individual by name – after all, they cannot see that you are talking to them. Never leave without saying goodbye: it is frustrating and embarrassing for a person to realise that they are talking to an empty space. Do not shout: many sight-impaired people have excellent hearing. Speak clearly and normally.

How easily someone who is deaf and blind can communicate depends on several factors. Firstly, how old they were when they lost their sight and hearing, secondly whether they lost both senses at once or one after another and thirdly

whether they have learned a language beforehand, either speech or sign.

Language and speech are not the same thing. Language is the ability to understand and communicate information. Speech is one method of doing this, gesture and touch are others.

People whose first handicap was deafness may know British sign language and finger spelling. They should not find it too difficult to use the deaf blind manual alphabet, as it is an adaptation of the deaf manual spelled out on the hand. An alternative is the Spartan alphabet, block capitals printed on the hand.

If the individual has enough sight you may try using a thick, black felt tipped pen and writing (on paper) in large print. Whatever method you choose, you must use it consistently. It is best to start off by linking it to essential information about some activity, such as meals, dressing or bathing.

Let them touch

When you approach someone who is deaf and blind let them know you are there without startling them, by tapping them gently on the forearm or wrist. To make sure they know who you are, let them feel a ring or a badge or a hair slide that you always wear. Or make an agreed movement on their hand such as tickling their palm gently.

Don't be put off if a deaf and blind person wants to use touch; remember it is the most important information sense they have left. Do use every opportunity to communicate and involve them in what is going on around them.

Guiding

Do ask first if a person wants assistance: no one likes to be grabbed and dragged. Let the person take your arm and walk slightly in front of them, watching out carefully for obstacles. If you need to walk in single file, through an open doorway

It helps to use the idea of a clock face to describe their plate of food to a blind person.

for example, indicate this by tucking your guiding hand behind your back.

Always stop at the beginning of stairs and steps and say whether they are going up or down and about how many there are. If there is a handrail put the person's hand on it to help them. Make sure you say when you are at the last step.

Help the sight-impaired person to sit down by putting their hand on the back of the chair. Leave the rest to them; never lower them bodily into a chair they have not inspected.

Mealtimes

Always ask what an individual likes and dislikes. There is nothing worse than putting an item of food into your mouth that you dislike. When serving a meal do remember to say that you have done so. Say what it is and the position it occupies on the plate and stick to the same system.

For example, always place meat at 12 o'clock, potatoes at 6 o'clock and vegetables at 3 and 9 o'clock (see left).

Do ask if help is needed, perhaps by cutting up the food. Providing a plate with an upturned rim will assist the sight-impaired person to feed themselves and reduce the risk and embarrassment of food sliding onto the table. When serving drinks say where you are placing them, and never over-fill cups or glasses; this will reduce the risk of spillage.

Dressing

Just because a person cannot see how they look does not mean to say that they do not want to look nice. Never let a sight-impaired person go about with odd coloured shoes on, laddered stockings, untidy hair or grubby clothing. They will rely on you to tell them tactfully if anything is amiss.

The environment

Make sure that the sight-impaired person knows the position of the call system, the radio, bedside locker and shaving points. Even people registered as blind may have some degree of sight. This does not mean that they are able to "see", but they may perhaps be able to distinguish between light and dark. Visual handicaps are so variable and the conditions that enable people to make the best use of their eyesight may vary considerably. Make sure the individual knows where the light switches are.

Make sure they know how to get to the bathroom, lavatory, day room and dining area. Try to mention easy to touch landmarks, such as pictures on the wall, or a change in surface from carpet to tiling underfoot. Watch out for hazards in their path such as hoovers, commodes, trailing flexes or tea trolleys. Always say if you have to leave something in the way, or if something must not be touched. If you move anything always put it back exactly in the same place.

Never put a sight-impaired person's belongings away before asking where they should go.

A little extra help

Do not worry about saying things like "Do you see what I mean?". Avoiding using such terms can often create more difficulties for everyone if a silence follows while you search for a different word.

Be natural. Your tone of voice and your manner is vitally important; it must convey what you intend it to. Sight-impaired people cannot see your face, whether you are smiling, worried or cross. Do not be afraid to touch. A friendly pat on the back or a squeeze of the hand can be reassuring and comforting.

But the greatest need for most deaf or blind people is for companionship. Someone to talk to them at their own pace. To tell them what is going on in the world outside as well as in the home. Remember that sight-impaired people are normal people who just can't see. Treat them as you would treat anyone else, except at those times when they need a little extra help. Just as you would in their place.

Points to remember

1. Older people may not complain of deteriorating sight because they think it is part of old age. But regular checks are important because loss of sight can some-times be halted.

2. When caring for people with impaired sight, address each individual by name and always introduce yourself. Stop and chat if you have time, and never leave without saying goodbye.

3. Don't be put off if a deaf and blind person wants to use touch.

4. Ask if someone wants assistance – never grab and drag.

5. At mealtimes, special help will be needed.

6. Don't let people go about looking grubby or untidy.

7. Make sure they know how to get to the bathroom, lavatory, day room and dining area.

8. Watch out for hazards and tell blind people about them.

9. Remember that their greatest need is for companionship.

Resources

National Deaf Blind Helpers League, 18 Rainbow Court, Paston Ridings, Peterborough PE4 6UP. Tel: 0733 73511. Information, advice and publications, including illustrated instructions for manual alphabets.

Royal National Institute for the Blind, 224 Great Portland St, London W1N 6AA. Advice, information and publications, especially Braille books, periodicals and music, and Moon books and periodicals.

NVQ Levels 2 &3 Core Units

O Promote equality for all individuals.
U4 Contribute to the health, safety and security of individuals and their environment.

Level 3 Core Unit

Z4 Promote communication with clients where there are communication difficulties.

Level 2 Direct care

Z6 Enable clients to maintain and improve their mobility.
Z9 Enable clients to maintain their personal hygiene and appearance.
Z10 Enable clients to eat and drink.

CHAPTER 23

Hearing difficulties and deafness

Alastair Kent

• How the ear works • Causes of hearing loss • Hearing aids and how to use them • Communicating with deaf and hearing-impaired people • Other aids and equipment

Losing your hearing is a very isolating experience because it cuts you off from much of everyday life. When hearing loss is accompanied by other problems associated with ageing the end result will, all too often, be an unhappy, lonely individual, cut off from family and friends.

Too often people make assumptions about people with poor hearing that increase this feeling of alienation. Many people try to hide their deafness, perhaps because it is assumed by others to go with loss of mental ability.

Hearing loss is remarkably common. The Institute of Hearing Research estimates that as many as 10 million people in the UK have a loss of hearing that will cause problems for them in some circumstances. The vast majority of these people are over retirement age. As many as 1 in 5 in this group have a significant hearing loss. If you work in a care home for elderly people, it is almost inevitable that some of your residents will have serious problems in hearing. This chapter aims to help you to help them.

How the ear works

The ear is divided into three parts - outer, middle and inner - each of which has a part to play in the process of hearing, and which will, if damaged or in some other way rendered non-functional, cause hearing loss or even deafness.

1) The Outer Ear

This part of the ear includes the *Pinna*, which is the visible part. This acts like a funnel, channelling sound into the *External Auditory Canal*. This canal is really just a tube in the side of the head at the end of which is a membrane called the *Ear Drum*. Sound waves entering the canal hit this membrane and make it vibrate. The higher pitched the sound, the faster the ear drum will vibrate.

2) The Middle Ear

This part of the ear is a small air-filled cavity inside the head. It is connected to the outside world by a narrow passage called the *Eustachian Tube*. This opens up in the nose and throat. Its function is to ensure that the air pressure on each side of the ear drum is the same.

In the middle ear are three little bones. These are linked together and connect the inside of the ear drum with another membrane, known as the *Oval Window*. This leads to the inner ear. The names of the bones are *Malleus, Incus* and *Stapes*. When the ear drum vibrates these bones transmit the vibrations across to the inner ear.

3) The Inner Ear

The inner ear is full of liquid. It consists of a complex system of passages and is in two parts: the *Cochlea* and the *Semi-Circular Canals*. It is the cochlea which is concerned with hearing, while the canals control your balance. In the cochlea is a very sensitive organ called the *Organ of Corti*. This can be likened to a piano keyboard,

but one with 17,000 keys!

Each "key" is a cell covered with tiny hairs, and each cell is connected to the *Auditory Nerve*. When the oval window is vibrated by the bones of the middle ear these vibrations are transmitted to the fluid which fills the cochlea. This then stimulates the hairs on the cells and, according to the frequency of the vibrations, a different combination of cells is caused to "fire" – or in other words, to send an electrical signal up the auditory nerve to the brain, where they are decoded and we are able to perceive the sound in our consciousness.

Causes of hearing loss

The ear is a very complex and sensitive organ which can easily be damaged. There are many conditions which can affect hearing, but generally speaking, they can be divided into three broad groups: *Conductive Deafness, Nerve Deafness* and *Old Age Deafness*.

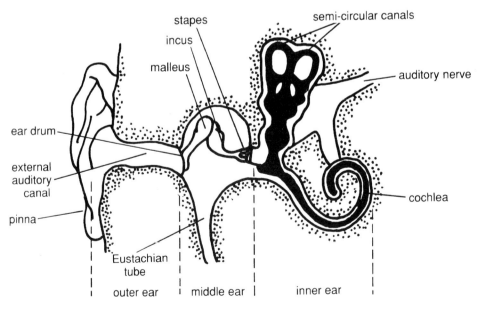

Anatomy of the ear.

172

1. Conductive Deafness

This may be caused by anything which prevents the conduction of sound from the outside world to the point where the vibrations can stimulate the hair cells in the cochlea. Some of the commoner causes of hearing loss in elderly people include:

a) Blockage in the external canal: This must be almost total before hearing loss is noticed. Normally the ear's own clearance mechanism prevents a build-up of wax. In some cases, however, it may be necessary to visit the doctor for the ears to be syringed. Poking with cotton buds usually makes the problem worse by pressing the wax down.

b) Otitis Externa: When the skin of the canal becomes irritated, it results in inflammation and sometimes infection. It may also affect hearing. Treatment is by careful cleaning and the application of ear drops.

c) Otosclerosis: This is the commonest type of conductive deafness. It is caused by an over-growth of bone in the middle ear, resulting in the link between the ear drum and the oval window becoming progressively more rigid and unable to transmit vibrations. It can be treated by surgery with a very good chance of improvement in the person's hearing.

d) Middle Ear Infections: These may be short term or long lasting, and may result in either temporary or permanent damage to hearing. They require medical treatment which varies according to the precise nature of the condition.

2. Nerve Deafness

Damage to the cochlea may occur as a result of illness, injury, exposure to some drugs or exposure to loud noises over prolonged periods. At present there is no known cure, and people with nerve deafness are dependent on others being aware of their problem and knowing what action

to take in the circumstances.

3. Old Age Deafness

Hearing, like any other sense, tends to become less acute as we get older. There is little or nothing that can be done to prevent this, and it is a very common problem among elderly people. Where hearing loss is suspected, and other causes have been eliminated, the quality of life of the elderly person with diminished hearing will be significantly affected by the attitude and approach of those around. Practical suggestions for help are outlined below.

Hearing aids

Hearing aids are supplied to those who have been assessed as needing them, by the NHS free of charge. NHS aids come in two broad types: those worn behind the ear and those which are body worn. Whatever type is supplied, it is important to ensure that they have been issued as a result of professional assessment, that they fit properly and that they are in good working order.

When a person uses a hearing aid it is important to check regularly that it is in full working order, and to ensure that it is **switched on** when needed. Models and types of hearing aids vary, but the following points are important:

• **Batteries**. These last between one and three months. When they run out they should be kept, and returned to the issuing audiology department where they can be exchanged free of charge.

If the aid whistles when switched on, and with the volume turned up, the battery is charged. If you cannot get a whistle, it is dead. Batteries should be checked every week and every day if the person is confused.

• **Volume**. To find the best volume setting, adjust the volume to the point just below where a whistle is heard. Check the whistle does not return if the person shakes their head. Ask and observe the person to see if they are comfortable with this volume.

• **Plastic tube**. The sound passes through this tube, so it must be kept clean, free of wax and flexible. It should be renewed regularly at the audiology clinic.

• **Ear mould**. This is made for the individual, and cannot be worn by anyone else. The small hole at the end is where the sound enters the ear. If this becomes blocked with wax, the aid is much less efficient.

It is therefore essential that the person's ears are checked for wax every six months. Care staff should check and remove any wax obvious in the *outer* ear every day.

• **Does the aid fit properly?** A high pitched whistling noise is a sign of feedback, showing that the aid is not properly fitted. This may be because the person has not put the mould snugly into his/her ear, or it may be an indication that the mould itself is poorly fitted and needs replacing. Also check the plastic tube is not split, as this too will often cause feedback.

Some people with impaired hearing seem unable to hear the high pitched whistle from feedback. It should not be ignored though, because it alters the hearing aid's ability to amplify other sounds that the hearing-impaired person can hear without distortion.

It is also extremely irritating to those around who can hear it, and may result in feelings of anger or unpleasantness towards the person whose aid is whistling!

• **Adjustment.** The controls on a behind-the-ear aid are very small and need a fair degree of fine finger control to adjust them. If a person is experiencing difficulty, they may find it easier to cope with a body worn aid. These have larger controls (they are similar in size to a personal stereo) which may be easier for stiff fingers to set.

Many people are issued with hearing aids but choose not to use them. Often this is because they feel embarrassed about owning up to their hearing loss. But hearing loss is widespread in the population over retirement age, and your sympathetic and matter of fact approach will help the person feel comfortable about admitting that they have a problem, and doing something about it.

It is also important to realise that a hearing aid will not "cure" deafness in most people. Hearing aids have a number of limitations:

• They are unselective – many will amplify all sound picked up by their microphone without differentiating between those things you want to hear and those which are just background noise. Some more sophisticated ones will amplify some frequencies more than others, but even the best are very crude compared to the human ear.

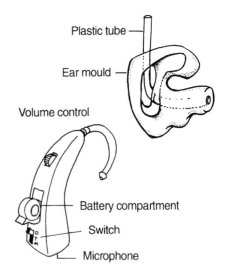

Diagram of a hearing aid.

• Hearing aids work best at the distance of normal conversation - between three and six feet. Closer in they may distort the sound, further away they may not pick up a sufficiently powerful signal to amplify it clearly.

• Hearing aids will not help in cases of nerve deafness. They can only amplify sound to compensate for problems associated with poor conductive mechanisms. They cannot make damaged nerves work again. People with nerve deafness need other kinds of help (see below).

What can you do?

There are a number of simple steps that you can take to help communication with the hearing-impaired person, whether or not they use an aid:

• **Control background noise.** If the radio is on, or the vacuum cleaner is going, then it will be much more difficult for the person with impaired hearing to understand you.

• **Avoid shouting.** If a person is using a hearing aid then the sounds which they can hear will be amplified as well as those sounds with which they have difficulty. They will be made very loud, they may be distorted by the amplifier in the hearing aid and they may even cause pain to the hearing aid wearer.

Shouting also distorts your face. If a person is trying to lip-read you, this will make it more difficult. Try standing in front of a mirror and speaking normally. Now shout the same words and notice how different your face looks. (NB It is best to do this when you are on your own!) Clarity of speech, not volume, is the main requirement, but again do not unnaturally emphasise words or articulate them in an exaggerated fashion as that will also change the shape of your face. Try this in the mirror too!

• **Give clues** to what you are talking about in your face and by your body movements. Let your feelings show in your expression and try to move so as to help convey your meaning.

• **Think about the lighting.** If a deaf person is to be able to lip-read you, good light levels are essential. Your face should be illuminated evenly, with no deep shadows. Do not stand in front of a window or a lamp, but turn so that the light falls onto your face. Do not get too close to the deaf person – about four to six feet is best, so that they can see all your face easily. Further away the elderly person will probably not see you clearly enough.

• Make sure that you have **attracted the deaf person's attention** and that they know you want to say something to them before launching into a conversation.

• **Talk in a normal rhythm**. Even if a person cannot hear or lip-read you very well, they may understand a lot from the context. If you speak in single words, rather than sentences, then the deaf person cannot get help from the flow of words.

• **Use different words.** If you seem to have a problem in helping the hearing impaired person to understand you, then try saying to him/her "I'm talking about..." If you get stuck with a particular word or sentence, say it again once or twice in the same words but do not repeat it over and over again. This will only cause embarrassment to both of you, and possibly result in anger or confusion. Try putting the same idea across in another way, using different words.

The person with impaired hearing is most likely to understand you if you face them and speak clearly and with a normal rhythm, so they can use both sight and hearing to best advantage.

One final point: a person can only lip-read if they can see your lips. Droopy moustaches, covering the top lip, make this really difficult. Two minutes once a week with a pair of nail scissors could make a really noticeable difference to your communication skills!

Other aids and equipment

You may have access to a very useful communication aid consisting of a microphone, into which you speak, connected to an amplifier which the patient holds to their better ear. This type of hearing aid is sometimes more useful than a conventional hearing aid because it does not pick up the same amount of background noise.

Other helpful devices include:

1. Special alarm clocks which flash a bright light or operate a vibrating pad under the pillow or mattress.

2. Doorbells connected into special electrical circuits to cause the lights to flash when someone wants to come in. This may use a special signal lamp or be connected to the main lighting for the room.

3. Help to hear the television without annoying the neighbours. This comes in a variety of forms, including:

• Headphones

• Specialist TV listening devices

• Induction loops - these transmit the sound from the TV into a wire loop set up round the room. The person wearing a hearing aid is able to adjust this to pick up the signal in the wire without interference from background noise.

• **Teletext.** Many TV programmes now are transmitted with sub-titles. To see the sub-titles it is necessary to have a special television or buy a de-coder to go with an existing set. These cost little more than a standard TV set and help many people to follow what is going on much more easily.

4. Help with the telephone. Telephones cause a serious problem for many hearing-impaired people. Inability to use the telephone results in people becoming much more cut off from family, friends and the outside world than they need be; but again, there are a number of items that may be helpful.

• The bell may be connected to a flashing light so that a person with impaired hearing knows that the phone is ringing.

• The earpiece may be fitted with an amplifier and /or an inductive coupler (or a miniature induction loop) to improve the transmission of sound into the ear.

When these devices are fitted to a telephone, they can make a great deal of difference. There are some people who are too deaf to use the telephone and their problems are more difficult to resolve. In such cases referral should be made to a specialist social worker with deaf people.

The aids and equipment mentioned above can make a major improvement in a person's ability to understand and take part in events going on around them. However they can only help if everyone - you, the resident, management, family and friends - know that the equipment is installed and working and also know how to use it! There is no equipment in the world that can work when packed away in a box on top of a wardrobe.

Conclusion

We are all bound, in whatever capacity, to come across people with impaired hearing at some stage in our lives. Yet, despite this, hearing loss remains one of the most misunderstood impairments to which people are prone. I have given a few suggestions to help break down the barriers between people with impaired hearing and the everyday life of the community in which they live. Awareness and sensitivity are two of the most important attributes that you can have to help in this process, as these will help you to recognise the hearing loss in the first place and then do something about it.

Resources

Social Services Departments usually employ specialist social workers for deaf people. They can be contacted through the officer in charge of the residential home where you work, or directly.

Royal National Institute for the Deaf, 105 Gower Street, London, WC1E 6AH (071 387 8033) offers advice, information and services to people with impaired hearing or those working with them.

British Association of the Hard of Hearing, 7-11 Armstrong Road, London W3 7JL (081 743 1110) runs local clubs in many parts of the country. It also provides information and a newsletter.

British Deaf Association, 38 Victoria Place, Carlisle (0228 48844). This organisation is mainly concerned with those born deaf and using sign language as means of communication. The BDA provides specialist services and deaf clubs for these people.

Local associations and societies in many parts of the country offer varying levels of service and support. Your local library should have this information.

NVQ Levels 2 & 3 Core Units

O Promote equality for all individuals.

U4 Contribute to the health, safety and security of individuals and their environment.

Level 3 Core Unit

Z4 Promote communication with clients where there are communication difficulties.

Level 2 Direct Care

Z9 Enable clients to maintain their personal hygiene and appearance.

CHAPTER 24

Confusion and dementia

Alan Crump

• What is confusion? • What is dementia? • The progress of dementia – changes in understanding, personality and behaviour • Building up a relationship of trust and respect • The right approach – clear communication, reducing frustration and risks

Caring for people with dementia is one of the most challenging areas of work. It can be both physically and mentally demanding, and at times it may feel that there are few rewards for your commitment, skill and patience. However, as a care assistant you have a key role to play in working with people with dementia. With the right attitude and approach you can make all the difference in their care.

What is confusion?

Confusion is a very broad term used to describe a situation where someone is unable to understand or function at the level you would normally expect of them. A person may not remember names, faces or previously well-known places. They may lose track of time or not understand relatively simple information.

Some people may become very anxious, believing there is a plot against them by their relatives or carers. Others become withdrawn and isolated. "Confusion" is not a single condition; rather there is a whole set of different behaviours which might be associated with someone who is confused.

We all get confused

There are times when we all get confused. We walk into a new building or a different street and think that an office or shop is to the left and end up getting lost and confused. All of us forget important information at some time. A name of a friend, an item from the shopping list or a special appointment. This is frustrating but we get around it, perhaps by using lists or a diary.

Illness can make people confused, both young and old. Severe influenza, a knock on the head, extreme anxiety or some medicines can cause some temporary confusion. Confusion for us is not a constant problem. It usually quickly disappears.

Older people can become confused when they get chest infections, urine infections or heart problems. Again these periods of confusion are short and can be easily treated. An older person who suddenly becomes confused will probably have a condition which is easily treated.

As a care assistant you will get to know residents well, and you will be able to spot and report any sudden unexplained changes. Your knowledge of the person will be essential. With appropriate treatment the suddenly confused older person will return to the able and orientated person that you know.

However for some people, those who have dementia, confusion is something that they and all those around them have to live with every day of their lives.

What is dementia?

Dementia is a term which describes a decline in the ability to think clearly and remember accurately. This decline results in a reduced ability to care for yourself and sometimes involves changes to your personality. All these changes lead to the person with dementia becoming "confused".

The confusion associated with dementia can take many forms. A person with dementia may show a range of behaviours or special needs. Although there may be some similarities, each person with dementia will have different losses and different abilities. Just as there is no condition which defines confusion there is no set of behaviours which defines dementia. In the early stages of dementia the periods of confusion may be only short or they may involve only minor lapses in concentration or forgetfulness. Often the changes will only be noticed when one looks back and is able to see a pattern of certain behaviours.

It is important to remember that if an older person forgets a name or an address this does not necessarily mean they have dementia. We all forget things and occasionally we all do unusual things. Being old is not the same as having dementia. Only five per cent of people over 65 have dementia. This only rises to twenty per cent of people over 80. The following are some behaviour changes that are common in dementia:

Memory loss
Memory loss will be most apparent at first with events and information that is recent. Forgetting that the kettle is on the stove. Losing important documents that were put into a "safe" place. Perhaps forgetting that they have just eaten and starting again, or asking the same question over and over again.

The usual pattern is that memories which are deeply embedded in the memory are the last to be lost. A person may have a very poor memory for the last thirty years, perhaps forgetting that a dearly loved spouse has died, but may have a very clear image of their early years of life.

Loss of understanding and reasoning
A person with dementia will begin to lose the ability to understand what is going on around them. For instance they may not see the importance of washing or dressing. They may not understand the need to have regular meals. If they go into shops they may make rash decisions, such as buying dog food when they do not have a dog!

An older person with dementia may be at risk when crossing busy roads. They may not understand the danger involved. On a cold day they may not realise that it would be sensible to wear a coat outside.

In the person with dementia, normal decision-making is altered. Being able to hold a couple of ideas at the same time becomes increasingly difficult and decision making is frustrating.

Restlessness and agitation
A person with dementia may begin to

The main aim of your care should be to develop a trusting relationship.

show signs of being restless. This restlessness may have no specific cause, and cannot be fully explained. They may wander around the house or garden without any apparent aim. Attempts to prevent them pacing may be met with anger and resentment. This restlessness may mean that their sleep pattern is altered, perhaps sleeping little at night and napping during the day.

Changes to the personality

A person with dementia may seem to have large changes in their personality. They may seem obstinate where once they were cooperative and helpful. This may be a result of the individual's desire to keep things as they are and not change anything, because this feels safer to them. They may become impatient and a little self-centred where once they were tolerant and generous.

They may start to depend upon one person for a sense of security, and become very anxious when that person is away. The person with dementia may develop ideas that someone is trying to harm them or steal from them. These ideas can become increasingly real for the individual and very difficult to change. Caring for a person with such strongly held ideas can be very difficult.

Physical and verbal aggression

The frustration and anxiety of the person with dementia can sometimes spill over into aggression. This might be shouting or strong language. Very occasionally it could result in physical blows. All these events may be completely out of the previously reported character of the patient. This can be particularly worrying for relatives.

Mood

Changes in mood are also possible, especially in the early stages of dementia. A person may seem distant and quiet. They may talk of dying and seem in low spirits. The person may realise that all is not as it should be and this may cause a great deal of distress. This kind of distress or depression may respond very well to medication. It will certainly respond well to warmth and genuine concern.

Loss of independence

Some people with dementia may slowly lose the ability to do the normal everyday activities like washing, dressing, preparing and eating food and using the toilet. It may also affect activities like walking and speaking. As the illness progresses the abilities of the person with dementia decline to the point where they may need help with every aspect of life.

A trusting relationship

The most important principle when working with a person who has dementia, is to limit their confusion or frustration. As a care assistant you may have to respond to a person who at times will believe they are living 30 years ago, and who believes they can cope without any help from "strangers".

The main aim of your care should be to develop a trusting relationship. A trusting relationship will mean that every other area of care will be that much easier.

Developing a trusting relationship is not easy. You may have to compete with some fixed ideas – for example they may believe you are stealing from them. Sometimes it is really difficult not to feel hurt and defensive. This kind of response creates frustration and even more feelings of insecurity. It will make every aspect of your care that much more difficult.

Patience

There are times when people with dementia test your patience to its very extreme. But rushing and being impatient are counter-productive. There will always be a more positive response if your care is measured, calm and patient.

Tolerance

Some of the behaviours of the person with dementia appear quite irrational. Some individuals do things, say things and believe things that are very unusual. You will have to learn how to tolerate unusual behaviours. It may be strong language. It may be inappropriate sexual advances. It may be severe frustration or aggression aimed at you personally. You may be the person who takes all the blame. The least helpful response would be for you to become angry or frustrated with the person who is confused.

Sometimes you will have to step back for a few moments and "count to ten" in order to continue. This is something every one has to do at times. Your tolerance in extreme situations will develop as you start to understand the frustrations of the individual with whom you are working.

Understanding and knowledge

Understanding and knowledge come with time, and help to build up the relationship. It helps a great deal if you try to understand the situation from the client's point of view. Try to feel the way they feel. We can never truly know what it is like to have dementia. However, with some knowledge of the condition, likely behaviours and causes, if we try to understand we can perhaps sense their frustration, their pain, loss and distress.

Sensitivity

Sensitivity is not the same as being very caring. It is about doing the right things at the right times. If a person with dementia was crying, a "caring" person might say "Oh, don't worry, it will all be all right". This is obviously not true, however, and could be called insensitive. The sensitive person would try and understand the frustration or the distress, and would not dismiss the feelings being expressed.

The "caring" person might see an individual struggling with shaving or washing and do it for them. This might save time but would take away the fragile independence of the person with dementia. The sensitive person would offer time, encouragement and support.

Taking risks

Similarly, a "caring" person might restrict someone's ability to move around because of a feeling that they are at risk. This will keep them safe but may take away one of the most important freedoms that remains. Sometimes in promoting safety we end up by promoting lethargy and helplessness. The sensitive person would weigh up the risks to find the most appropriate solution.

Humour

This does not mean deliberate attempts to make someone feel small by laughing at them. It is about always being able to see the lighter side. Humour can be used to build relationships. Laughing with people develops understanding and shared feelings. Working with people who have dementia can sometimes seem very hard without much feedback. Watching someone smile and smiling with them can add something to the relationship that could not be offered in any other way.

Respect

When all the other qualities set out above are brought together, then the final quality will shine through. Respect comes when you can accept the person just as they are. It is the quality that is most difficult to define but which is crucial in building up a working relationship with the person with dementia.

The right approach

It is important to remember that a confused person will perform at their best when they are relaxed and free of frus-

tration. To help with this you could consider the following:

Communication

At all times this needs to be as clear as possible. Avoid saying things in a complex way; keep sentences short. Use the same language that the individual uses: if he says TV for television then use TV, if he uses bathroom to talk about the toilet then you should say bathroom.

If you have said something that is important and does not appear to have been understood, repeat it. Perhaps use simpler words. When the individual says they understand, get them to repeat it back to you in order to check. Many of the frustrations and anxieties for the person with dementia come from misunderstanding information.

Always bear in mind the use of a hearing aid or spectacles. Make sure the batteries are fresh and the ear piece is free of wax. Clean spectacles. These could help vastly in any aspect of communication. (See also chapters 6, 22, and 23.)

Names

How you address someone is important. If you call everyone "Gran" or "Dear" this will not show any respect or sensitivity. People have preferred names and titles. Using these will show that you have thought about what you are doing. It gives the impression that the person to whom you are talking really counts. Nicknames and terms like "Sweetie" or "Lovey" are patronising, and the person may not understand that you are talking to them.

Avoiding confrontation

When working with a confused person never confront them with painful truths or harsh realities. Confrontation will cause anxiety and distress for the person with dementia. It will make your job that much more difficult.

If an individual talks about his deceased wife as though she were alive it is insensitive to confront him with the painful truth that she is dead. It would be more appropriate to talk about his feelings – how he is missing her.

Staying calm

Being calm is important. A person with dementia might be angry with you. Staying calm will give you the best chance of persuading them, for example to get washed or dressed. If they are very angry, and perhaps you have to change soiled clothing, then calmness remains the most appropriate approach. Often in these circumstances a "running commentary" will help, telling the confused individual what you are doing as you do it. Your unhurried and patient approach will show that you still care.

Making the environment less confusing

It is important that a person with dementia is given every chance to be as independent as possible for as long as possible. As memory fails, even a familiar environment can become confusing and frightening. A person might forget the location of the toilet, or their bedroom. Simple signs on doors may be all that is needed to prompt them.

Reducing some of the risks

Be alert to possible dangers in the home, and report them or take action yourself. (See chapter 11.)

Creating a supportive routine

A regular routine during the day will help reduce confusion. It can help to make people feel more secure because they know what is going to happen.

Supporting carers

Care assistants working with people with dementia will also get to know residents' relatives and/or friends who visit. These are the people who know your resident best – they may have spent years caring for them at home (or perhaps they still do, if an individual has been admitted for respite care). It is an important part of your work to give them friendly support (see chapter 8).

Activities

Activities are what make us different. They are what mark us out as an individual and give us our character. Young or old, there are some things that we all do but it is the way in which we do those things that make us special. And we are all special. People with dementia are just the same. They do not arrive in our care without their own likes and dislikes. They have a history. They may have been a great one for putting on their best clothes every Wednesday and going out to the local dance or club. They may have been the one that sat at home and watched all the soaps curled up with the gas fire on and a good book. They may have been the one that was the respected shop steward, always out at meetings in smoke-filled rooms.

When considering activity we often think immediately of games or making something or being part of a group. We should remember that for some the act of getting up and dressed is a major and important activity in itself. It may take a long time, bathing, choosing the right clothes and putting those clothes on.

This should not be seen as a task to get through but an important time in the day (see chapters 19 and 20). When we get up or plan to go out this very act can cause several changes of clothes until the "right" look is achieved. Everyday activity should not be underestimated. If we can value the normal activities and make them special, then finding meaningful pastimes for people with dementia will be that much easier.

The largest hurdle to overcome is our own reluctance to get started. Sometimes our own motivation for activity is less than that of the patient! We put excuses in the way, "there isn't any time" or "the sister/manager wouldn't like it" or "we don't have the resources". We've all done it.

The shock comes when an activity happens and not only do you find it interesting but so too do the people in your care. They blossom before your very eyes. The person you thought could do nothing for themselves knows all the words to "Abide with Me". The person who needs help to do their buttons up is also the same person who can handle dominoes like he was still in the tap-room. Activity makes residents into people. It makes them special.

Get to know them

The really important point to remember about all activity is that different people need and enjoy different types of activity. Not all men enjoy football and not all women enjoy knitting. It would be a dull world indeed if we all enjoyed the same things. The message therefore is to get to know the people who you care for and discover their interests. A knowledge of someone's previous background and history will give clues to what they will enjoy doing now.

By working with people and helping them to do the activities which give them pleasure however small (or large) you will really make a difference. Sometimes it is difficult to see how our care can make a difference but by making activity a regular event, the difference quickly becomes apparent.

Points to remember

1. We all get confused. Just because someone is confused it does not necessarily mean they have dementia.
2. Sudden confusion is usually the result of a treatable condition.
3. Dementia is a condition which results in a gradual decline in the ability to think clearly and remember accurately.
4. The qualities you should try to develop include:

• Patience
• Tolerance
• Understanding
• Sensitivity
• Humour
• Respect.

5. The right approach will help you to develop a good working relationship with the patient. Bear in mind the following areas:

• Good clear communication
• Using appropriate names and titles
• Avoiding confrontation
• Staying calm
• Making the home less confusing
• Reducing some of the risks
• Creating a supportive routine
• Supporting relatives.

This chapter applies to all NVQ units. The following are particularly relevant.

NVQ Level 2 & 3 Core Units
O Promote equality for all individuals.
Z1 Contribute to the protection of individuals from abuse.
Level 2 Core Units
W2 Contribute to the ongoing support of clients and others significant to them.
W3 Support clients in transition due to their care requirements.
Level 3 Core Units
Z3 Contribute to the management of aggressive and abusive behaviour.
Z8 Support clients when they are distressed.

CHAPTER 25

Care of the dying person

Sheila Mackie Bailey

*• Our experience of death and dying • Differences of culture and beliefs
• Choosing for ourselves • The dying process: denial, anger, bargaining, depression, acceptance • Physical care • Tactics staff use to avoid distress • Staff training and support • Spiritual care • The closest relationship*

When caring for a dying person your main task is to ensure that they experience an "appropriate" death. By this I mean the kind of death they would have chosen for themselves if they had the opportunity and were able to choose. The way in which such a preference can be expressed will be discussed later. However, when a person is dying others are affected, especially close relatives, partners, close friends and those who are caring for them.

Experience of dying

Up until very recent times not only did both birth and death take place in the home, but after someone had died the body remained in the house until the funeral. As a result people grew up with first-hand experience of dying and death.

Not only that but the death rate among all age groups was high, either due to infectious disease or conditions for which there was no known cure. Nowadays the infant mortality rate is much lower, and generally speaking people are living much longer.

But perhaps a more significant change is the fact that most people die in hospitals or nursing homes. Even if someone dies at home, their body is taken to the undertakers where it remains until the funeral. As a result most of us grow up with little or no experience of dying and death, making it difficult when we first encounter death at work.

Working with a dying person is always distressing. It reminds us of our own mortality, that one day we will ourselves die.

In order to protect ourselves from the anxiety and stress which contact with dying causes us, we use a variety of coping tactics, as do the dying person and others close to them. These tactics will be discussed later.

But even in everyday life death and dying is difficult for people to talk about, and the words dying and death are rarely used. Instead we use euphemisms, disguising an unpleasant event with milder words and phrases, such as "he's on the way out; he's slipping away; he won't last much longer; he's snuffed it; he's passed away; she's lost her husband" – you can probably think of others.

Choosing for ourselves

Death used to be accepted as the natural conclusion of life, the ultimate experience. Nowadays, however, many of us fear and resent it.

Elderly people approach death in a variety of ways. Some certainly do resent it, while for others it is a welcome release. The important thing is that nether staff nor family should assume that they know what the dying resident thinks and what they would like to assist them in an appropriate death. They should ask and talk about it. A document relating to resident choice in this area, which has recently appeared in this country, is an *Advance Directive*, or as it is more popularly known, a *Living Will*.

A Living Will is a document which attempts to set out the kind of health care a resident wishes to receive at a time when they are unable to be involved in the actual decision making, for example if they are unconscious, delirious, or otherwise incapacitated. It is an attempt to allow residents the right to refuse treatment in advance, in case they are too ill to choose for themselves, or become unable to express that choice as their condition deteriorates.

The subject of Living Wills has been extensively discussed by the Royal College of Nursing, the British Medical Association and the Law Commission. Although Living Wills are still not legally recognised, doctors and nurses have agreed that where they exist they will be taken into consideration in relevant decision making.

The dying process

In the late 1960s Dr Elisabeth Kubler-Ross described five stages of dying: *denial, anger, bargaining, depression, acceptance,* which not only residents but also those closest to them, and care staff, may experience. Each stage is a way of coping, and care staff need to learn to recognise the stages people are at, and provide the appropriate support.

However what Kubler-Ross does make clear is that people do not go through the stages in a neat sequence but may move backwards and forwards between them, and that the acceptance stage may not be reached at the time of death. Also the resident and those who care about and for them may not experience the same stage at the same time. So care staff have to be very sensitive to what is happening.

Denial

In this stage the resident denies what is happening. He needs support, but care staff should neither encourage nor contradict what he is saying about his illness. This stage gives the resident time to get used to the idea that they are terminally ill, and will die soon.

At this stage the resident or those close to him may try to "shop around", to get another opinion. Staff should realise that this is a normal coping mechanism and should offer people realistic hope, but not lie to them.

Anger

This stage is probably the most difficult for care staff to deal with: the "Why me?" or "Why my mother?" "It's not fair" stage. The anger may be understandable but the abuse is frequently directed at those closest to the resident, including the care assistant. During this time those close to the resident and care staff feel guilty because they feel helpless and frustrated and this makes them angry as well.

It is important that care staff understand that any abuse and anger is not directed at them personally, but rather at the impending death. All care at this time should be concerned with supporting the dying resident, meeting all their physical needs and maintaining a pleasant attitude – without being too jolly, as this is likely to provoke further anger.

Bargaining

During this stage, which is often quite short, the resident and sometimes those close to him seek ways of postponing the death: "If only I can live long enough to see my grandchild born...If only she can live long enough to see one more Christmas..."

These and other similar remarks are not uncommon, but most common is to try to bargain with God. "If God lets me/my husband/my mother live I'll be a better person...pray more regularly...go to church..." or something similar. Again the responsibility of care staff is to encourage the resident and others in their realistic hopes, and to make other members of the health care team concerned aware of what has been said. But staff should try to prepare the resident to cope with the disappointment if the bargains, especially those with God, are not apparently kept. The assistance of the resident's priest or minister may be helpful at this time.

Depression

This may be quite a long stage as the resident, and those close to him, realise that the bargaining has failed, and that the impending death is getting ever closer. Often residents are very quiet during this stage, and just sitting with them and holding their hand is all they need you to do, and the same can be done when those close to them visit.

Crying is a healthy sign as this usually shows that the person is coming to accept the closeness of their death. They should not be told off for crying but rather assured that it is okay to cry. They should be comforted while they weep, and there is no shame in staff having a weep along with them. This is a time when the care assistant should be aware of the resident's spiritual beliefs and needs and make sure they are visited by a priest or representative from their religion if that is important to them.

Acceptance

This is a time of contentment for residents and of sharing with those close to them; a time for tying up loose ends, putting their house in order and saying their farewells. It is often a surprise for those caring for even quite young children who are dying, how quickly they accept the imminence of their death and how practical they are, such as organising what should happen to their favourite toys and their pocket money.

At this time an important part of caring is to make physical contact. Touching is very therapeutic; a simple gesture like holding a resident's hand and stroking their forearm is very comforting.

It is also important to respect the resident's wish to be silent and not to chat, if this is the case. When those close to the resident visit they should also be encouraged to touch and stroke, as it is good for them as well as for the resident. The use of complementary therapies, especially aromatherapy and massage, can be very helpful.

It is important to remember that these stages are *unconscious* coping mechanisms. Not only that, but a resident who is dying does not necessarily go through them in the order set out here, but may move or jump between them. Anger may return at intervals, and some stages may last a lot longer than others.

Finally, it should be remembered that at the time of the death the resident may not have reached the stage of acceptance and neither may some of those who care about him. For all those affected by the death there follows a period of bereavement, which may last up to two years, and they may go through the same stages as experienced during the time before the death as described above.

There are times when staff involved in caring for a resident who is terminally ill may need support, especially when they were close to and fond of the resident.

Sudden death

When the death is sudden and unexpected, then the period immediately following can be very traumatic. Care assistants may face extreme reactions of denial and anger by relatives or partner, and this requires the attention of very experienced staff. But an older care assistant with life experience can sometimes be a more suitable person to deal with the situation than a young and inexperienced staff nurse.

Physical care

The main problems when caring for a dying resident are management of pain, control of sickness, care of the skin, control of constipation and respiratory secretions, all of which will cause the resident and visitors distress.

Some of these aspects of physical care are discussed in other chapters, others will be detailed on the individual's care plan. Remember that carrying out activities such as washing, care of the skin, change of position, which must be carried out in private, provide ideal opportunities to talk to the resident, to offer comfort and support, and to find out more about his feelings, hopes and fears.

Psychological care

Death may be the loneliest experience human beings face. How we care for somebody who is dying can make this experience worse, or better. Many people who are dying feel abandoned; they are physically cut off from those around them, either because they are in a room on their own or because they have curtains or screens pulled round them. The only time they receive any attention is for cleansing, toileting and feeding.

Some elderly people already feel that their bodies have let them down; that they are worthless and have nothing to contribute to their family or society, and this belief is reinforced by the isolation which they experience when they are dying.

Some people, if asked, would say they prefer to be alone, but they are probably in a minority. Care staff should try to find out what each individual would like. One danger is that the routine of the home determines the care a dying person receives, rather than that care being of their choosing, and planned to meet their needs.

Ways of telling

But how do care staff find out what the dying person would like? A direct question would probably be inappropriate, but if you listen to what someone says about other people's deaths, you may learn a great deal:

"It's a shame his children weren't here..."

"She shouldn't have been alone like that"

"I can be doing without all that nonsense"

"If they do that to me I'll come back and haunt them."

There are many ways in which people make their wishes clear. We must listen and then discuss with them what we have heard. A simple response to any of the statements above, such as "What would you like if it was you?" is frequently all that is needed. Then any preferences expressed should be discussed with other members of staff and the person's family, and noted on the person's case notes, or in a file kept for that purpose.

It is perhaps a privilege of old age that one is able to express a choice, both about the way you would like to die and funeral arrangements, including a preference for burial or cremation.

Again, neither of these are subjects that can easily be discussed, but frequently can be deduced from comments about other people. Alternatively the family may be aware of what is wanted because of what has happened to other close relatives. Close friends should also be consulted as often this is something discussed with friends but not with family.

Sometimes people will make a note in their Will of special wishes they have for the disposal of their body or the style of funeral, but unfortunately unless somebody made aware of these special wishes they are often not known until too late. For example, although an elderly person's organs are not generally suitable for transplantation, the cornea may be useful. If it is to be used, however, it must be removed soon after death. Donor cards may be a useful way of encouraging the elderly person to discuss their wishes about the events of their death.

Stress for care staff

Sometimes caring for a dying person causes care staff distress, and there are a variety of tactics we may adopt to help us cope with the stress. These include:

Avoidance: Care staff may avoid going anywhere near the dying person. If contact cannot be avoided, then the staff member does the very least that is necessary when carrying out a task, but ignores the person.

Passing the buck: The care assistant doesn't answer any "awkward" questions, but brushes them aside, by saying things like "You'll have to ask the doctor or the nurse" and at the same time doesn't look at the resident or visitor asking the question. A kinder response would be to say "I don't know but I will ask your nurse to come and speak to you."

Miracle cures: Staff hope that some miracle cure will become available to save the resident's life, perhaps especially if they are young, or when the dying process is going to be prolonged and possibly painful.

Careful conversation: The care assistant avoids asking the sort of questions which would encourage the resident to discuss how they feel about their forthcoming death. For example rather than asking "How are you feeling?" the care assistant says "You're looking better today" or "You're feeling better, aren't you?" then quickly changes the subject before the resident can answer.

Isolation: The dying person may either be nursed in a single room (on occasions this is necessary because of the nature of their illness) or they are hidden from other residents by drawing the curtains. This means visitors are also isolated and care staff are protected from coming into contact with them.

Selective hearing: The care assistant only hears the most comfortable things the resident says. For example if he says "I'm frightened, the pain is getting worse" then the care assistant will respond to the second part of the statement, perhaps by offering to make enquiries about pain-relieving drugs, and avoid the first part of the statement, the resident's expression of their feelings of fear.

Denial: When talking to the dying resident the care assistant will deny that death is the probable outcome, by saying such things as, "Don't be silly, you're good for another twenty years" or "Don't talk nonsense, whatever gave you that idea?" in response to an awkward question, then continuing the conversation by talking optimistically but unrealistically of the future.

Resident awareness: In some circumstances the care assistant may assume that a resident is unaware of what is going on around them. The care assistant therefore talks freely to a colleague or visitor about the resident and what is wrong with them, or even jokes with a colleague at the resident's expense. Inability to respond does not mean that the resident cannot hear, and even if they cannot, it is still disrespectful to speak in their presence in a way that you would not if they were fully conscious.

It is important to recognise that these tactics are adopted unconsciously; they are the way our minds protect us from a situation that might otherwise be difficult for us to deal with. However, it is vital that these behaviours are recognised and changed, as they prevent us from giving of our best and assisting the resident to an appropriate death.

Training and support

Training courses are available which prepare staff to cope with death and dying, including dealing with awkward questions and difficult moments.

In addition it is useful to hold regular meetings at which issues relating to care of the dying are discussed, or staff support sessions led by a trained counsellor. Such meetings allow staff to discuss their feelings and experiences and to offer each other mutual support and an opportunity to share. Being able to discuss your feelings about death and dying reduces the stress and unhappiness you may experience.

Spiritual care

We live in a diverse society and it is essential that care staff should be aware of the spiritual beliefs of all those they care for, but especially those who are dying. In particular they need to know what influence the resident's spiritual beliefs may have on their attitude to dying, and what relevance this has on the ritual which has to be observed at the time of death, including rituals such as Last Offices which have to be performed and care of the body (which is important, for example, in the Jewish religion).

A simple solution is to have a set of guidelines and a copy of Jennifer Green's book[1] available. In addition many religious groups have leaflets to assist care staff, and are always willing to discuss the details with them.

It is also important to remember that some people are atheists or agnostics and their values, beliefs and wishes must also be respected. What would be insulting and disrespectful would be, for example, to ask a minister to visit them when they are near to death, because that is what you would want for yourself.

If a funeral service is to be held at a crematorium there is a great deal of freedom for the order of service to be in accordance with the wishes of the person who has died. It may be helpful to the resident if you show that you are aware of this and give them an opportunity to discuss what form of service they would prefer. They should be encouraged to discuss this with the one closest to them if they have not already done so.

Whatever your personal religious

beliefs, it is important that you do not impose them on the dying resident, or those close to them, but rather respect their expressed spiritual needs. A mistake at this time could cause the dying person, and those close to them, much distress.

The involvement of a representative of the resident's religion, as soon as they request it, is very important. They then become part of the caring team, offering support to residents, those close to them, and staff.

Close relationship

Perhaps the first thing to remember is that not every elderly person is loved or cared about by their family, and this feeling may be mutual. In some cases a close friend (or friends) is more important to the dying person than their family. This friend or whoever it is that they are closest to, should be allowed to be as involved in the caring as they and the dying person wish them to be. This may mean assisting with quite intimate aspects of care, or simply being allowed to sit and keep the dying person company. Family and friends should be included as part of the caring team. To shut them out at this time is cruel and may cause both them and the dying person a great deal of distress and misery.

Both the dying person and the people they care about most should be supported in their grief, especially at the time of death. If they have not previously witnessed a death then it is helpful if somebody – perhaps a nurse or religious minister – describes for them what it might be like. Being present at the death helps the survivors to come to terms with what has happened, and to begin the next stage of their grieving. If they are not present then every effort should be made to ensure that they view the body as soon as possible, in the company of someone they know well, preferably a member of the caring team. At times it may be that care staff and those just bereaved have become close, and it is fine if they want to share their grief with each other, perhaps even crying or praying together.

In conclusion

Death is the inevitable end of life. According to Henry Fielding, "It is not death, but dying which is terrible." The responsibility of care staff is to ensure that the dying person's experience is not terrible, but that they experience an "appropriate" death, where they have been involved in the decision making and planning, and where their wishes and beliefs are known and respected.

Points to remember

1. Try to discuss with residents, while they still can, their notion of an appropriate death, but be sensitive to some people's reluctance to talk about dying.
2. Staff need to be supported while caring for a dying person, and in their grief after the death of a resident they were fond of.
3. The dying person's spiritual beliefs and needs should be respected, whatever they may be.

Reference
1. Jennifer Green (1991). *Death with Dignity*. A *Nursing Times* Publication.

NVQ Level 2 Core Units
O Promote equality for all individuals.
W2 Contribute to the ongoing support of clients and those significant to them.
W3 Support clients in transition due to their care requirements.
Level 2 Direct Care
Z7 Contribute to the movement and treatment of clients to maximise their physical comfort.
Z9 Enable clients to maintain their personal hygiene and appearance.
Z10 Enable clients to eat and drink.
Z19 Enable clients to achieve physical comfort.

CHAPTER 26

Rules and regulations

Deirdre Wynne-Harley

• The law that affects you • Registration and inspection of homes
• Keeping accurate records • Residents' rights • Complaints
• Health and safety at work • Employment legislation

This chapter is about the law as it relates to people in residential care and nursing homes.

The most important thing to remember is that whatever dependency, disability or illness your residents suffer from, they are individual people first and foremost with all the normal rights of citizenship. Care workers have a duty to protect these rights and ensure that residents' autonomy and civil liberty is not infringed by the care and treatment given.

The legislation which regulates life and work in homes falls into three broad categories:
• registration
• residents' rights
• employment and health and safety.
Each of these topics is discussed below.

NOTE: The legislation quoted applies specifically to England and Wales. Requirements in Scotland and Northern Ireland are similar and the acts are listed at the end of the chapter.

The legislation

The Registered Homes Act 1984 governs residential care and nursing homes. This Act, together with the regulations and guidance, sets out the requirements for registration and operation of homes. Some homes are "dually registered": that means they have beds both for residential care and for nursing care.

The law requires that all care homes with more than three residents and all nursing homes regardless of numbers must be inspected and registered by the appropriate authority. Until 1991 this has normally been the local social services department for residential care and the health authority for nursing homes.

From April 1994 Inspection Units have had a duty to inspect and register **all** homes. There are special requirements and arrangements for the inspection of care homes for under four residents. Under the 1990 Community Care Act multi-disciplinary inspection units have taken on this responsibility for residential homes. They are still locally based and work closely with the health authority.

The registration covers client groups and the numbers of residents who may be cared for in the establishment. Sometimes registration will be refused or cancelled; in these cases the proprietor may appeal to the Registered Homes Tribunal, which will either confirm the decision of the registration authority, uphold the appeal against this decision, or vary the conditions of the registration. The registration authority must comply with any directions made by the Tribunal.

How it works

1. Starting up
Anyone wishing to open or take over an existing home MUST apply for registration.

2. The Certificate
When a registration certificate is granted, the home must abide by its conditions as to number and type of resident/patient. When registration authorities consider applications, they will specify certain criteria regarding the suitability of the applicants and the premises. They will also issue guidelines about the services and facilities to be provided and the level of staffing. Criteria and guidelines will be based on the 1984 Registered Homes Act and Regulations, *Home life: a code of practice for residential care*, the NAHA Handbook on Registration and Inspection of Homes (1985) and guidance from the Department of Health. The certificate must be displayed in a prominent place.

3. Inspection
Inspection is an essential element of the registration process and includes continuing checks on standards. The Registration or Inspection Officer will visit the home at least twice a year and one of the visits is likely to be unannounced. The formal annual inspection is likely to take at least one whole day and may involve more than one officer from the Inspection Unit. During the visit they will meet and talk with all (or most) residents and staff. The manager of the home will receive a written report after the inspection.

The registering authority will also require that the home continues to comply with the demands of the fire department, environmental health department and the Building Regulations. These requirements will be reviewed from time to time and the registration officer will check that they are up to date.

4. Records
When the home is registered and operating normally, certain records must be kept, and be available at all times for inspection by authorised officers of the registration authority.

These records must include:

• A statement of the aims and objectives of the home, of the care and attention to be provided in the home and of any arrangements for the supervision of residents, which has been supplied to the registration authority and has been agreed with that authority. In practice this means that staffing levels, therapeutic and rehabilitation facilities and services agreed must be provided.

• A daily register of all residents (excluding persons registered or persons employed at the home and their relatives) which must include the following particulars:
(a) the name, address, date of birth and marital status and whether the person is the subject of any court order or other process
(b) the name, address and telephone number of the resident's next of kin or of any person authorised to act on his behalf
(c) the name, address and telephone number of the resident's registered medical practitioner and of any officer of a local social services authority whose duty it is to supervise the welfare of that person
(d) the date on which the resident entered the home
(e) the date on which the resident left the home
(f) if the resident was transferred to a hos-

Enabling people to have as much choice as possible in their daily life and activities will ensure that their rights as citizens are protected.

pital or any other home, the date of and the reasons for the transfer, and the name of the hospital or home to which the resident was transferred

(g) if the resident died in the home, the date, time and cause of death

(h) if the resident is an adult who is subject to the guardianship of a local social services authority, the name, address and telephone number of that authority and of any officer of the authority whose duty it is to supervise the welfare of that resident

(i) the name and address of any authority, or organisation or other body which arranged the resident's admission to the home.

• A case record in respect of each resident shall include details of any special needs of that resident, any medical treatment required by the resident, including details of any medicines administered and any other information in relation to the resident as may be appropriate, including details of any periodic review of the resident's welfare, health and progress

• A record of all medicines kept in the home for a resident and of their disposal when no longer required

• A record book in which shall be recorded the dates of any visits by persons authorised to inspect the home, that is any registration or inspection officer, fire officer or environmental health officer

• Records of the food provided for residents in sufficient detail to enable any person inspecting the record to judge whether the diet is satisfactory, and of any diets prepared for particular residents

• A record of every fire practice drill or fire alarm test conducted in the home and of any action taken to remedy defects in fire alarm equipment

• A statement of the procedure to be followed in the event of fire

• A statement of the procedure to be followed in the event of accidents or in the event of a resident going missing

• A record of each person employed at the home to provide personal care for residents, which shall include that person's full name, date of birth, qualifications, experience and details of that person's position and dates of employment at the home, and the number of hours for which that person is employed each week

• A record of any relatives of the registered persons or of persons employed at the home who are residents

• A statement of the facilities provided in the home for residents and of the arrangements made for visits by their relatives, guardians, friends and other visitors

• A record of the fees applicable from time to time including any extras for additional services not covered by that scale and of the amounts paid by or in respect of each resident

• A record of all money or other valuables deposited by a resident for safe keeping or received on the resident's behalf, specifying the date on which such money or valuables were deposited or received and the date on which any sum or other valuables was returned to a resident or used, at the request of the resident, on the resident's behalf and the purpose for which it was used.

This may all seem to be very complicated, but is usually made easier by the use of standard recording systems.

Care staff will often be involved in providing some of the necessary information. Through recording in a day book their observations of the residents' health, activities, appetite and so on, a valuable contribution may be made. It is very important to ensure that any accidents to residents or staff or incidents such as a missing resident, or sounding of the fire alarm (whether this is a false alarm or not) are recorded. It should be standard practice in all homes for staff to exchange information when shifts change, so that staff coming on duty understand any notes in the incident book or in the residents' records.

Residents' rights

It is important to remember that the legal rights of residents in residential care and nursing homes are exactly the same as those of any other citizen, and staff must always bear this in mind in their day-to-day duties. It is all too easy when caring for people to diminish an individual's basic rights without being fully aware of doing so. This happens most commonly through the use of forms of restraint, through medication and health care, by withholding information, and most of all by the erosion of choice in daily life and activities.

Sometimes it will be necessary for decisions to be made on behalf of an individual who has become incapable of doing so themselves. The legal position is often unclear as physical and mental conditions may change dramatically or almost imperceptibly over a long period. There are often also variations, ups and downs which can create uncertainty about a resident's true mental state.

The common law test of "capacity" is to the effect that the person concerned must at the relevant time understand in broad terms what he is doing and the likely effects of his action. Thus, in principle, legal capacity depends upon understanding rather than wisdom: the quality of the decision is irrelevant as long as the person understands what he is deciding.

The Mental Health Act 1983 itself contains three different approaches. The first in Parts II and III governs compulsory admission to hospital and guardianship, the second in Part IV governs consent to particular forms of treatment for mental disorder, and the third in Part VII governs the management of property and affairs.

Whatever the situation, care staff should never make decisions or even assumptions about a resident or patient's mental capacity without guidance from the home's medical advisers.

Managing finances

Many older people have informal arrangements for the management of their finances and property. Often these will be handled by a close relative or friend. Sometimes a solicitor or bank manager will act on their behalf.

On no account should care or nursing staff become involved in residents' financial affairs. Where an individual has no one to assist with their affairs, the registration authority should be asked to recommend someone to act as his or her agent. There is an increasing number of advocacy groups which offer specially trained volunteers to help elderly people in this way. Social services, Age Concern and Citizens Advice Bureaux will usually know of local advocacy schemes.

Some residents will be under the jurisdiction of the Court of Protection and all their affairs, property and money will be managed through the Court.

Increasingly, as people get older, they are making Enduring Powers of Attorney (EPA). This means that they give someone else the power to represent and act for them in matters of property and finance at some time in the future if the need arises. If they become unable to make decisions for themselves the EPA is registered with the Court and the named representatives takes over. No one connected with the home should be appointed an attorney.

Restraint

Physical restraint should never be used in residential care in any form - including restraining chairs. If it appears that restraint is necessary, the home is clearly not an appropriate place for that resident to be, either in terms of staffing or in the facilities and environment provided. Restraint in this situation is an assault on the person and consequently could give rise to legal action against the manager or member of staff involved.

Restraining chairs cannot be a substitute for adequate and appropriately trained staff cover and therefore should never be used in care homes. The use of cotsides is more likely to cause accidents than provide protection as residents may fall while trying to get out.

Consent to treatment

Admission to a home does not change an individual's right to choose their own general practitioner. Neither does it change the rules on consent to treatment. The law provides that no medical treatment can be given to any person without his valid consent. Any breach of this rule will result in the person concerned being liable to legal proceedings.

For consent to be valid, the patient must be given information about the proposed treatment or medication, be competent to give consent and give consent voluntarily. If the resident has difficulty in understanding or communicating in English, every effort must be made to find an interpreter to explain the purpose and effect of the treatment.

When a resident or patient is not able to understand because of their mental state, treatments prescribed by the GP or consultant must be in the best interests of the individual but keeping in mind any strongly held views they have expressed in the past.

Medication

No drugs except simple "household remedies" should be given without a doctor's prescription. Whether residents retain and administer their own medicines or these are kept by the manager, proper arrangements must be made for safe keeping. All medicines must be in individual containers, clearly labelled with the name and dosage. When held by the home, they must be administered ONLY by a responsible person authorised by the manager.

Staff responsibility does not include insisting, forcing or tricking residents into taking medication. If residents refuse, this should be noted and the GP informed. Medication must not be used for control or punishment. As with restraint, inappropriate or forceful administration of any medicines is in effect a physical assault.

Access to information

Changes in the law over the past few years have given people greatly increased rights to know what is said about them in personal records. This applies to residents also. Therefore, subject to adequate safeguards and counselling where necessary, individuals should be able to see the records about themselves kept by the home. Any decision to withhold information should only be taken at a senior level in the organisation and the reason for doing so explained to the satisfaction of the registration authority. All residents' records should be kept securely with strictly limited access.

Residents' finances are often a matter of concern and a recent amendment to the legislation [Residential Homes (Amendment) Regulations 1988] requires that homes keep detailed records for each resident of any money or valuables (including social security benefits) received on his or her behalf and indicating how this was spent or disposed of. Residents or their representatives must have access to these records.

Complaints

Residents and their families have a right to know how and where to contact the registration authority if they wish to make a complaint or discuss some matter which has not been resolved between them and the management. Information about who to contact, and where, must be displayed clearly, preferably near to the registration certificate.

Health and safety and employment legislation

The Health and Safety at Work Act 1974 obliges all employers to ensure as far as reasonably practicable the health and safety at work of all employees, by providing any information, training and supervision necessary. Employees have a duty to take reasonable care to protect their own health and safety, and that of other people, who could be affected by their actions or omissions at work. (There are new additional regulations on health and safety at work. Those relvant to care work are covered in chapter 11, Safety and security.)

The Control of Substances Hazardous to Health Regulations (COSHH) (1988) requires employers to assess the risks created by work when a hazardous substance is used. If you use a dangerous substance, you must know:
• What the risks are
• How the risks are controlled
• What precautions you have to take.
Your employer is obliged to give you training in all aspects of handling hazardous substances.

Manual Handling Operations Regulations (1992). These regulations apply to any lifting that may be part of your duties. Where there is the risk of injury, every effort should be taken to redesign or avoid the task so that the risk is reduced or removed. For example, it may be possible to show a person how to move themselves, or to arrange for bath aids, equipment or a portable hoist to be installed.

Your employer must provide training and guidance on manual handling and assess the likely risks of injury in every situation. For further information on safe lifting, see chapter 16, Lifting and handling.

Accident prevention

Safety is also covered in the 1984 Registered Homes Regulations. This states that "the person registered shall, having regard to the size of the home and the number, age, sex and condition of the residents, take adequate precaution against the risk of accident, including the training of staff in first aid". Inspectors from registering authorities will enquire into accident prevention arrangements, when making visits. The home will also receive occasional visits from the health and safety or environmental health officers who are responsible for enforcing the Health and Safety at Work legislation. Properly authorised inspecting officers have legal rights of access to homes.

In matters of safety, staff must be alert, observant and careful. Accident prevention in residential homes, as in our own homes, is often a matter of common sense. Legislation and special precautions will be ineffective if equipment is not used correctly or defects reported. All accidents in the house or grounds, however minor, affecting residents, staff or visitors should be recorded in detail without delay. Any witnesses should also make and sign written statements. This is very important and should be done immediately.

Policy statement

Where five or more people are employed, the employer must have a written policy statement regarding safety at work, including arrangements for carrying out that policy. All staff must be made aware of this policy and any subsequent changes that are made to it.

For staff in residential and nursing homes, special risks may be associated with lifting and helping residents to move. These risks are to residents as well as staff and illustrate the importance of having a clear safety policy and appropriate accompanying arrangements for training. Every home must have at least one first aid box clearly marked. All staff should know where this is kept.

Emergency procedures

Emergency procedures must also be clearly stated and understood by all staff. These should cover
- procedure in the event of a fire
- procedure in the event of accidents
- procedure if a resident is missing

Food hygiene

Food hygiene is another aspect of safety which may involve care staff, especially in small homes where job specifications are more flexible.

The Food and Drugs Act 1985 and the Food Hygiene (General) Regulations 1970 apply in residential and nursing homes and it is the responsibility of the manager to see these are observed. Staff must be aware of regulations which affect them directly, like the requirement for wearing clean washable over-clothing when handling, preparing and serving food. Any members of staff who have kitchen or dining room duties should follow the basic rules of hygiene displayed in the kitchen. The Food Safety Act 1990 requires that all staff who handle food attend approved training courses in basic hygiene.

Health

There are also health requirements and staff must inform their employer if they are suffering from or are a carrier of:
- typhoid
- paratyphoid
- other salmonella infections
- amoebic dysentery
- bacillary dysentery
- any infections likely to cause food poisoning, eg septic cuts, boils, burns, sore throats or nasal infections.

Any of these infections will have to be reported to the local medical officer for environmental health who will advise the person in charge about necessary precautions.

Your employment

Employment law is very complex. Both

employer and employee have rights and duties and these should be clear to both parties when the appointment is made. The Employment Protection (Consolidation) Act 1978 provides that all new employees (who work over 16 hours a week) should be given a written statement of terms and conditions of employment within 13 weeks of starting. This statement must give the names of employer and employee and the date when the employment starts. It must also detail:

- job title
- rate of pay and whether this is weekly or monthly
- hours of work
- holiday entitlement, including public holidays
- arrangements for such pay
- notice period
- pension schemes

Information about disciplinary rules, grievance procedures, and persons to whom application should be made if the employee is dissatisfied with any disciplinary action against him should be available in the contract or a separate specific reference document.

If any terms or conditions change, the employee must be informed in writing within one month what the changes are.

Trade unions

In law every employee has a right to membership of an independent trade union; they also have an equal right not to belong to a union. This is regardless of whether or not the employer recognises the union. An employer may not prevent or deter employees from being members of independent trade unions or compel them to join one.

The employer is free, however, to choose whether or not to recognise a union. "Recognition" means the employer recognises the right of the union to represent its members in collective bargaining.

The relevant legislation is The Employment Act 1980.

Rehabilitation of offenders

Under the Rehabilitation of Offenders Act 1974 a person who received a non-custodial sentence of not more than 30 months, and is not convicted during a specified period, becomes a rehabilitated person. His conviction then becomes "spent", in other words it is regarded in law for most purposes as never having occurred.

There are, however, certain types of employment (listed in the 1975 Order) where this does not apply, provided that when asked about previous convictions, the person is told that by virtue of the Order spent convictions must be declared. The exceptions include occupations concerned with carrying on an establishment required to be registered under the Registered Homes Act 1984.

Data protection

Many homes now use computers for keeping personal records of staff and residents. Under the Data Protection Act 1984 anyone storing personal information about other people must register with the Data Protection Registrar. The onus is on the computer users to declare themselves. As with the residents, staff have a right of access to information about themselves held by the employer.

Conclusion

This chaper has highlighted the areas of legislation which are most likely to affect care staff directly or are concerned with the registration of the home.

There may be occasions when a member of staff becomes aware of acts or incidents which breach some aspect of the law. These may be minor and perhaps arise from a genuine oversight or of a much more serious nature. Whatever position an individual holds, they have a duty to residents and colleagues to take action. The first course would normally be to discuss the matter with the head of home and in the case of a safety hazard to alert colleagues until the danger is removed.

If the matter appears to concern the work of a senior colleague and affects the residents' well being, the advice of the registration officer should be sought. The registration authority has a duty to investigate any possible offences against the Registered Homes Act. Similarly serious concern about matters of health and safety should be reported to the Environmental Health Officer if no action is taken by the Head of Home.

Fortunately staff are rarely in a situation where they have to report incidents or practices in a home. However, if this does happen, they should not be deterred from taking the correct course of action through fear of the consequences.

Work with people who are mentally frail or have dementing illness can be very stressful and it is often easier to provide a regime which assumes a generally low level of ability in all residents. But each resident is a different person and, however ill, will respond differently. By treating each one individually, however severe their dementia, their rights as citizens will be protected and maintained to the greatest degree possible. This will also be seen to enhance the work of the carers and the quality of life of the home as a whole.

Points to remember

1. Residential care and nursing homes must be registered and work within the terms of their registration.

2. Proper resident records must be kept on the premises and any accident or incident should be recorded immediately by care staff in the day book.

3. Residents' property must be safeguarded and a record kept of all valuables

deposited for safe keeping.

4. Staff of homes should never take responsibility for residents' finances or accept a power of attorney.

5. Physical restraint of residents is an assault and may give rise to legal action.

6. Residents and their families must be given information about how to make a complaint.

7. Think safety – staff should always be alert and observant.

8. Be aware of emergency procedures.

9. Staff must report accidents or incidents which they believe are wrong or illegal.

10. However frail the resident, their civil rights must be protected. Personal and nursing care should not reduce their rights or dignity.

Main legislation quoted

Registered Homes Act 1984 and Regulation 1984, amendments 1988 (England and Wales).

Nursing Homes Registration (Scotland) Regulations 1988 (came into force November 23 1988 and covers both residential and nursing homes).

Health and Personal Social Services order (Northern Ireland).

Health and Safety at Work (etc) Act 1974 (whole of UK).

Employment Acts 1980, 1982, 1988.

Employment Protection (Consolidation) Act 1987 (whole of UK).

Data Protection Act 1984.

Home life: a code of practice for residential care, Centre for Policy on Ageing, 25-31 Ironmonger Row, London EC1V 3QP. Tel: 071 253 1787.

NAHA Handbook – Registration and Inspection of Nursing Homes, 1985 published by the National Association of Health Authorities.

NVQ Levels 2 & 3 Core Units

O Promote equality for all individuals

U4 Contribute to the health, safety and security of individuals and their environment.

U5 Obtain, transmit and store information relating to the delivery of a care service.

Z1 Contribute to the protection of individuals from abuse.

Level 3 Core Unit

Z3 Contribute to the management of aggressive and abusive behaviour.

CHAPTER 27

National Vocational Qualifications

by Judith Roberts

What are NVQs and what use are they to you? • The way training and assessment works • How you can get started

National Vocational Qualifications (NVQs) are a country-wide system of qualifications related to job skills and occupations. In Scotland they are called Scottish Vocational Qualifications (SVQs). NVQs/SVQs apply not only to the care sector, but are also available in many other fields of work, from horse grooming to hairdressing, motor vehicle repair to management.

All NVQ awards are based on the idea of competence – the ability to perform in the workplace, to the standards that the occupation requires.

An NVQ is gained when the candidate is assessed performing in a real work situation, doing a real job, to the required standards. But skills on their own are not enough. The worker has to show that they understand why they are doing the task in

The benefits of NVQs

• NVQs allow you to build up parts of the award, or "credits", gradually. It doesn't matter when you do them or how long it takes. This helps people fit in training around domestic or work commitments.

• There is open access: anyone can apply to be assessed.

• Assessment can be obtained and achieved independently of the time or methods of any accompanying learning. Distance or Open Learning becomes a practical solution for people who work unsocial hours.

• NVQs do not demand time away from the workplace, and their development and the assessment process is directly relevant and meaningful to the worker.

• It is learning by doing, an active process that for many people makes the learning process more enjoyable, more relevant and more effective.

Why get involved?

Candidates who have achieved NVQ awards in Care have said that the process of becoming qualified has meant:

• They are more aware of their clients' needs and rights, especially their emotional, social and cultural needs.

• They feel they now give more individualised care, and are more useful to other members of the team.

• They are now more aware of the "How?" and "Why?" of their practice, and are able to describe their experience using a more "professional" vocabulary.

• They consider themselves to be better informed, more assertive and confident, and better able to challenge inadequate practice.

• They found the support and recognition offered to them by their work based assessor valuable, and often developed more effective working relations with others.

that way; in other words some "under-pinning knowledge" is necessary.

Standards have been decided on, after years of work developing and testing them, by representatives from each field of work, called Lead Industry Bodies (LIB). The LIB for the care sector is the Care Sector Consortium.

NVQs are awarded by organisations called Awarding Bodies. Examples are City and Guilds, the Central Council for Education and Training in Social Work (CCETSW), and BTEC.

Levels of awards

All NVQs are graded, rising from Level 1 to Level 5. The higher the level, the greater the breadth and complexity of the qualification. This allows the worker to progress within the qualification structure as their skills, knowledge and responsibilities increase and broaden.

Level 1 Foundation/ basic work activities
Level 2 A broad range of skills and responsibilities
Level 3 Complex/skilled and/or supervisory work
Level 4 Managerial/specialist
Level 5 Professional/senior managerial

The NVQ framework

NVQ awards have a common structure. Each different **level** is made up of a number of **units**. These units are in turn split into several **elements** of competence.

Each element contains **performance criteria** (details of what is expected of you as you perform the task), **range statements** where you need to show competence in a range of care situations, and details of the **underpinning knowledge** you are required to show.

Taking one **element** at a time, the worker is assessed working in each of the situations specified in the element. Their standard of competence is assessed against the **performance criteria** and **underpin-**

ning knowledge that element requires. Through this process the worker can slowly build up their qualification. This is called "credit accumulation".

NVQs Awards in Care: the Integrated Standards

NVQs in both social care and nursing settings have been brought together, and there are qualifications available at Levels 2 and 3. These awards give care workers more choice and opportunity for progression in jobs across both sectors, and represent more closely the wide range of client groups, roles and responsibilities.

To the structure of units and elements described before, **endorsements** are added. These are units grouped together because they relate to the specific role of the candidate. In addition there is **Unit O – Promote equality for all individuals –** that is assessed during every assessment.

For example, care assistants working with elderly people need some of the same skills and knowledge, and some different skills and knowledge, from care assistants working in postnatal departments. So both will work through the same Core Units as described earlier, plus the Endorsement for their work area.

People involved in the assessment process

A *candidate* is the worker being assessed for an NVQ.

An *assessor* is the person who carries out the assessment of the candidate. The assessor is usually a more senior colleague who has a broad expertise in the work. Increasingly it is expected that the assessor will also have proved they are competent to assess the work of others.

The assessor's decisions are checked by a person called the *Internal Verifier* (IV) whose role is to make sure that the assessments carried out by the assessor meet the NVQ standards and the Awarding Body assessment requirements. This per-

How to start

There are three main processes involved:

1. Collect information so that you can see which Levels and Endorsements would be best for you.

2. Identify your training requirements and how you can obtain any necessary training.

3. Find out how, and by whom, you can be assessed in the workplace. It is possible that your employer is already associated with an assessment centre.

Remember, without the opportunity for assessment, and verification of the assessment, you will not get your qualification.

1. Information gathering

You will need to find out:

• Is your workplace considering getting involved with NVQs? Whom should you contact, where and when? This is not always easy if you work nights or weekends, but persevere. It is likely that other care assistants, the matron or manager will know more.

• More information about NVQs, and especially about NVQs in Care. This information should be available from your training department, but it also could be obtained from the Career Service, the local Training and Enterprise Council (TEC), the National Council for Vocational Qualifications, your union or local colleges, or the awarding body. The UK Central Council for Nursing and Midwifery has decided that possession of a Level 3 Care NVQ could be a possible entry qualification into Nurse Education – but it is **not** automatic. Each school of health may have additional requirements.

• Which level of award and choice of endorsement would be appropriate for you? This will be decided in discussion with your immediate line manager and the training centre.

• What existing knowledge could you be accredited with, and what additional training might you require?

• When are you likely to be accepted onto an NVQ programme and offered assessment? There may be some delay, so it could be useful to see if there are any appropriate programmes or short courses you could attend while waiting. Accreditation of Prior Learning should be available, so this would not be wasted.

• What costs, if any, might you have to pay towards your assessment? Ask whether your local TEC is sponsoring NVQs, especially if there is any financial support.

• Where will any training occur? Will you have to do it in your own time? Is attendance at the training sessions compulsory?

• How quickly will they expect you to complete all your assessments? (Less than six months is unrealistic unless you and your assessor are very committed and your establishment not too busy.)

• Is there open access? Do you have to be employed for a certain length of time? Will they only assess day staff? (They shouldn't – this could contravene their equal opportunities policy.)

• Do you have to be recommended by your line manager?

• Will they expect you to stay in employment for a stated length of time following completion – or pay any fees back?

• Will you be allowed to progress to Level 3? This will depend upon your role – you cannot do a Level 3 qualification unless you are doing the relevant work, as you would not be able to be assessed otherwise.

2. Undertake any training or development required

This could be through a variety of routes and take varying lengths of time. It is recommended that for a Level 2 award training should take between six and ten months, and for a Level 3 award about one year. Obviously it depends on your previous knowledge, and how recently any training took place. This handbook would be a very useful resource for your training. When enquiring about your training, find answers to the following questions:

• Does your workplace offer training on site or do you have to go elsewhere for it?

• How many actual hours of tuition will you receive? How big are the classes?

• Is there access to a library? Are any other resources available?

• What methods will be used to deliver the "underpinning knowledge"? Will any specialists be teaching you? How much tutorial support will you be offered?

3. Getting assessed in the workplace

This will depend upon the policy of your employer. You should be able to find out who is to be your assesssor, so make time to get to know them (although it will probably be someone you have already worked with).

Don't forget that at first both you and your assessor may be anxious or uncertain. You may have to develop a working relationship that suits you both.

The "Standards" may look like a foreign language, but after time and lots of reading they do become more "user-friendly". So once you are given the Standards, do start to read them. Ask if you do not understand a word or phrase – others are probably wondering too!

Start taking notice of your practice and the practice of others, reflect on what you observe and discuss it if you can with your assessor or tutor. Trust yourself: you may have things to learn, but don't forget you are already doing the job. You probably know more than you think.

son may come from a different work setting or section from the assessor.

Finally the work of the Internal Verifier is checked by an *External Verifier*, who is appointed by the Awarding Body and has no connection with your workplace.

Your assessment

The assessment methods are designed to be flexible and easily organised, with the assessment timetable being devised and controlled by the candidate. This is called "Assessment on demand".

The commonest method of assessment, particularly in care, is assessment by direct observation of the candidate's work. However, another eight methods are also acceptable, These can include simulations (role playing), oral or written questions, assignments, completion of work products such as reports or records, testimony of others (clients, other workers), or the candidate's explanation of the process or review of work. These other assessment methods are particularly useful when candidates do not regularly work with their assessor.

However, often for NVQ Level 2 Care Awards, direct observation is the most practical. A typical assessment might run as follows:

1 A worker checks the assessment requirements of the element. They check to see if they have sufficient underpinning knowledge and skills. They may ask the opinion of an impartial adviser to help decide this. They may decide to undertake training or support. The training could be "in house", from a more senior colleague or training officer, or from a planned programme.

2 Following training the candidate checks that they now have the required knowledge and skills, and they are ready for assessment.

3 The candidate approaches their assessor, and requests assessment. The assessor talks about the impending assessment, checks the candidate is fully aware of the assessment requirements, and might offer to do a "practice assessment". They will discuss any queries, and only when they *both* feel confident that the worker is ready to be assessed will they arrange a date that suits them both.

In the case of the care awards, they also approach a suitable client or clients, to ask if they would agree to be involved. It is vitally important that the client gives informed consent, and is not coerced in any way. If a client is confused or has limited understanding, the family should be asked for permission if at all possible.

4 The assessment day. The candidate will confirm with the client that they

---

Awards in Care
NVQs/SVQs Level 2

Level 2 Core

O Promote equality for all individuals

Z1 Contribute to the protection of individuals from abuse

W2 Contribute to the ongoing support of clients and others significant to them

W3 Support clients in transition due to their care requirements

U4 Contribute to the health, safety and security of individuals and their environment

U5 Obtain, transmit and store information relating to the delivery of a care service

Direct Care Endorsement

Z6 Enable clients to maintain and improve their mobility

Z7 Contribute to the movement and treatment of clients to maximise their physical comfort

Z9 Enable clients to maintain their personal hygiene and appearance

Z10 Enable clients to eat and drink

Z11 Enable clients to access and use toilet facilities

Z19 Enable clients to achieve physical comfort

These are the Units you need to work through to achieve NVQ Level 2 in Care with the Direct Care Endorsement.

are still happy to be involved and the assessor will confirm that the candidate is ready. Throughout whatever activity is taking place the assessor will observe the candidate, as unobtrusively as possible.

After the observation of the candidate's practice the assessor will question the candidate, and may ask to see any relevant documentation or reports. This helps the assessor to check on any aspects of the assessment process and helps to make sure that the candidate has the understanding and knowledge specified in the standards. Then, and only then, will the assessor confirm to the candidate their decision: either the candidate is competent or not yet competent.

Once the decision has been recorded, the assessor will explain to the candidate, in as much detail as is required, why they made that decision, if necessary giving comments or advice that will help the candidate improve their future practice.

At the end of the process they will make an appointment for the assessment of a new element, or if necessary a re-assessment. All necessary documentation is completed and made available for the Internal Verifier to see.

5 Once the assessor has completed a few assessments the IV will be invited to check on the documentation and the candidates' records of evidence.

6 Finally when all the units of the award have been assessed and the candidate is declared competent, the External Verifier will be invited to visit the assessment centre to view the assessment records (probably those of other candidates as well). They will make their decision based upon the evidence they check. Once the assessments have External Verifier approval the candidates will receive their qualification certificates.

See page 207 for useful addresses.

Relationship between chapters and NVQs in Care (Direct Care)

NVQ Unit	Main Chapter/s	Additional Information
O Promote equality for all individuals	4 Homes are for individuals 5 Multicultural care needs 6 Talking and listening	Aspects of this unit are integral to every other chapter
Z1 Contribute to the protection of individuals from abuse	3 Attitudes, feelings and the risk of abuse	5 Multicultural care needs 6 Talking and listening 24 Confusion and dementia 26 Rules and regulations
W2 Contribute to the ongoing support of clients and others significant to them	7 Interests and activities 8 Relatives and carers	3 Attitudes, feelings and the risk of abuse 5 Multicultural care needs 10 Health promotion 14 Keeping older people mobile 16 Safe lifting and handling 24 Confusion and dementia 25 Care of the dying person
W3 Support clients in transition due to their care requirements	2 Coming into care	3 Attitudes, feelings and the risk of abuse 5 Multicultural care needs 24 Confusion and dementia 25 Care of the dying person
U4 Contribute to the health, safety and security of individuals and their environment	10 Health promotion 11 Safety and security 12 Health, hygiene and infection 13 Accident and emergency	9 Nutrition 14 Keeping older people mobile 16 Safe lifting and handling 26 Rules and regulations
U5 Obtain, transmit and store information relating to the delivery of a care service	26 Rules and regulations 4 Homes are for individuals	All other chapters detailing possible information to be recorded.
Z6 Enable clients to maintain and improve their mobility	14 Keeping older people mobile	10 Health promotion 15 Care of the feet 16 Safe lifting and handling
Z7 Contribute to the movement and treatment of clients to maximise their physical comfort	16 Safe lifting and handling 17 Pressure area care	11 Safety and security 14 Keeping older people mobile 26 Rules and regulations
Z9 Enable clients to maintain their personal hygiene and appearance	19 Personal hygiene 20 Personal grooming and dressing	5 Multicultural care needs 12 Health, hygiene and infection control 15 Care of the feet 17 Pressure area care 22 Sight problems and blindness 25 Care of the dying person
Z10 Enable clients to eat and drink	9 Nutrition	5 Multicultural care needs 10 Health promotion 12 Health, hygiene and infection control
Z11 Enable clients to access and use toilet facilities	18 Promoting continence and stoma care	9 Nutrition 12 Health, hygiene and infection control 14 Keeping older people mobile 22 Sight problems and blindness
Z19 Enable clients to achieve physical comfort	21 Physical comfort, rest and sleep	11 Safety and security 16 Safe lifting and handling 17 Pressure area care 24 Confusion and dementia 25 Care of the dying person

Useful addresses

All these organisations welcome a stamped, self-addressed envelope sent with your enquiry.

Action for Dysphasic Adults, Canterbury House, 1 Royal Street, London SE1 7LN, Tel: 020 7261 9572.

Action on Elder Abuse, Age Concern England,, Astral House, 1268 London Road, London SW16 4ER, Tel: 020 8679-8000.

Afro Caribbean Mental Health Association, 49 Effra Road, Brixton, London, SW2 1BZ, Tel: 020 7737 3603.

Age Exchange Reminiscence Centre, 11 Blackheath Village, London SE3 9LA, Tel: 020 8318 9105.

AIDS Helpline National, Healthwise Helpline Ltd, 1st floor, Covern Court, 8 Matthew Street, Liverpool L2 6RE, Ethnic minority language lines also available, Tel: 0151 227 4150, Tel: 0800 567123 (free line).

Alcoholics Anonymous, PO Box 1, Stonebow House, York, YO1 7NJ, Tel: 019046 44026.

Alzheimer Scotland – Action on Dementia, 22 Drumsheugh Gardens, Edinburgh EH3 7RN. Tel: 0131 243 1453.

Alzheimer's Society, Gordon House, 10 Greencoat Place, London SW1 1PH, Tel: 020 7306 0606.

Arthritis and Rheumatism Council (ARC), Copeman House, St Mary's Court, St Mary's Gate, Chesterfield, Derbyshire, S41 7TD, Tel: 01246 558033.

Arthritis Care, 5 Grosvenor Crescent, London, SW1 7ER, Tel: 020 7235 0902.

Association For Continence Advice, Winchester House, Cranmere Road, Tel: 020 7820 8113.

Association of Blind Asians, 65 Bolsover Street, London, W1P 7Hl, Tel: 020 7226 1950.

Association Of Continence Advisers, The Disabled Living Foundation, 380-384 Harrow Road, London, W9 2HU, Tel: 020 7289 6111.

Breast Care and Mastectomy Association of Great Britain, 15-19 Britten Street, Anchor House, London, SW3 3TZ, Tel: 0808 800 6000 (free line).

British Association Of Cancer United Patients (BACUP), 3 Bath Place, Rivington Street, London, EC2 3JR, Tel: 020 7696 9003.

British Association of the Hard of Hearing, 7-11 Armstrong Road, London, W3 7JL, Tel: 020 8743 1110.

Dementia Services Development Centres

SCOTLAND
Dementia Services Development Centre, University of Stirling, Stirling SK9 4LA, Tel: 01786 467740.

NORTH-EAST/CUMBRIA
Dementia North, Centre for Health Services Research, University of Newcastle, Tel: 0191 222 7045.

REPUBLIC OF IRELAND
St James' Hospital, Dublin 8, Tel: 003531 453 7941.

SOUTH-WEST ENGLAND
Dementia Voice, Blackberry Hill Hospital, Fishponds, Bristol, Tel: 0117 975 4863.

OXFORD
Oxford Dementia Centre, Headington Hill Hall, Oxford Brookes University, Oxford OX3 0BP, Tel: 01865 484706.

LONDON
London Centre for Dementia Care, Department of Psychiatry and Behavioural Sciences, University College London, Wolfson Building, 48 Riding House Street, London W1N 8AA, Tel: 020 7679 9588.

WALES
DSDC Wales: Cardiff – Tel: 029 2049 4952; Bangor – Tel: 01248 383719.

NORTH-WEST
North-West Region Dementia Services Research and Development Centre, School of Psychiatry and Behavioural Sciences (Medical School), University of Manchester, Oxford Road, Manchester M13 9PL. Tel: 0161 275 5250.

Each of these centres is a resource for local information on best practice, training and resources for dementia care. Centres in other areas of the country are planned (network coordinated by the Alzheimer's Society, 0120 7306 0606). Latest information from the Journal of Dementia Care (020 7720 2108).

Also: Bradford Dementia Group, School for Health Studies, University of Bradford, Bradford BD5 0BB, Tel: 01274 233996.

Research, training (including Dementia Care Mapping) and publications.

British Colostomy Association, 15 Station Road, Reading, RG1 1LG, Tel: 0800 3284257 (free line), Tel: 0118 939 1537.

British Complementary Medicine Association, Kensington House, 33 Imperial Square, Cheltenham, GL50 1QZ, Tel: 011628 25511.

British Deaf Association, 1-3 Worship Street, London, EC2A 2AB, Tel: 020 7588 3520.

British Dental Health Foundation, Unit 6 Eastlands Courts, St Peters Road, Rugby, Warwickshire, CV21 3QP, Tel: 07788 54635.

British Diabetic Association, 10 Queen Anne Street, London, W1M 0BD, Tel: 020 7323 1531.

British Dietetic Association, 5th Floor, Elizabeth House, 22 Suffolk Street, Queensway, Birmingham B1 1LS, Tel: 0121 616 4900.

British Digestive Foundation, PO Box 251 Edgware, Middx HA8 6HG.

British Epilepsy Association, New Anstue House, Gateway Drive, Yeden, Leeds, L519 7XY, Tel: 011321 08800.

British Federation of Care Home Proprietors, 840 Melton Road, Thurmaston, Leicester LE4 8BN. Tel: 01162 640095.

British Heart Foundation, 14 Fitzhardinge Street, London, W1H 4DH, Tel: 020 7935 0185.

British Institute Of Learning Disabilities, Information and Resource Centre, Wolverhampton Road, Kidderminster, Worcs, DY10 3PP, Tel: 01562 850251.

British Red Cross Society, 9 Grosvenor Crescent, London, SW1X 7EJ, Tel: 020 7235 5454.

BTEC (Business & Technology Education Council), Central House, Upper Woburn Place, London, WC1H 0HH, Tel: 020 7413 8400.

Cancer Care Society, 11 The Cornmarket, Romsey, Hampshire, S05 18DB, Tel: 0117 942 7419.

Carers National Association, Ruth Pitter House, 20-25 Glasshouse Yard, London EC 4JT, Tel: 020 7490 8818.

Central Council for Education and Training in Social Work (CCETSW), Derbyshire House St Chad Street, London, WC1H 8AD, Tel: 020 7278 2455.

Centre for Policy on Ageing, 25-31 Ironmonger Row, London EC1V 3QP, Tel: 020 7253 1787.

Chartered Society of Physiotherapy, 14 Bedford Row, London WC1R 4ED, Tel: 020 7242 1941.

Chest, Heart and Stroke Association, CHSA House, 123-127 Whitecross Street, London, EC1Y 8JJ, Tel: 020 7566 0300.

Chinese Mental Health Association, Oxford House, Derbyshire Street, London, E2 6HG, Tel: 020 7613 1008.

Christian Council on Ageing, Mrs Margaret Young, New Cottage, The Square, Parwich, Derbyshire DE6 1QJ. Tel/fax 01335 390484.

City And Guilds, 1 Giltspur Street, London, EC1 9DD, Tel: 020 7294 2468.

Citizens Advice Bureaux, Myddleton House, 115-123 Pentonville Road, London, N1 9LZ, Tel: 020 7833 2181.

CNEOPSA (Care Needs of Minority Ethnic Older Persons Suffering from Alzheimer's Disease), University of Bradford, Bradford BD7 1DP.

Counsel and Care, Twyman House, 16 Bonney Street, London NW1 9PG, Tel: 0207485 7585, Advice Line 0845 300 7585.

Cruse Bereavement Care, Cruse House, 126 Sheen Road, Richmond, Surrey, TW9 1UR, Tel: 020 8940 4818.

Department Of Health, Richmond House, 79 Whitehall, London, SW1A 2NS, Tel: 020 7210 4850.

Disabled Living Foundation, 380-384 Harrow Road, London W9 2HU, Tel: 0870 603 9177.

Disability Alliance, Universal House, 88-94 Wentworth Street, London, E1 7SA, Tel: 020 7247 8763 (Mon-Sat 2-4pm).

English National Board for Nursing, Midwifery and Health Visiting, Victoria House, 170 Tottenham Court Road, London, W1P 0HA, Tel: 020 7388 3131.

Equal Opportunities Commission, Arndale House, Arndale Centre, Manchester, M4 3EQ, Tel: 0161 833 9244.

Health and Safety Executive (HSE), Broad Lane, Sheffield, S3 7HQ, Tel: 0114289 2500.

Help the Aged, 16-18 St James Walk, Clerkenwell Green, London EC1R 0BE, Tel: 020 7253 0253.

Hospice Information Service, St Christopher's Hospice, 51-59 Lawrie Park Road, Sydenham, London, SE26 6DZ, Tel: 020 8778 9252.

Ileostomy Association, PO Box 23, Mansfield, Notts, NG18 4TT, Tel: 01724 720150.

Jewish Care, Stewart Young House, 221 Golders Green Road, London NW11 9DQ, Tel: 020 8922 1998.

Laryngectomy Clubs (national association), Ground Floor, 6 Rickett Street, Fulham, London, SW6 1RU, Tel: 020 7381 9993.

Limbless Association, Roehampton Disability Centre, Rehab Centre, Roehampton Lane, London, SW15 5PR, Tel: 020 8788 1777.

Listening Books, 12 Lant Street, London SE1 1QH.

Marie Curie Cancer Care, 28 Belgrave Square, London, SW1X 8QG, Tel: 020 7235 3325.

Medic Alert Foundation, 1 Bridge Wharf, 156 Caledonian Road, London, N1 9UU, Tel: 020 7833 3034.

MENCAP (Royal Society For Mentally Handicapped Children And Adults), 123 Golden Lane, London, EC1Y 0RT, Tel: 020 7454 0454.

MIND (National Association for Mental Health), Granta House, 15-19 Broadway, Stratford E15 4BQ, Tel: 020 8519 2122, Info line: 020 8522 1728.

Mobility Information Service, National Mobility Centre Unit 2, Atcham Industrial Estate, Shrewsbury, SY4 4UG, Tel: 01743 761889.

Motor Neurone Disease Association, PO Box 246, Northampton, NN1 2PR, Helpline: 08457 626626.

Multiple Sclerosis Society, 25 Effie Road, Fulham, London, SW6 1EE, Tel: 020 7610 7171.

Muscular Dystrophy Group, 7-11 Prescott Place, London, SW4 6BS, Tel: 020 7720 8055.

National Association for Colitis and Crohn's Disease, PO Box 205, St Albans, Herts, AL1 1AB, Tel: 01727 844296, Info Line: 01727 830038.

National Asthma Campaign, Providence House, Providence Place, London, N1 0NT, Helpline: 0845701 0203, Tel: 020 7226 2544.

National Autistic Society, 393 City Road, London, EC1 V1G, Tel: 020 7833 2299.

National Back Pain Association, 16 Elmtree Road, Teddington, Middx, TW11 8ST, Tel: 020 8977 5474.

National Care Homes Association, 3rd Floor, Martin House, 84-86 Grays' Inn Road, London WC1X 8BQ. Tel: 020 7831 7090.

National Council for Vocational Qualifications, 29 Boltan Street, Piccadilly, London, W1Y 7PD, Tel: 020 7509 5555.

National Deaf Blind League, 18 Rainbow Court, Paston Ridings, Peterborough PE4 6UP, Tel: 017333 58100.

National Schizophrenia Fellowship, 30 Tabernacle Street, London, EC2A 4DD, Tel: 01761 432472/020 7330 9100.

National Society for Epilepsy, Information Department, Chalfont St Peter, Buckinghamshire, SL9 0RJ, Tel: 01494 601300.

Pain Society, 9 Bedford Square, London, WC1B, Tel: 020 7636 2750.

Parkinson's Disease Society, United Scientific House, 215 Vauxhall Bridge Road, London SW1V 1EJ, Tel: 020 7931 8080.

PAT Dogs (Pet Aided Therapy Scheme), Rocky Bank, 4 New Road, Ditton, Kent ME20 6AD. Tel: 01732 848499.

Royal College of Nursing, 20 Cavendish Square, London W1M 0AB, Tel: 020 7409 3333.

The Royal College of Speech and Language Therapists, 2 White Hart Yard, London, SE1 1NX, Tel: 020 737 81200.

Royal National Institute for the Blind, 224 Great Portland Street, London, W1N 6AA, Tel: 020 7388 1266.

Royal National Institute for the Deaf, 19-23 Featherstone Street, London EC1Y 8SL, Tel: 020 7296 8000.

Samaritans, 10 The Grove, Slough, Berkshire, SL1 1QP, Tel: 01753 532713, Fax: 01753 819004.

Social Care Association, Thortan House, Hook Road, Surbiton, Surrey, KT6 5AN, Tel: 020 8397 1411.

Schizophrenia Association of Great Britain, Bryn Hyfryd, The Crescent, Bangor, Gwynedd, LL57 2AG, Tel: 01248 354048.

Spinal Injuries Association, 76 St James Lane, London, N10 3DF, Tel: 020 8444 2121, Helpline: 020 888 34296.

SPOD (Sexual and Personal Relationships of Disabled People), 286 Camden Road, London, N7 0BJ, Tel: 020 7607 8851.

St John Ambulance, 1 Grosvenor Cresent, London, SW1X 7EF, Tel: 020 7235 5231.

The Stroke Association, Stroke House, 123-127 Whitecross Street, London EC1Y 8JJ, Tel: 020 7566 0300.

TFH, 76 Barracks Road, Sandy Lane, Industrial Estate, Stourport on Seven, Worcestershire, DY13 9QB, Tel: 01299 827820. Games, puzzles, pastimes etc for disabled/older people.

United Kingdom Central Council For Nursing, Midwifery and Health Visiting, 23 Portland Place, London, W1N 3AF, Tel: 020 7637 7181.

University of the Third Age, 26 Harrison Street, London, NWC1, Self help educational activities for older people, Tel: 91207837 8838.

VOICES (Voluntary Organisations Involved in Caring in the Elderly Sector), c/o The Association of Charity Officers, Beechwood House, Wyllotts Close, Potters Bar, Herts EN6 2HN. Tel: 01707 651777.

Further details of these and other organisation, including links to their web sites, can be found at www.careinfo.org.

Glossary of terms

Abuse. Physical, verbal or emotional mistreatment or exploitation of another person against their best interests.

Accreditation of Prior Learning (for NVQ). The assessment of an individual's past achievements against national standards.

Acute. Used to describe an illness or condition that is of relatively short duration, and usually severe.

Advocate. A person who supports, encourages, defends and negotiates on behalf of another by representing them where they are unsure or unable to represent themselves.

Agitation. An extreme state of upset where the person may experience physical signs of restlessness and feel uneasy and tense.

AIDS (Acquired Immunodeficiency Syndrome – see also HIV). A condition caused by a virus called Human Immunodeficiency Virus (HIV). It damages the defence system so that the body cannot fight infection. AIDS can cause people to develop certain forms of cancer, and to get serious infections of the lungs, digestive system, the brain and skin. It is passed on by exchanging body fluids such as blood, semen and vaginal fluids.

Allergy. A reaction to a substance to which a person is sensitive. Examples include fur, dust, alcohol, certain foods, insect stings and medicines. Usually causes skin rashes, but can be more severe causing difficulty with breathing due to swelling of the throat and airway. Death can occur. (See also Anaphylaxis).

Alzheimer's disease (see also Dementia). A form of dementia characterised by changes to the brain, although the particular cause is unknown. Disorientation, loss of memory and intellectual function, apathy and difficulty with coordinating movement, speech and thoughts, and disorientation, are common features.

Amnesia. Loss of memory.

Anaemia. Shortage of the oxygen-carrying part (haemoglobin) of the blood's red cells. This may be because the body is losing too much haemoglobin (eg due to bleeding) or because it is not making enough (eg due to a shortage of iron in the diet).

Anaesthetic. A substance that can cause temporary loss of the sensation of pain or consciousness. As a "local" anaesthetic it numbs a specific part of the body only. As a "general" anaesthetic it causes the patient to lose consciousness.

Analgesics. Medicines that provide relief from pain.

Anaphylactic shock. A severe reaction causing swelling of the airway and possible respiratory and cardiac arrest. It can occur when a medicine or injection is given. It can also occur if people are allergic to a particular food or are bitten or stung by an insect.

Angina. Chest pain due to oxygen shortage in the heart muscles. Caused by narrowing or blockage of the coronary arteries which supply the heart muscle with oxygen.

Anorexia. This is the loss of desire to eat. Emotional disturbances, such as depression, may induce a chronic state of anorexia.

Antibiotics. Medicines which either kill bacteria or stop them multiplying. They have no effect on a virus.

Anticonvulsant drugs. Medicines which are used to treat epilepsy.

Anti-depressant drugs. Medicines that are used in the treatment of depression. These drugs act upon and stimulate parts of the nervous system.

Anti-emetics. Medicines that are used to prevent nausea and sickness.

Anti-histamine. Medicines and creams used to counter the symptoms of an allergic reaction, eg irritation and itching of the skin.

Anus (see also Colon and Rectum). The muscular ring at the end of the intestinal canal.

Anxiety state. A condition in which the individual is so worried about a certain situation, that their life is severely restricted. The main characteristic is the inability to relax.

Arteriosclerosis. A gradual loss of elasticity in the walls of arteries due to thickening and the build up of calcium and cholesterol deposits. This may cause decreased blood flow and oxygen supply to essential parts of the brain and body.

Artery. A blood vessel carrying blood containing oxygen around the body.

Arthritis (see also Osteoarthritis and Rheumatoid Arthritis). Inflammation causing pain, stiffness or swelling in one or more joints. There may be serious deformity, (eg of the hands) and disability. There are several different types including osteoarthritis and rheumatoid arthritis. Main causes are inflammation, and the effects of wear and tear.

Aseptic. Free from germs and bacteria that cause infection.

Assessment. The systematic collection of information by observing, interviewing and examining an individual and their social environment in order to develop a plan of care.

Assessment (for NVQ). The process of collecting evidence and making judgements on whether national standards have been met.

Assessors (for NVQ). Individuals approved by assessment centres to judge evidence of competence.

Asthma. A condition in which the tubes of the lung have a fluctuating and reversible tendency to narrow causing breathlessness, coughing, wheezing or chest tightness. It may be triggered by an allergy.

Audiometer. A machine used to test a person's ability to hear normally.

Audit (see also Standards and Quality Assurance). A methodical process of examining (for example, practical care, record keeping and client satisfaction with services) against agreed standards.

Autopsy. See post mortem.

Awards in care. A set of 20 NVQs at Level 2 and 3 with wide availability across health and social care.

Barrier cream. A cream, usually water based, that is applied to the skin to prevent drying or damage where for example a person may be incontinent.

BCG. A vaccine given to prevent people contracting Tuberculosis (TB). See also Immunisation.

Benign. When describing a tumour means favourable, non-cancerous, usually contained within a capsule and not spreading to other parts of the body.

Bereavement. The human response to loss, usually as a result of a person dying. It also occurs when a person has lost something personal and important to them, such as their home, or a limb.

Blood pressure. The force of blood in the arteries measured in millimetres of mercury by a machine called a sphygmomanometer. Blood pressures are written down as two figures. The top figure is called "systolic" and the bottom figure is called "diastolic". How high or low the blood pressure is depends on the strength of the heart beat and the condition of the arteries.

Bradycardia. A marked slowing of the rate of the heart.

Braille. A system of writing and printing by means of raised points representing letters which allows blind and partially sighted people to read by touch.

Bronchitis. Inflammation of the air tubes of the lungs. It may be "acute" due to infection, or "chronic" due to excessive production of mucus caused by many factors including pollution and smoking.

Bronchodilators. Medicines used to widen the lung airways.

Cancer. A large group of diseases which are linked together. In each case there is uncontrolled new abnormal tissue growth of the affected part/s of the body. The outlook for each cancer sufferer is dependent upon the site and type of the growth.

Capillaries. Tiny blood vessels that lie between arteries bringing blood to the tissues, and veins taking blood away.

Cardiac arrest. Used to describe a situation in which the heart suddenly stops beating.

Cardio-pulmonary resuscitation (CPR). The technique used to try and restart a heart after a person has had a cardiac arrest. It includes breathing into the person's lungs and externally massaging the heart in a regular and systematic way.

Carer. The term usually applied to a person who provides care at home without receiving a salary or wage. Most often it is a female relative of a dependent person.

Cataract. A clouding of the lens of the eye preventing light passing through it. Vision becomes very dim or is lost altogether.

Catheter. A tube which is passed into the body to drain away fluids. The most common is the urinary catheter for draining the bladder.

Cerebrovascular accident (CVA). See stroke.

Cervix. The neck of the womb.

Chemotherapy. The treatment of disease by medicines or chemicals. The term is often used for cancer treatment, which can make the person feel very unwell, nauseous and cause hair loss.

Chronic. A term used to describe a long standing and continued disease process. There may be progressive deterioration (sometimes despite treatment).

Cognition. Consciously knowing, understanding and having insight into personal and environmental events. The person may not necessarily be able to take action.

Colic. A sharp pain resulting from spasm of a muscle, commonly the stomach and gut.

Colon (see also Anus and Rectum). A part of the large intestine that absorbs nutrients and fluid from the diet. It ends at the anus.

Colostomy. See Stoma.

Compliance aid. A storage box for tablets. Contains sections for each day and the time that the medicine should be taken. Helps to remind people of when to take medicines.

Competence (for NVQ). The ability to perform an activity to the agreed standard. The assessment of competence forms the basis for NVQs and SVQs.

Compress. Soft pad of gauze or cloth used to apply heat, cold or medications to the surface of the body.

Concussion. A temporary loss of consciousness due to a knock on the head. The person becomes pale, has a feeble pulse and shallow breathing.

Confusion. Conditions in which consciousness is clouded, so that the individual is unable to think clearly or act rationally.

Confusional states may be temporary, due to acute illness (toxic confusional states), or long term and irreversible.

Connective tissue. The supporting tissues of the body, found under the skin, between muscles, and supporting blood vessels and nerves. Their functions are mainly mechanical, connecting other active tissues and organs.

Constipation. Incomplete or infrequent action of the bowels, due to lack of muscle activity, insufficient fluids or inadequate diet.

Continence (see also Incontinence). The ability to control the functions of passing urine or faeces when desired.

Contra-indication. A reason for not doing something, such as giving a medicine as this could have an adverse affect on the person.

Coronary artery disease. Narrowing or blockage of the arteries supplying the heart with oxygen. Usually due to blockage of the coronary arteries. Also known as coronary heart disease or coronary vascular disease.

Counselling. A skilled method of listening to and talking with a person or a group of people, to enable them to overcome a problem, make a decision or accept their circumstances.

Cramp. Painful contraction of a muscle, associated with salt loss. Failure to replace salt or fluids, a lack of oxygen reaching the muscle, or poisons of various kinds may be the cause.

Culture. The values, attitudes, lifestyle and customs shared by a group of people and passed from one generation to the next.

Cyanosed. Bluish discolouration of the skin, particularly the lips, due to shortage of oxygen supply.

Cytology. The microscopic study of the cells of the body.

Defaecation. The act of opening the bowels.

Dehydration. Excessive loss of fluid from the body caused by vomiting, diarrhoea or sweating or because of inadequate fluid intake.

Dementia (see also Alzheimer's disease). An organic mental illness caused by changes to the brain. This may be a result of disease or damage. The principal changes include inability to learn and retain information, inability to recall recent events, and feelings of anxiety and depression. This leads to disorientation and confused behaviour.

Depression. A profound sadness, distinct from normal bereavement or loss. Its features include reduced enjoyment, slowness and a lack of interest in life or the lives of others.

Dexterity. The ability to use fingers and hands to undertake everyday activities.

Diabetes. Failure of the pancreas in the body to produce insulin, or failure of the body to use the insulin correctly. Insulin breaks down sugary foods, allowing the body to use it for energy. Diabetes results in too much sugar circulating in the blood. Normal body functioning, for example wound healing, is affected by the condition. It is treated by diet alone, medicines or insulin.

Digoxin. One of the earliest discovered medicines which was found to have a beneficial effect on the failing heart.

Disorientation. A state of confusion in which an individual has lost a sense of where they are, what time it is and what they are doing.

Diuretic. A medicine which stimulates the kidney to produce more urine.

Diverticulitis. A condition in which there is inflammation of small pockets (diverticulae) of large bowel which stick through the muscle surrounding the bowel at weak points. Generally caused by long-standing constipation.

Down's syndrome. A congenital disorder caused by an extra chromosome. The person may have marked learning difficulties and heart problems.

Dysarthria. A speech disorder caused by poor muscle movement or poor muscle co-ordination, often following a stroke.

Dyslexia. Difficulty with reading and writing.

Dysphagia. Difficulty with swallowing.

Dysphasia. A language disorder which may affect understanding, speaking, reading and writing (often due to a stroke).

Eczema. A condition of the skin causing dryness, flaking and extreme itching.

Elimination. The removal of waste matter from the body.

Encephalitis. Inflammation of the brain, usually due to a virus.

Enema. Procedure involving the introduction of a fluid into the rectum for cleansing or therapeutic purposes.

Enteral feeding. Provision of nutrients through a tube directly into the stomach when the person cannot chew or swallow food but can digest and absorb the nutrients.

Epilepsy. A condition in which excessive or unregulated electrical activity in the brain causes fits. These may involve the whole body with loss of consciousness – "grand mal" – or parts of the body, involving perhaps a short loss of full consciousness, known as "petit mal" fits. "Focal fits" are said to occur when only one part of the body, eg arms or legs, is affected.

Ethnicity (see also Culture). A group's sense of identity associated with race, heritage, upbringing and values.

Evidence (for NVQ). Proof in support of the judgement made by an assessor that a candidate is competent.

Exertion. The amount of effort a person puts into carrying out a task. This may be physical, in walking or getting out of bed. It can also be mental, for example struggling to remember recent events.

Faeces. Waste matter which is indigestible such as fibre, excreted by the bowel.

Fainting. A temporary loss of consciousness due to a fall in blood pressure. The person usually falls to the floor, as this is the way in which the body attempts to restore the blood circulation, so that oxygen can reach the brain.

Fatigue. State of extreme exhaustion or loss of strength.

Fibre (in diet). Used to describe food that is high in roughage, indigestible, and which stimulates the action of the intestine (bowel).

Flatulence. Excessive wind, usually causing discomfort and pain.

Fracture. A broken bone. The signs and symptoms include pain, swelling, loss of power and shortening of the affected limb.

Gangrene. Death of body tissue usually due to loss of blood supply.

Genital. Relates to the sexual organs of the man or woman.

Glaucoma. An illness in which abnormally high fluid pressure inside the eye can cause permanent damage.

Guardian. A person who assigns themselves or is appointed legally to look after and take responsibility for another.

Guarding. A defensive action that a person may take to safeguard themselves or to prevent any pain. It may include not wishing to talk about difficult subjects or holding oneself in a comfortable position that prevents physical pain.

Haemorrhoids. Piles.

Health education. Educational activities aimed at enhancing or maintaining the health and wellbeing of others.

Heart attack. Damage to an area of the heart muscle due to obstruction of the artery supplying this area with blood. Usually preceded by extreme chest pain.

Heart failure. The failure by the heart to pump blood around the body efficiently. The most common symptoms are breathlessness, tiredness and swollen ankles.

Hemiplegia. Paralysis of one side of the body. Usually caused by stroke or as a result of injury or disease to the brain.

Hernia. Protrusion of an organ from its normal position in the body into another. The most common is the inguinal hernia in which bowel pushes through defects in the muscle of the groin. Also known as a "rupture".

HIV (Human Immunodeficiency Virus). The virus that causes AIDS. It is not one virus, but a family of many similar viruses. It weakens the body's defence system by entering and destroying white cells that normally protect our body from infection.

Hydrocephalus. Accumulation of fluid in and around the brain.

Hypertension (see also Blood pressure). A condition in which the blood pressure is higher than it should be for an individual person. Blood pressures are written down as two figures. The top figure is called the "systolic" and the bottom figure is known as the "diastolic".

Hypotension. A condition in which the blood pressure is lower than it should be.

Hypothermia. Body temperature below the usual value of 37 degrees centigrade. At about 35 degrees centigrade confusion and listlessness may begin. Below 33 degrees centigrade the breathing and pulse rate and blood pressure may start to fall. If prolonged, death may occur.

Ileostomy (see Stoma).

Immunisation. The process by which a small safe dose of an infectious disease is given to build up body immune resistance.

Impairment. A reduction or weakening of any body function.

Incontinence (see also Continence). The inability to control the passage of urine or faeces until a suitable time and place is found. Urinary incontinence may occur when abdominal pressure, through coughing or lifting heavy weights, causes urine to leak from the bladder and urethra. Faecal incontinence is caused by a loss of control of the anus. Disorientation may also cause incontinence.

Infarct. An area of the body which is damaged or dies as a result of not receiving enough oxygen from its arteries. This supply failure is usually due to a blockage of or haemorrhage from the artery. Frequently used as "coronary" or "myocardial" infarct to describe the damage done to heart muscle after a heart attack.

Infusion. Introduction of a substance, such as a medicine in fluid form, directly into a vein or under the skin. May be attached to a mechanical pump to ensure that the correct amount is given over a period of time.

Insomnia. Difficulty getting to sleep or staying asleep for a long time.

Intestine. The bowel.

Intractable. Commonly used in reference to pain, that is difficult to control or cure.

Larynx. The voice organ. Vocal cords of elastic tissue are spread across it. The vibrations and contractions of these produce the changes in the pitch of the voice.

Laxative. A medicine to encourage passing faeces.

Legislation. Acts of Parliament passed by the Government that must be upheld under the law.

Local authority. A body responsible for a range of public services, such as housing and recreation provided in a given area, usually a geographical Borough or Council.

Malabsorption. The failure of the gut to absorb nutrients and food. It can lead to malnutrition.

Malignant. A type of tumour that spreads and grows uncontrollably.

Malnutrition (see also nutrition). Under-nourishment due to poor diet or disease that prevents absorption of essential nutrients.

Medication (see also Sedation and Tranquilliser). Used to describe tablets, liquids or injections used with the aim of improving a person's physical or mental condition.

Melaena. The production of black, tarry stools containing blood from the upper part of the gut.

Meningitis. A serious infection of the tissues surrounding the brain.

Metabolism. The sum total of the chemical processes that occur in living organisms, resulting in growth, production of energy, elimination of waste material.

Micturition. The act of emptying the bladder of urine.

Monitored drug dosage system. A system of providing medicines that are dispensed and sealed by the pharmacist in weekly or monthly packs.

Motor neurone disease. A disease in which there is progressive destruction of some of the nerves responsible for stimulating muscles. This causes weakness and problems with movement, breathing and swallowing. The cause is unknown.

Motor strength. The strength of the muscle which stimulates the limbs and body to move.

Mucous membrane. A mucus-secreting membrane that lines body cavities (eg lungs) or passages that are open to the external environment (eg mouth, nose, vagina).

Mucus. The slimy protective secretion of the mucus membranes.

Multiple sclerosis. An often fluctuating, sometimes progressive disease of the brain and spinal cord in which plaques replace normal nerve tissue. This can cause a range of symptoms, including difficulty with coordinating movement, incontinence and problems with vision and speech.

Muscular dystrophy. A group of muscle disorders which are usually passed on through families and become apparent in childhood and adolescence.

National Council for Vocational Qualifications (NCVQ). Sets out the structure and framework of vocational qualifications for England, Wales and Northern Ireland. (SCOTVEC is the equivalent for Scotland.)

Nausea. The sensation of feeling sick.

Nebuliser. Equipment that adds drops of water or medicine to compressed air or oxygen so that it can be absorbed more effectively or dislodge mucus in the air passages and lungs.

Neurological. Relating to the body's brain and nerves.

Neuro-transmitters. Chemical substances that help to pass a signal down a nerve.

Nutrition. The intake of nutrients (in food and drink) and their assimilation into body tissue.

NVQs – National Vocational Qualifications. Practical work-based qualifications. See chapter 27.

Occupational therapist. A health care practitioner who is qualified to diagnose and teach people with an illness or disability to use aids and adaptations for everyday living and working.

Oedema. Excess tissue fluid, often around ankles, at the base of the spine or in the heart and lungs.

Osteoarthritis (see also Arthritis & Rheumatoid arthritis). A form of arthritis occurring in the joints of older people. It is usually very painful. There is destruction of the spongy pads between bones, and small bony growths at the edges of the bone joint.

Palliative. Treatment that relieves or reduces uncomfortable symptoms, such as pain, but does not provide a cure.

Paralysis. Loss of movement (but not sensation) in a muscle or group of muscles normally under the person's control. May be due to damage to the muscle itself or to its nerve supply.

Parkinsonism. Symptoms such as shaking or trembling, rhythmical muscular tremors, rigidity and a mask-like face that shows no emotion. Thumb and fore fingers may move in a "rolling" fashion. It can be caused by tranquillisers.

Peak flow. The measurement of air as it is expelled from the lungs.

Performance criteria (for NVQ). A set of outcomes related to an element of performance by which an assessor can judge that a candidate can work to the required standard.

Personality. The mental make-up of a person. The way that they respond is influenced by life events and experiences, and their attitudes to situations.

Pharmacist. Practitioner trained to make up prescribed medicines and provide advice and information on side effects and contra-indications.

Photophobia. Intolerance to light.

Physiotherapist. A health care practitioner who is qualified to diagnose, teach and apply therapies, usually involving muscles and bones, to people who are ill, have an injury or disability, in order to restore them to health.

Pneumonia. Inflammation of the lungs due to bacterial, viral or fungal infections.

Prescription. A legal document that must be used and signed by a doctor for issuing medicines. It must contain the name, dose and frequency of the medicines.

Pressure sore. An area of skin and underlying tissues which dies as a result of pressure persistently preventing the flow of blood through its blood vessels. It can cause an ulcer or sore to develop, particularly if the skin is broken.

Prognosis. The outlook for a person with a disease, in terms of disability and death.

Prostate. A gland at the base of the bladder in men. It may become enlarged due to disease or old age, causing difficulty in passing urine.

Prosthesis. Manufactured substitute for a part of the body (for example an artificial leg, false teeth, breast).

Pruritus. Itching.

Pulse. The regular expansion and contraction of an artery produced by waves of pressure as blood is pumped from the heart.

Pyrexia. Raised body temperature.

Quality Assurance (see also Audit and Standard). A system of evaluating and auditing the standards of a service to ensure that the best possible service is provided in terms of value for money and client satisfaction.

Racism. Discrimination against a person on the grounds of skin colour and/or ethnic origin.

Range statements (for NVQ). The breadth of contexts in which a candidate is expected to demonstrate competence (linked to an element of competence).

Reality orientation. The way in which older people with mental illness are helped to keep in touch with the world around them. This may be through the use of large clocks, signs on doors, and newspapers.

Recovery position. The safest position in which to place a person who is unconscious. See chapter 13.

Rectum (see also Colon). The lower end of the bowel leading out to the anus.

Rehabilitation. The process by which a team of workers restores a person who has had a serious illness or injury to as near as possible their previous state of health.

Reminiscence therapy. Active participation by individuals or groups, using past life events to understand the reasons for their mental health problems. The past can also be used as a basis to share concerns and anxieties, since people with dementia are more likely to have a better memory for long term events than for more recent events.

Respiratory arrest. Used to describe a situation in which a person stops breathing, but before the heart stops beating. There can be more than one cause.

Respite. Temporary relief services for the main carer of a dependent person in the home or other setting.

Rheumatism. The term is loosely applied to any pain of unknown cause in the joints or muscles. Small swellings may appear under the skin, particularly around bony ridges. There may be fever, sweating and pain and stiffness in the joints.

Rheumatoid arthritis (see also Arthritis and Osteoarthritis). Arthritis occurring in the small and large joints of people of all ages. The cause is unknown.

Role reversal. A situation in which a person exchanges a pattern of behaviour with another. For example a daughter may have to take on a mothering role to her own mother if she requires care.

Sacrum. Part of the lower end of the spine.

Sedative (see also Medication and Tranquilliser). Having a calming or soothing effect.

Sexuality. A part of the human personality that relates in physical, emotional and social dimensions to the way a person identifies and values themself. It includes their gender, appearance and sexual preferences.

Sharps. Any piece of equipment used that could cause injury by stabbing or cutting a person if not disposed of safely.

Shock. This may arise out of fear or pain, it may also be the result of loss of blood, as a reaction to medicines, or contact with electrical currents. It is the condition in which there is a sudden fall in blood pressure, which if untreated will lead to a lack of oxygen in the tissues.

Social services. A department of the local authority that employs social care workers to enable people to live independently at home by providing practical help and advice. Examples include social workers, welfare rights officers, disablement officers and care assistants.

Social worker. A professional trained to counsel clients and families, helping them seek community and financial resources to enable them to live independently in the community or other setting.

Sphincter. A muscular ring which surrounds the opening of a hollow organ, such as the bladder. It controls the escape of the content of the organ until a suitable time.

Spina bifida. A congenital disease in which there is a defect in the bones of the spine. This can be mild and cause no symptoms. In more serious forms the spinal cord can be damaged causing paralysis of the legs and incontinence of urine and faeces, often accompanied by hydrocephalus and mental retardation.

Sprain. An injury to a ligament when the joint it is supporting is forced through a range of movements greater than normal, without dislocation or fracture.

Sputum. Excess secretion from the lungs that contains mucus and saliva. It may also contain bacteria.

Standard. A guide that serves as a basis for measuring how good or bad a particular service or practice is. (See also Audit and Quality Assurance.)

Stereotype. A commonly held belief about a behaviour, individual or group that is not always true.

Stethoscope. A device for listening to sounds within the body, such as heart beat, bowel sounds and breathing, that cannot otherwise be heard by the human ear.

Stoma. A surgical procedure in which an opening is made on the abdominal wall to allow the passage of intestinal contents (colostomy and ileostomy) or urine (urostomy) from the bladder.

Stool. Formed faeces passed from the bowel..

Stress. Stress reactions, both physical and mental, occur when the individual is unable to cope with all the demands made upon them. If extreme, it may be called "burn-out".

Stroke (see also Cerebrovascular accident). A rapid brain disorder usually caused by a blockage in or haemorrhage from one of the main arteries of the brain. Speech and movement are commonly affected. Other functions may be damaged depending upon which artery is affected. Recovery depends on the extent of the damage.

Subcutaneous. Relates to an injection or infusion given into the skin tissue at a 45 degree angle, rather than into the muscle (intramuscular).

Syringe driver. A battery-driven device for giving drugs (usually pain killers) over a period of time via a subcutaneous needle under the skin.

Systole. The maximum level of blood pressure measured between heart contractions.

Tachycardia. A marked increase in the rate of the heart.

Thrombosis. The formation of a blood clot on the lining of an artery or vein which may partially or completely block the blood flow through it.

Thrush. A fungal infection usually affecting the mucous membranes such as the mouth and vagina.

Toxin. Any poisonous compound. It may be caused by bacteria multiplying in the body.

Tracheostomy. A temporary or permanent surgical opening above the Adam's apple. It allows a person to breathe when the throat or upper airway is diseased or damaged.

Tranquilliser (see also Medication and Sedation). Medicines that allay anxiety and have a calming effect on the person. They may also prevent them from feeling pain.

Trauma. A wound or injury, physical or emotional. Emotional trauma can be a cause of mental illness.

Tumour. A lump or swelling in the body that is not inflamed. A benign tumour does not grow in other parts of the body. A malignant tumour may spread to other organs.

Ulcer. An erosion and inflammation of the skin or mucous membranes. Examples include venous leg ulcers, caused by poor skin condition and poor return of blood to the heart. Arterial leg ulcers are caused by poor blood supply.

Universal precautions. The wearing of gloves and protective clothing, and correct cleaning and disposal of waste, to prevent the spread of infection from blood and body fluids.

Ureters. The tubes which drain urine from the kidneys into the bladder.

Urethra. The tube that carries urine from the bladder to outside the body.

Urine. Waste products in liquid form that are produced in the kidney and emptied from the body via the bladder.

Urinary tract infection. An infection that affects the bladder or the urethra. It may result in the person wanting to pass urine frequently, cause pain and a stinging sensation.

Urostomy See Stoma.

Value base unit (for NVQ). This is the "O" Unit which embeds in NVQ awards in care the principles of good practice: anti-discrimination, confidentiality, rights and choice, respect for beliefs and identity and effective communication.

Varicose veins. A condition, usually of the lower leg, in which the veins are swollen and may be twisted due to structural changes in the walls or valves of the vessels. These veins have difficulty returning blood back to the heart . Knocks to varicose veins commonly cause leg ulcers in older people which can be painful.

Vascular. Relating to blood vessels, usually arteries or veins.

Vein. A vessel carrying blood from the capillaries back to the heart after oxygen has been removed by the tissues and organs that need it.

Vertigo. A feeling of dizziness accompanied by a feeling that either oneself or one's surroundings are spinning.

Visual acuity. A measurement of how much a person can see at a particular distance, usually six metres, to identify whether they are short- or long-sighted.